Educating the Young Child

Advances in Theory and Research, Implications for Practice

Volume 17

This academic and scholarly book series will focus on the education and development of young children from infancy through eight years of age. The series will provide a synthesis of current theory and research on trends, issues, controversies, and challenges in the early childhood field and examine implications for practice. One hallmark of the series will be comprehensive reviews of research on a variety of topics with particular relevance for early childhood educators worldwide. The mission of the series is to enrich and enlarge early childhood educators' knowledge, enhance their professional development, and reassert the importance of early childhood education to the international community. The audience for the series includes college students, teachers of young children, college and university faculty, and professionals from fields other than education who are unified by their commitment to the care and education of young children. In many ways, the proposed series is an outgrowth of the success of *Early Childhood Education Journal* which has grown from a quarterly magazine to a respected and international professional journal that is published six times a year.

More information about this series at http://www.springer.com/series/7205

Angela Eckhoff

Editor

Participatory Research with Young Children

 Springer

Editor
Angela Eckhoff
Old Dominion University
Norfolk, VA, USA

ISSN 2543-0610   ISSN 2543-0629   (electronic)
Educating the Young Child
ISBN 978-3-030-19364-5   ISBN 978-3-030-19365-2   (eBook)
https://doi.org/10.1007/978-3-030-19365-2

This Springer imprint is published by the registered company Springer Nature Switzerland AG.
The registered company address is: Gewerbestrasse 11, 6330 Cham, Switzerland

Preface

Over the past few decades, a methodological revolution has been changing the face of qualitative research within fields devoted to childhood studies and education. Scholars across various fields within the social sciences are appropriating theoretical frameworks and qualitative methodologies that serve to support children's involvement in research as valued collaborators. My own introduction to these ideas came from William Corsaro's seminal works exploring children's friendships and peer culture in the mid-1980s and early 1990s. As a doctoral student training in ethnographic methods, I found Corsaro's emphasis on the necessity of interpreting children's behaviors from their own perspectives (1985) both commonsense and seemingly impossible. While I had read many ethnographies that emphasized adult perspectives, Corsaro's works were the first that I'd encountered where young children were presented as capable of such engagement. My experiences of teaching and working with young children for many years informed an intuitive reaction that such participation was certainly possible if children were provided sustained and personally meaningful opportunities for collaboration. From my own experiences, I knew that such engagement happened every day in classrooms and learning environments where adults respected, honored, and believed in children as knowledgeable beings.

However, the constraints to such practices often come from those outside the world of participatory research where children are viewed as *becomings* rather than as knowledgeable, powerful *beings*; where the language around children's abilities is focused on readiness, appropriateness, and typicalness; where research mentors expect to see adult commentary as necessary data sources to supplement children's work and words in order to satisfy long-held understandings of what constitutes valuable data in early education settings; or, where ethics review boards wonder how to protect children whose voices and faces appear in the photos or videos they themselves create during the day-to-day life of a classroom. While there is an increasing interest in creating spaces of participatory collaboration with young children in research, much of what is currently written involves older children and teenagers, providing little guidance related to children in the early childhood years. The unique issues that arise during participatory work with young children – ethical considerations, limitations in individual agency, power inequities, and emerging communication abilities – warrant a volume dedicated to exploring participatory practices as applied in a variety of early learning settings.

The inspiration for this volume arose from numerous conversations with colleagues, students, and the children that we, as a collective, work with in an attempt to support authentic views of participatory research as it unfolds in complex early learning environments. This volume features the work of researchers collaborating with young children across a wide landscape of early learning settings but, as a point of commonality, all of us hold true to the understanding that young children are capable, knowledgeable collaborators. Our collective intention with this volume is to contribute to the existing knowledge base on participatory research by presenting detailed descriptions of our work alongside young children as we navigate learning settings that often emphasize the *becoming* view of children rather than the *knowledgeable being* view. As a primary aim, this volume serves to demonstrate the ways in which we, as early childhood scholars and qualitative researchers, problematize, adapt, and overcome the challenges that are inherent to participatory work with young children.

Participatory research with young children is, for a lack of a better word, complicated. Participatory researchers must be open to shared decision making and the ways in which children's participation evolves over time. This means that participatory researchers must hold a deep level of trust in children – trust that children are capable, knowledgeable, and collaborative. The chapters within this volume hold these fundamental viewpoints of young children while also presenting honest accounts of researchers struggling with the messiness and uncertainty of participatory research when undertaken in real-world classrooms and schools. In addition to views into authentic learning environments, the chapters in this volume also draw upon on a wide range of children's knowledge and learning experiences. The diversity of our underlying research aims and focus across a range of educational content areas also serves to share a variety of researcher voices, from emerging to established scholars, in order to broaden the methodological conversation within and invite readers to connect to the multiple ways of exploring and understanding shared within this text. In this sense, *Participatory Research with Young Children* works to place the field of participatory research within the context of contemporary early learning environments.

Structure of the Text

Participatory Research with Young Children presents a guiding framework for designing and supporting work with young children that is grounded in contemporary understandings of child development and the rights of every child. The volume shares detailed approaches to research designs that support collaborative work with young children, teachers, and families in a wide range of early learning environments. *Participatory Research with Young Children* seeks to empower and inform readers about the conceptual understandings and methodological approaches that can be used to support participatory research investigations where the young is viewed child as knowledgeable and capable of sharing unique opinions, interpretations, and understandings of her experiences as embedded within social, cultural, and political worlds. Throughout this volume the authors set the stage for early childhood researchers and educators to develop new understandings grounded in post-developmental, post-structural, and social constructivist theories while exploring supportive methodological approaches.

Participatory Research with Young Children:

1. Introduces the conceptual foundations of participatory work with young children
2. Describes the ethical considerations that underlie all collaborative work and participatory research with young children
3. Connects participatory research approaches with young children in a variety of early learning environments to meaningful research questions and projects which view the child as capable and competent
4. Provides descriptive accounts of contemporary participatory research with children from study design through dissemination
5. Explores the obstacles and affordances that emerge during the data generation, analysis, and dissemination phases of participatory research with young children

The text is presented in four parts – *Conceptual and Ethical Considerations for Participatory Work, Exploring Children's Agency Through Engagement in Participatory Research Practices, Participatory Research and Challenges to Accepted Practices and Understandings of Young Children*, and *Analysis and Dissemination of Participatory Work with Children*. The chapters in each part are designed to scaffold and extend understandings of participatory research through authentic, illustrative descriptions of work with young children. Each chapter also includes a listing of questions designed to engage the reader in a collaborative dialog with the chapter author(s) regarding the themes and ideas presented within.

Part I: Conceptual and Ethical Considerations for Participatory Work

This part features three chapters that explore the conceptual and ethical issues encountered during participatory research endeavors. With the increasing use of participatory approaches in work with young children and the support underscored in international legislation advocating for the rights of the child, problematizing research ethics is key responsibility of participatory researchers. Grounding participatory research in conceptual understandings of the roles that children can enact to support their own agency during research interactions is central to uncovering the process and outcomes of such work. Additionally, the chapters within this part all position participatory work with young children within a strengths-based theoretical or conceptual framework. Eckhoff (Chap. 1, this volume) presents and applies two conceptual frameworks that are useful for understanding and situating the range of participation that can be supported when researching with young children. In addition to conceptual supports for participatory work, participatory research must take efforts to ensure that the research practices employed support children's views and perspectives, empower engagement, and ensure their right to be heard. Truscott, Graham, and Powell (Chap. 2, this volume) present a reflective account of their own ethical thinking during research design, recruitment, informed consent, field work, and the analysis and dissemination of research findings. Their account clearly situates the participatory researcher in a space outside that of a traditional developmental or post-developmental approach. The role described by Truscott et al. and later by Pase (Chap. 3, this volume) describes the tensions with researcher positioning in participatory work as it gives rise to varying possibilities for more respectful, genuine interactions between adults and children.

Part II: Exploring Children's Agency Through Engagement in Participatory Research Practices

The four chapters in this part explore the development of research practices and designs that support the direct and meaningful involvement of children within a variety of learning settings. Classrooms, schools, and child care settings for young children are dynamic, demanding, and challenging environments for research. In spite of the challenges, these spaces offer researchers opportunities to explore children's perspectives on their experiences which can, in turn, inform adult understandings and decision-making for both large-scale policy and individual practices. Central to this work is an emphasis on supporting authentic routes for children to enact choice-making over their experiences and activities. Each chapter within this part explores the considerations participatory researchers encounter as they develop the contexts and supports necessary to promote young children's agency within early learning environments. In Chap. 4 of this volume, Griffin presents her experiences as a participatory researcher working in early-grades classrooms utilizing four different participatory interviewing practices with young learners and discusses the implications of interviewing practices on children's engagement. Through work within the content area of language arts, Ness (Chap. 5, this volume) explores the relationship that can be supported between participatory research design and participatory classroom pedagogical practices. In her work, Ness connects inquiry-based classroom practices to active student engagement in the development of content knowledge and pedagogical practices. Offering additional understandings of children engaged in both curriculum and research, Husbye (Chap. 6, this volume) explores the duality of children's engagement in the creation of video data as their work ultimately created the space(s) for both inquiry and agentic positioning within their learning environment. Another important consideration to children's agency within early learning spaces is the child's role in documentation and reflection. Kumpulainen and Ouakrim-Soivio (Chap. 7, this volume) explore various supports and challenges to children's agency when engaged in the cultivation of digital portfolios and documentation.

Part III: Participatory Research and Challenges to Accepted Practices and Understandings of Young Children

A central idea within participatory work is that participants are empowered to develop deeper understandings of their lives or enact possibilities for change within their experiences and their collaborative involvement. This part presents two chapters exploring the ways in which participatory research with young children can serve to challenge accepted practices or understandings in early childhood. Accounts of participatory research with young children with special needs are quite rare in the participatory research landscape. In Chap. 8 of this volume, Urbach and Banerjee examine the methodological, ethical, and theoretical issues inherent to engaging children from special populations in participatory work. They offer a constructive analysis of the issues surrounding children's participation and offer recommendations for equitable, authentic research practices for children from special populations. As participatory research has the potential to provide opportunities to share the authentic voice of children participating as researchers, it can serve to challenge the dominant understandings and beliefs about young children. Leafgrean (Chap. 9, this volume) details her work with counterstorytelling a key component of critical race theory (CRT), an accessible, yet powerful approach to participatory work with marginalized children of color. In this work, the children's counternarratives disrupted the dominant narrative of school experiences and offered a new space for the children's own words and stories.

Part IV: Analysis and Dissemination of Participatory Work with Children

The final part of this volume features three chapters that explore children's engagement in the latter stages of participatory research – analysis and dissemination. These stages are often the least included components of participatory research with young children. The chapters in this part explore various means of supporting the meaningful engagement of young children during the processes of analysis and dissemination while also problematizing the challenges inherent to such engagement. Eckhoff (Chap. 10, this volume) explores the possibilities for young children's engagement in the local display and public dissemination of their work. The children's engagement in a *Photovoice* project offered new opportunities to support children during the analysis and dissemination phases of research highlighting the possibilities that can exist for young children to share their insights and experiences through their own work. Pinter (Chap. 11, this volume) shares her work with an exploratory project working together with mixed ability and linguistically diverse primary-grades children. Serving as first-time researchers, Pinter recounts the children's experiences navigating throughout all phases of research and suggests the need for further research exploring children's sustained engagement in participatory work. In Chap. 12 of this volume, McClure Sweeny shares a critical, reflective account of her work engaged in arts-based participatory research with young children in an early care setting. McClure Sweeny offers an account that captures intra-active, collaborative nature of digital art-making and documentation as it occurred between children, teachers, and family members and highlights the forms of dissemination that were collaboratively developed.

Concluding Thoughts

While analytic findings drawn from the work of young children have filled volumes of early childhood research for decades, the children themselves have been largely absent from this same body of literature. It is our intention to promote deeper, authentic understandings of young children's engagement in participatory research within the complex, often restrictive, spaces of learning inhabited by young children and early educators. Through careful attention to the experiences of children in our research, we invite all concerned with early care and education to consider the practices involved in participatory research in order to support the ethical, authentic inclusion of children as key collaborators working alongside adults.

Norfolk, VA, USA   Angela Eckhoff

Reference

Corsaro, W. (1985). *Friendship and peer culture in the early years*. Norwood, NJ: Ablex.

Contents

Part I
Conceptual and Ethical Considerations
for Participatory Work

Chapter 1
Participation Takes Many Forms: Exploring the Frameworks Surrounding Children's Engagement in Participatory Research

Angela Eckhoff

The Roots of Participatory Work

As awareness of children's participation rights increased in the 1990s following ratification of the United Nations Convention on the Rights of the Child (1989), academia's attention to participatory-based methodological approaches to researching with children began to emerge and gain increasing understanding and acceptance. While utilized more frequently in health education, community research, and educational research with older children, participatory research with young children is an emerging paradigm in qualitative research approaches. Such practices are designed to provide an authentic look into children's thoughts, insights, and interpretations of their lived experiences. Participatory research practices coincide with contemporary theoretical views of children and childhood. Within the early childhood field, approaches to designing collaborative work and participatory research are informed by theoretical understandings of the child as competent and capable as proposed by Loris Malaguzzi and scholars from Reggio Emilia, Italy in the early 1990s (Edwards, Gandini, & Forman, 1993) and further explored by scholars acknowledging and empowering children as experts on their own lives (Christensen & Prout, 2002; Kellett, 2011; Mayall, 2000). Additionally, a substantial, yet growing, body of participatory literature seeks to reposition the role and participation of young children in educational research, ethics, policy, and practice (Cannella, 2014; Christensen & Prout, 2002; Dahlberg & Moss, 2004; Davies, 2014; Eckhoff, 2015; Einarsdóttir, 2007; Hatch, 2014; Kellett, 2011; Sellers, 2013; Water, 2018).

Researchers undertaking participatory research with children will find themselves confronting cultural perspectives and institutional policies that typically work to do things *to* children rather than working *alongside* children (Runeson, Enskar, Elander, & Hermeren, 2001; Sandbaek, 1999). A core principal of

A. Eckhoff (✉)
Old Dominion University, Norfolk, VA, USA
e-mail: aeckhoff@odu.edu

© Springer Nature Switzerland AG 2019
A. Eckhoff (ed.), *Participatory Research with Young Children*, Educating the Young Child 17, https://doi.org/10.1007/978-3-030-19365-2_1

participatory research is that the process ultimately generates knowledge for both participants and researchers rather than serving as a process to gather knowledge from groups of passive research participants. Traditional research practices place responsibility for the design, implementation, analysis, and dissemination of research almost exclusively on the adult researcher. Such designs are aligned with developmentalist views of child development that maintain that young children are emotionally, socially, physically, and cognitively immature. A view that limits children's power and decreases adults' willingness to take seriously their ideas and understandings (Oakley, 1994). Traditional qualitative research paradigms involving young children have also relied upon the collection of supplemental data from the significant adults or professionals involved in children's lives inferring that data generated from the children themselves would not be sufficient in and of itself to respond to research questions. These practices and assumptions place children in a position of *less than* and work to inhibit adults' understandings of their perspectives, ideas, and considerations. Conversely, participatory practices aim to highlight the research spaces that expand children's active engagement in research and in turn, provide rich insight into the lives of children and encourages to them to be viewed as experts in their own lives (Gallagher, 2008).

As a researcher dedicated to understanding the lives of children, I begin each new invitation to research examining the roles, rules, rights, and responsibilities of collaborative work with young children. My own research begins with contemporary understandings of participatory work as grounded within a community of learners where adults and children alike are learners as they engage together in inquiry, reflection, experimentation, advice, and support (Howes & Ritchie, 2002; Lave & Wenger, 1991; Sellers, 2013). Partnerships can be defined as "a social practice achieved through and characterized by trust, mutuality and reciprocity" (Kruger, Davies, Eckersley, Newell, & Cherednichenko, 2009, p. 8). Collaborative research relationships and participatory paradigms position children in the forefront as integral partners in the development of research questions, descriptions, interpretations and analyses. Collaborative work affirms the role of children as children at different points in the research process and acknowledges that children are competent beings living within complex social and cultural settings (Clark & Moss, 2001; Lansdown, 2005). As such, children are understood and treated as competent to share their thoughts and opinions in a variety of verbal and visual forms. Participatory research and collaborative work with children are ethical practices involving unique roles and responsibilities for both children and adult researchers. As with any partnership, the adult researcher must value children's understandings of cultural norms and related expectations as collaboration cannot be achieved in a setting dominated by a singular or outside cultural orientation.

Frameworks Supporting Understandings of Children's Participatory Engagement

Within this participatory view of children engaged within the process of research, I present Fielding's (2001) four level model of student participation which delineates the nuances within the roles of children and adults engaged in participatory work within educational settings. Fielding's model distinguishes between the participation roles of students as sources of data, students as active respondents, students as co-researcher, and students as researchers (Fig. 1.1). Within Fielding's model, the 4th level – students as researchers -is conceived as the most intensive and, ultimately, the rarest form of participation with students.

Fielding's 1st level – Students as Data Source – occurs in work that involves students as recipients of adult actions and interactions. Within this first level, researchers and educators are interested in exploring student understanding and perceptions in order to more effectively work with students. Data in this level is generally dictated by adults and takes the form of student work samples and examples of past student performance. Examples of early childhood research involving students as data sources include research investigations exploring student work products and other aspects of curriculum learning. A key distinction of this level is that student involvement is best described as non-direct in that their work informs understandings but the students are not in active/reactive roles.

Fielding's 2nd level – Students as Active Respondents – involves students as discussants that have valuable information to share with adults. At this level, adults ask questions and listen carefully to students in order to better understand how children learn and ways to enhance teaching and learning. When students take on the role of active respondents, they have opportunities to share insights, ideas, and understandings within a research agenda determined by the adult researcher(s). Surveys, interviews, and focus groups are just a few examples of approaches to data collection with young children that fall under this level of participation.

In Fielding's 3rd level – Students as Co-Researchers – adults recognize the need to engage students as partners in the learning process in order to deepen and support their learning. Adults work to listen and enact dialogue with students as both parties work collaboratively to research aspects of teaching and learning. This level of

Fig. 1.1 Fielding's (2001) four level model of student participation

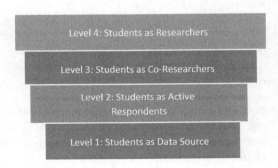

Level 4: Students as Researchers

Level 3: Students as Co-Researchers

Level 2: Students as Active Respondents

Level 1: Students as Data Source

participation involves more collaborative processes than the previous two levels which indicates more of a give-and-take relationship between the adult(s) and children as decision-making and power-sharing becomes consistent components of the research process.

In Fielding's 4th level – Students as Researchers – students take initiative in researching how best to support their learning and understanding in the classroom. Adults take on the task of listening to students in order to find ways to contribute to the student's learning process. Within the Students as Researchers role, Fielding underscores that all involved parties work to develop true partnerships where each are respected and valued for their expertise. Improvement through involvement is a means to enhance the communication and learning outcomes for all students through direct and supported action. It is not until Fielding's 4th level that the adult researcher or educator truly makes the paradigm shift from their actions as a means to 'do to' children to an understanding that they can 'work with' children.

As Fielding's model indicates, the involvement of children in participatory research can range from superficial inclusion to collaborative, personally significant engagement. As part of token or superficial inclusion, children can be encouraged to consult with adult researchers as their perspectives and ideas are viewed as valuable but this type of involvement differs from meaningful engagement in collaborative work. To clarify these differences Lansdown's (2005) framework is particularly useful in differentiating the degrees of children's participation within educational and social experiences – consultation, participatory processes, and self-initiation.

When adult researchers invite children into work through a consultation role they are acknowledging that children have important perspectives and unique experiences to share that can inform adult understandings. The process of consultation in work involving children and adults is generally characterised as adult initiated, organized and managed. Children engaged in consultation typically respond to a preconceived, adult agenda but they lack any real possibility to control the outcomes of the work (Lansdown, 2005). Consultation experiences can involve responding to research questions or prompts through surveys, interviews or non-traditional sources of data including drawing, performances, or digital media.

In Lansdown's model, children involved in work characterized as participatory move past the bounds of the consultation role and engage in experiences that underscore the collaborative nature of a project. Participatory processes in work involving children and adults are generally characterized as adult initiated but also empower children to influence or shape the work and any potential outcomes (Lansdown, 2005). Importantly, participatory processes allow for increasing levels of self-directed action by children over a period of time. In this sense, children are encouraged to use their experiences to deepen and extend their involvement over the course of the project. Over time, children may take on more responsibility and assert their agency to make decisions based upon the knowledge and experiences gained during earlier phases of the work. This is an important consideration for researchers interested in supporting children's participation as research involves a variety of skills that can be developed over time with careful scaffolding and targeted supports for young children.

Lansdown's third category of involvement – self-initiated processes- differs from participatory processes in that children define their work and are not merely responding to an adult agenda. In this role children select areas or ideas of interest and determine which methods of investigation and inquiry will be used. Self-initiated processes in work involving children and adults are generally characterized as focusing in on issues of concern identified by children themselves where they also determine the pace, direction, and outcomes of the work. In this category, adults serve as facilitators rather than leaders as children develop and negotiate their own opportunities for engagement and exploration. The processes of participation and self-initiation in Lansdown's framework require the adult researcher to have given significant thought, time, and effort to the understanding that participatory work requires more than a mere desire to provide a platform for children to share their voices. These levels of work require the adult researcher to attend to issues of children's agency in such a way as to directly confront preconceived understandings children's capabilities. Such confrontation is necessary in order to examine the validity of the research methodologies that create opportunities for children to take an active role in the "…process of influencing decisions, policies and services that impact on their lives" (Lansdown, 2005, p. 69).

The frameworks developed by Fielding (2001) and Lansdown (2005) provide useful entry points for researchers interested in supporting young children's engagement during research in early learning environments. Additionally, the frameworks identify particular areas of concern for early childhood researchers as young children typically have less experience with the processes of research than older children and adults. Engaging young children in participatory research will require researchers to work within a continuous cycle of observation, reflection, and adaptation alongside children and to document the children's engagement in order to make informed decisions about the supports children may need throughout the investigation. Even as we develop and support participatory experiences that attend to the particular needs of young children, we must also accept that our interactions with young children in research will often be unequal and that developing and presenting an accurate representation of their 'multi-voicedness' will pose numerous challenges for early childhood researchers (Horgan, 2017).

Understanding Children's Experience of Place: Out-of-School Learning

As children's perspectives of their own experiences and understandings are fluid and performative (Warming, 2011), participatory engagement in researching with children requires an emphasis on building research relationships with children over time rather than a more traditional protocol where researchers move into and out of children's spaces quickly. In the remainder of this chapter I present an illustrative research vignette interwoven with identified conceptual connections to participatory engagements outlined by Fielding (2001) and Lansdown (2005). The vignette documents the experiences of a group of preschool children as they use digital media to capture their actions during an informal class field trip. The vignette is drawn from a multi-year project investigating preschoolers' use of digital media during their school experiences as the media was embedded into the everyday experiences in their classrooms. This research aimed to explore, through children's imagery, their evolving understandings of place-based learning over an extended period of time. The presentation of this this vignette below includes research aims, data collection methods, methods of analysis, and ethical issues interspersed with a discussion highlighting the roles of the child, teacher, and place in learning.

Research Perspectives

Since the early 1930s with Lucy Mitchell's seminal writings, the field trip has been viewed as an essential element of children's early school experiences (Mitchell, 1934). Taking a class walk or a field trip in the community can encourage children's learning and engagement in ways that are a far cry from the scripted lessons and paced curriculums used in many classrooms. Many researchers have investigated students' knowledge gains and content learning that occurr during adult-led, highly structured field trips (Davidson, Passmore, & Anderson, 2010; DeMarie, 2001; Matthews, 2002; Saul, 1993; Taylor, Morris, & Cordeau-Young, 1997; Zoldosova, & Prokop, 2006). However, given contemporary, re-conceptualized understandings of the young child as competent and complex social learners, the highly structured field trip does not align with, nor recognize, the many modalities by which children learn, express, and communicate. Within a participatory framework, field trips can be viewed as experiential, authentic group events that encourage and promote new ways of knowing or experiencing an object, concept, or operation (Scarce, 1997) In this sense, and consistent with the field trip described here, informal field trips are typically teacher-initiated but are less structured in order to offer children opportunities for choice concerning their activities or actions within the environment.

Informal, field-based experiences defy traditional notions of what teaching and learning look like in school settings as the traditional roles of teachers and students become blurred when they engage together in new experiences beyond the scope of the classroom. Tal and Morag (2009) present an understanding of field trips as out-of-the-classroom experiences at interactive locations designed for educational purposes. The notion of experience and interactivity is a central component of social-constructivist understandings of knowledge development and learning within a group context. Experiential-learning theory highlights the central role of experience within the learning process (Kolbe, 1984). Placing primary importance on experience in learning brings the child and notions of playful, engaging learning to the forefront. Additionally, contemporary conceptions of learning emphasize the contextual nature of learning as any educational experience is always situated within a particular time and place (Lave & Wenger, 1991). Through this lens, a child's learning and knowledge development involves the entirety of the experience and inextricably links the learner and learning environment. In the research study described within this chapter, the environment explored, captured, and researched by the children is central to understanding the understandings held within the children's photographic images.

Methods of Data Collection

This research is framed by a participatory methodology as the children in this project created and collected all data utilized in this study. As the principal investigator, I utilized a participatory lens in this research as the project sought to explore locally-held knowledge and experiences of a particular group – young children – through digital imagery. In this view, cultural practices, meanings and experiences are visible in what group members propose, recognize and act on, socially accomplish, and signify as socially significant (Bloome, Katz, & Champion, 2003). Thus, the child captures particular images or events and, in turn, makes visible the social patterns, practices, and interests of their social group to outsiders viewing their imagery. Given that the project was researcher-initiated but the children made all decisions about where, when, and what images to create, collect, and share, the conceptual level of student as co-researcher (Fielding, 2001) is the most appropriate designation for student involvement. In addition, the project involves the upper degrees of Lansdown's (2005) framework of children's participation – participatory processes and self-initiation at various stages in the work which are detailed below.

Participants

This case study is drawn from a larger, multi-year project which included over 75 participating children ages three to five enrolled in a full-day early childhood child care program the campus of a large metropolitan university in the Southeastern USA over a 3-year time span. At the time of the study, all participants attended the child care program daily and represented nearly the entire population of the program's three, mixed-age classrooms for children ages 3–5 years. Many children participated in the project for several years as they remained in classrooms from the ages of three to five. Throughout the course of the study, children's participation was voluntary and they were free to choose to engage and disengage from image-making as they desired. Specific to the intent of this writing, the children's interactions with the digital media during informal field trips took place over 12 scheduled, out-of-the- classroom activities which included outdoor, informal walks and teacher-planned visits to sites on the university campus and in the neighborhoods surrounding the university where the child care program was located. On each of these occasions I accompanied the class on their walks and fieldtrips and provided the children with digital cameras for use if they so desired. These opportunities yielded hundreds of field trip photos taken by the children during the various trips taken over the course of the study. The vignette featured in this writing is drawn from a class visit to the university's baseball fields. The children captured images during the walk to and from the ballfield as well as during their experiences at the ballfield.

Child Roles Throughout the Project The children in this project were introduced briefly to the general operation of the digital cameras which captured both still and video images. Following parental assent to participate in the project, I shared with the children that they would be able to use the cameras or not use the cameras any time they were available to them. The children could also request to use cameras at any time if they spoke with myself or the classroom teacher. The rules for camera use were presented to the children in order to assist in the negotiation of camera use between the children themselves. In each classroom the ratio of cameras to children was one camera per three children. The children could express their interest in the camera use and request to "be next" to a teacher, another child, or myself. Children were encouraged to use the camera for as long or as little as they wished but would never be forced to share the camera after a pre-determined time had passed. This rule was set into place to encourage the use of the camera as an arts media where time and reflection of one's own work is viewed as central to the aesthetic and artistic exploration of a media. The children were shown how to view their photos on the camera as well as how to save or delete images or videos. During the child assent process, I discussed the understanding that any images or video that the child created was their own and they held the ultimate decision on what could be done with the image. Images and video could be captured, deleted, and shared with others through viewing on the camera's screen. I shared with the children that I would look at any images and video left on the cameras at the end of the day so that they could decide for themselves if they wanted to leave their images on the camera for my viewing. I also shared that the general aim of working with the cameras was part of a project that hoped to see the children's experiences through their eyes and that they were encouraged to photograph or video anything they found worthy of interest as long as any other children or adults consented to be a part of their image-making.

Adult Researcher Role Throughout the Project The adult researcher role in this project was collaborative in intent and nature but guided by the aims of the research. Over the course of the field trip, the classroom teachers and I rarely stopped children during their image-making unless safety reasons were determined (e.g. stopping photographing while crossing a busy street). I shed the more expected and accepted researcher roles in order to adopt become a collaborator in a variation of "least-adult role" (Mandell, 1988, p. 435). As such, I was responsive, interactive, and fully involved in the children's activities as a guide and collaborator. This role required me to align my engagement in the processes of image making and exploration to the children's engagement. In order to accomplish this, I needed to move out from behind my own documentation tools. Practically speaking, embracing a participatory, collaborator role necessitated the abandonment of traditional qualitative research tools – cameras, recorders, and field notes – as those tools would have inhibited my opportunity to fully engage alongside the children in the processes of play, image making, and image sharing. Engaging in traditional field note taking and researcher documentation would have placed me in a more traditional role of an adult or teacher for the children and would have limited opportunities to fully engage in the work alongside the children in the roles of facilitator and collaborator as presented in Lansdown's participatory and self-initiated processes (2005). During the field trip, I was present to assist the children with any technical support as well as engage in play and image making alongside the children if afforded the opportunity though child-initiated invitations. However, I remained a guest in the participating classrooms and, as such, had a role that was relatively undefined. As part of the research process using a participatory approach, I worked to understand the classrooms' norms and expectations but was not responsible for the children in the way that is typically associated with teachers' roles and responsibilities. Ultimately, I was also solely responsible for the analysis of all of the images and video shared by the children following each field trip as the children were not involved in the analysis phase of the project designating their participation level at student as co-researcher (Fielding, 2001). For participatory work to be to reach Fielding's 4th level of student as researcher (2001) participating children need to be engaged throughout all research phases.

Methods of Data Analysis

The analysis protocol for this research is based upon the visual materials conceptual framework from Rose (2007) and utilized content analysis procedures for all child-created visual imagery. The sole use of child created visual imagery as data in this research requires an analytic approach that considers the agency of the image, the social practices surrounding its creation, and the interpretation and practices of viewing. Rose's framework brings understanding to the meanings of an image or set of images from three sites- the sites of production, the image itself, and the viewing or audience context- and there are thee modalities to each of these sites: technological, compositional and social (2007). The site of production encompasses the idea that all visual images are made in a specific way and the circumstances of their production may contribute towards the effect they have. The site of the image encompasses the idea that every image has a number of formal components related to production tools and the social practices surrounding it. The site of audiences encompasses the idea that social practices are an important component in understanding the viewing context of the images. The consideration of the three sites is important to recognize that, as an outsider to the children's experiences, you will view, analyze and discuss their work through your own experiential lens.

Images were analyzed using thematic content analysis methods which involve an inductive, reflexive process which focuses on the emergence of understandings and thematic structures (Hsieh & Shannon, 2005). To begin analysis, myself and another coder evaluated a random subset of the hundreds of photographs created during the field-based experiences recording their initial observations. Upon completion of this initial coding sample, we met to discuss relevant themes and compared and condensed the two coding frames into a unified coding frame which was used to code all of the remaining images. This process yielded three overarching themes in the participants' experience of image making during field trip experiences: Inquisitiveness, Artistic and Aesthetic Exploration, and Social.

Findings Overview

The three key themes discussed below will be presented with corresponding images from one of the twelve documented field experiences – a trip to the university's baseball field complex. The images from this particular field trip experience were selected for use in this vignette because they represent both the range of field experiences and the thematic content explored in the project as a whole. The teacher-planned field trip involved a brief walk from the children's school to the university's baseball field. Once on site, several baseball team members taught the children the basics of throwing, catching, and hitting while the children explored the field and practiced the mechanics of baseball. The images shared here were created by the children on the walk to and from the baseball field or during their time on the field. Eight digital cameras were shared among two classes of students during the field trip. The children chose what, when, and how to photograph the images shared in this writing. In addition, by choosing to save the images on the cameras, they also held the decision to share their work. The children's increasing decision making over the course of the project and field trip can be labeled as engagement at the participatory process degree of Lansdown's model (2005).

The first theme, Inquisitiveness, incorporates images from the children where they used photography as a tool to aid in their exploration and curiosity as they attempted to build their understanding of an object, phenomenon, or concept. As an example, Fig. 1.2, was taken as the children sat in rows watching and waiting their turn as classmates received one-on-one batting instruction. The image captures a child-level perspective of an action shot. The intent of the photograph is clear as the image crisply captures the momentary action of a child successfully hitting a ball while the baseball team member hurries to retrieve it. Figure 1.3 is representative of many photographs taken by the children on this particular field trip and documents the children's view of their own shadows. The overhead sun, clear skies, and large, open field created a wealth of shadows that were captured by several students during their time on the ball field.

The second theme, Artistic and Aesthetic Exploration, incorporates images captured to explore apparent patterns, scenery, architecture, and images of interest with

Fig. 1.2 Child's view of batting instruction

Fig. 1.3 Shadows on the field

varying levels of abstractness. The levels of abstractness seen in these images are a result of the children's routine practice of zooming in to take close-up images of a larger object or scene of interest. The images in this theme most often show a part of the whole but rarely capture the complete object or scene. This practice of zooming the camera lens or physically moving their own bodies to gain closer look at a particular object was, in itself, an exploratory exercise. Figure 1.4 was created on the children's walk from their school building to the campus practice ball fields. As the children passed the university library, a bicycle is chained to a light pole. This image captures the place at which the bicycle is chained against the light pole and, in doing so, documents the point of interest for the child. Figure 1.5, a close-up of

Fig. 1.4 Locked bicycle

Fig. 1.5 Painted street line

the painted lines on the street the children crossed, also represents the theme of Artistic and Aesthetic Exploration. The cracked and worn yellow paint against the dark, paved roadway creates a visual contrast that draws the viewer into the child's observation and appreciation of the everyday.

The third theme, Social, incorporates images of enjoyment created by the children of their classmates, friends, and teachers. This category of images was generally unrelated to the teacher-intended purpose or aim of the field trip experience. The images in the Social category involved playfulness and were regularly interspersed throughout the various images created by the children. These images reflect the actions and interest of a child as he or she shifted their attention between the site of the field trip and the experience of sharing the field trip with friends. This category illustrates children's engagement at the Lansdown's 3rd degree of participation – self-initiated processes - as the imagery documents the children's experiences as they followed their own interests during the field trip. Figure 1.6 is an image captured of a child making a funny face to his classmate with the camera. The image was captured while the children were sitting on the ball field watching the ballplayer's hitting demonstrations. The images captured by the photographer just prior to Fig. 1.6 were images of the ballplayers working with classmates. There were eight funny face photographs of this child in a series captured prior to the photographer shifting attention back to capturing images of the hitting demonstration. The images that make up the Social category underscore the collective and playful approach to learning and exploration that can occur given a supportive, field-based environment where children enact choice, agency, and interest. Figure 1.7 is an action shot of the children directly in front of the photographer as they make their way across campus and back to their classroom. The teacher in this class assigned the children to walk with a classmate which sometimes resulted in the pair holding hands throughout the walk as captured in Fig. 1.7. The children captured many images of these small but important actions providing the viewer with an insight into the social values and culture in this particular classroom.

The themes uncovered during the analytic process revealed the elements of the field trip experience that captured the children's attention and imagination – content, social, and environmental explorations. When explored with a critical lens, these field trip elements can highlight the spaces in which young children are questioning, exploring, wondering, and experimenting. In participatory work, the photographs created by young children can be used to begin dialogues between teachers and students as part of the process of developing emergent curriculum and inquiry-focused learning. Exploring the themes of the children's photographs as outsiders to the experience, we gain insight into how the children balanced experiencing the

Fig. 1.6 Funny face

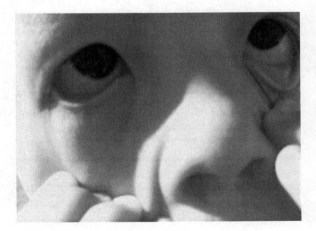

Fig. 1.7 Buddy walk

content of the trip alongside the social nature of being in a group during an out-of-school experiences. The children's images reflect both their playful engagement during the course of the field trip and their experiences of the field trip as a highly social experience. As early childhood educators are faced with push-down curricula and scripted, inflexible approaches to teaching, it is important to explore the ways in which we can support children's playful engagement in learning about and with their surrounding environment. The informal field trip experience can be seen as providing the critical space for young children to explore, experiment, question, and play alongside their peers in such a way as to honor their individual ways of understanding. Additionally, the use of digital media in this research provided the children with opportunities to create documentation of their experiences that demonstrate the educational and social significance of such learning.

This research documented the use of digital photographic arts media investigations during informal, field-based experiences and yielded interesting views of young children's school lives and experiences as they pushed image making in unexpected, yet interesting directions. Analysis of their work provides greater understandings of the importance and interests with which children view unstructured opportunities for learning as part of a group where their experiences are inextricably tied to the social nature of experience. Consideration of these ideas can serve to extend conceptions of the nature of teaching and learning as teachers and children work together to create emergent experiences for exploration.

Problematizing Children's Participation

This project used only the images created by the children as the sole data source and data analysis was my responsibility as the principal investigator. Including student voice to accompany the images – through post-field trip interviews as the children reviewed their images and helped to choose images for inclusion in analysis – would ultimately bring a higher and more meaningful level of child participation and collaboration to the research. At the time of the project and continuing on into the time of this writing, I remain unconvinced that the young children I worked with held an understanding of what would happen to the images and video they chose to save on the cameras as data to be analyzed. In fact, how could they understand the analysis and dissemination phases of the project when they weren't actively involved? They enacted high levels of choice-making while interacting with the cameras – choosing to create images or video, selecting the subjects of their work, sharing their work with their immediate peers– but their involvement in the research ended when they handed the cameras and their images over to me. As young children just beginning to process understandings of time, they could not know that I would spend years viewing, analyzing, and publishing the results of their work. Involvement in the analysis process, even to a minor degree, could help to bring a deeper understanding of the research process as well as provide a space to reflect upon their individual understandings of their experiences. Supporting opportunities for children's reflective experiences surrounding the data they generated could help to push their engagement to the higher level of Fielding's model (2001) and support their roles as co-researchers throughout the entire research process.

Questions for Reflection
- What concerns would you have in providing digital media for young children to use in documentation experiences? What steps could you take as a researcher or classroom teacher to best support children's use of expressive media as a language?
- How could children's engagement be extended past the data collection phase and into data analysis? What could the researcher have done to better support children's understandings of the longevity of their images in her work?
- What ethical issues do you feel could arise from the student use of digital image making in early childhood research? What steps could you take to mitigate such issues?

References

Bloome, D., Katz, L., & Champion, T. (2003). Young children's narratives and ideologies of language in classrooms. *Reading and Writing Quarterly, 19*, 205–223.

Cannella, G. (2014). Critical qualitative research and rethinking academic activism in childhood studies. In M. N. Bloch, B. B. Swadener, & G. S. Cannella (Eds.), *Reconceptualizing early childhood care and education. A reader* (pp. 15–52). New York, NY: Peter Lang Publishing.

Christensen, P., & James, A. (2000). *Research with children: Perspectives and practices*. London, UK: Falmer Press.

Christensen, P., & Prout, A. (2002). Working with ethical symmetry in social research with children. *Childhood, 9*(4), 477–497.

Clark, A., & Moss, P. (2001). *Listening to young children: The mosaic approach*. London, UK: National Children's Bureau.

Dahlberg, G., & Moss, P. (2004). *Ethics and politics in early childhood education*. London, UK: Routledge.

Davidson, S. K., Passmore, C., & Anderson, D. (2010). Learning on zoo field trips: The interaction of the agendas and practices of students, teachers, and zoo educators. *Science Education, 94*(1), 122–141.

Davies, B. (2014). *Listening to children: Being and becoming*. London, UK: Routledge.

DeMarie, D. (2001). A trip to the zoo: Children's words and photographs. *Early Childhood Research & Practice, 5*(1), 1–26.

Eckhoff, A. (2015). Ethical considerations of children's digital image-making and image-audiancing in early childhood environments. *Early Child Development and Care, 185*(10), 1617–1628.

Edwards, C., Gandini, L., & Forman, G. (1993). *The hundred languages of children*. Norwood, NJ: Ablex.

Einarsdóttir, J. (2007). Research with children: Methodological and ethical challenges. *European Early Childhood Education Research Journal, 15*(2), 197–211.

Fielding, M. (2001). Beyond the rhetoric of student voice: New departures or new constraints in the transformation of 21st century schooling. *Forum, 43*(2), 100–110.

Gallagher, M. (2008). Foucault, power and participation. *The International Journal of Children's Rights, 16*(3), 395–406.

Hatch, A. (2014). Reconceptualizing early childhood research. In M. N. Bloch, B. B. Swadener, & G. S. Cannella (Eds.), *Reconceptualizing early childhood care and education. A reader* (pp. 45–52). New York, NY: Peter Lang Publishing.

Horgan, D. (2017). Child participatory research methods: Attempts to go 'deeper'. *Childhood, 24*(2), 245–259.

Howes, C., & Ritchie, S. (2002). *A matter of trust: Connecting teachers and learners in the early childhood curriculum*. New York, NY: Teachers College Press.

Hsieh, H. F., & Shannon, S. E. (2005). Three approaches to qualitative content analysis. *Qualitative Health Research, 15*(9), 1277–1288.

Kellett, M. (2011). Empowering children and young people as researchers: Overcoming barriers and building capacity. *Child Indicators Research, 4*(2), 205–219.

Kolb, D. A. (1984). *Experiential learning: Experience as the source of learning and development*. Upper Saddle River, NJ: Prentice-Hall.

Kruger, T., Davies, A., Eckersley, B., Newell, F., & Cherednichenko, B. (2009). *Effective and sustainable university–school partnerships: Beyond determined efforts by inspired individuals*. Canberra, Australia: Teaching Australia: Australian Institute for Teaching and School Leadership.

Lansdown, G. (2005). *Can you hear me? The right of young children to participate in decisions affecting them* (Working papers in early childhood development, no. 36). The Hague, Netherlands: Bernard van Leer Foundation.

Lave, J., & Wenger, E. (1991). *Situated learning: Legitimate peripheral participation*. Cambridge, UK: Cambridge University Press.

Mandell, N. (1988). The least-adult role in studying children. *Journal of Contemporary Ethnography, 16*(4), 433–467.

Matthews, K. (2002). Building a community of experience. *Young Children, 57*(6), 86–89.

Mayall, B. (2000). Conversations with children: Working with generational issues. In P. Christensen & A. James (Eds.), *Research with children* (pp. 120–135). New York, NY: Falmer Press.

Mitchell, L. S. (1934). *Young geographers: How they explore the world and how they map the world.* New York, NY: Bank Street College.

Oakley, A. (1994). Women and children first and last: Parallels and differences between women's and children's studies. In B. Mayall (Ed.), *Children's childhoods: Observed and experienced* (pp. 13–32). London, UK/Washington, DC: Farmer Press.

Rose, G. (2007). *Visual methodologies: An introduction to the interpretation of visual materials* (2nd ed.). Thouasnd Oaks, CA: Sage.

Runeson, I., Enskar, K., Elander, G., & Hermeren, G. (2001). Professionals' perceptions of children's participation in decision making in healthcare. *Journal of Clinical Nursing, 10,* 70–78.

Sandbæk, M. (1999). Children with problems: Focusing on everyday life. *Children & Society, 13*(2), 106–118.

Saul, J. D. (1993). Ready, set, let's go! Using field trips in your curriculum. *Early Childhood Education Journal, 21*(1), 27–29.

Scarce, R. (1997). Field trips as short-term experiential education. *Teaching Sociology, 25*(3), 219–226.

Sellers, M. (2013). *Young children becoming curriculum: Deleuze, Te Whāriki and curricular understandings.* London, UK: Routledge.

Tal, T., & Morag, O. (2009). Reflective practice as a means for preparing to teach outdoors in an ecological garden. *Journal of Science Teacher Education, 20*(3), 245–262.

Taylor, S. I., Morris, V. G., & Cordeau-Young, C. (1997). Field trips in early childhood settings: Expanding the walls of the classroom. *Early Childhood Education Journal, 25*(2), 141–146.

United Nations Human Rights, Office of the High Commissioner. (1989). *Convention on the rights of the child.* Retrieved from https://www.ohchr.org/EN/ProfessionalInterest/Pages/CRC.aspx

Warming, H. (2011). Getting under their skins? Accessing young children's perspectives through ethnographic fieldwork. *Childhood, 18*(1), 39–53.

Water, T. (2018). Ethical issues in participatory research with children and young people. In I. Coyne & B. Carter (Eds.), *Being participatory: Researching with children and young people* (pp. 127–146). Cham, Switzerland: Springer.

Zoldosova, K., & Prokop, P. (2006). Education in the field influences children's ideas and interest toward science. *Journal of Science Education and Technology, 15*(3–4), 304–313.

Chapter 2
Ethical Considerations in Participatory Research with Young Children

Julia Truscott, Anne Graham, and Mary Ann Powell

Introduction

The participation of children in research has grown considerably over the past 30 years, legitimizing child-centered, participatory methods (Gallacher & Gallagher, 2008; Graham, Powell, & Truscott, 2016). A broad suite of creative methods are now commonly adopted by researchers and approved by institutional ethics research committees, from involving children in art or play activities to child-framed photography or baby head cameras (see, for example, Clark & Moss, 2001; Robson, 2011; Sumsion, Bradley, Stratigos, & Elwick, 2014). The development of these techniques has been ethically and epistemologically motivated to facilitate children's participation in research, diffuse inherent power dynamics between children and adults, and assist researchers to 'tune in' and 'listen' to children's voices. However, concerns have been raised they may be seen as ethically 'fool-proof' (Gallacher & Gallagher, 2008, p. 513). Indeed, participatory methods cannot, in and of themselves, ensure a project is intrinsically ethical, nor safeguard ethical practice for the duration of a study (Bitou & Waller, 2017; Horgan, 2017).

Mitigating these risks has been increased discussion of the socio-relational dilemmas and ethical moments that arise in research practice long after formal ethical clearance (Pálmadóttir & Einarsdóttir, 2016; Salamon, 2015; Sumsion et al., 2014). Terms such as 'situated' ethics, 'in-situ' ethics and 'ethics in practice' have been used to distinguish the on-going, 'messy' reality of ethics in the field from compliance-oriented procedural ethics (Bitou & Waller, 2017; Ebrahim, 2010). Reflecting upon dilemmas encountered, researchers have continued to problematize broader ethical issues such as competency, power and 'voice' (Holland, Renold, Ross, & Hillman, 2010; Palaiologou, 2014; Pálmadóttir & Einarsdóttir, 2016; Salamon, 2015). Alongside this literature, considerable attention has been focused

J. Truscott · A. Graham (✉) · M. A. Powell
Southern Cross University, Lismore, Australia
e-mail: info@cyraservice.com; Anne.Graham@scu.edu.au; maryann.powell@scu.edu.au

© Springer Nature Switzerland AG 2019
A. Eckhoff (ed.), *Participatory Research with Young Children*, Educating
the Young Child 17, https://doi.org/10.1007/978-3-030-19365-2_2

on the ethical processes associated with participatory research, such as the development of creative approaches to seeking children's informed consent (for example, Dockett, Perry, & Kearney, 2012). Collectively then, these efforts have created an evolving and expanding culture of ethics surrounding early childhood research and practice (Graham et al., 2016).

In this chapter, we draw upon our experience in undertaking the international Ethical Research Involving Children (ERIC) project; a major initiative to help inform considerations of good practice in research involving young children. The chapter introduces the ERIC project, including how the concept of ethics was theorized within this, and provides a brief overview of the emergent conceptual framework of 'Three R's' (Rights, Relationships and Reflexivity). Working from an understanding that ethical research requires careful attention to ethics throughout every aspect of the research process, we then draw upon the ERIC framework of 'Three R's' to unpack key ethical considerations surrounding research design, recruitment and informed consent, research practice in the field, and the dissemination of research findings. We illustrate these concepts with extracts from a case study research project (Truscott, 2018), which sought to explore children's nature-based play within the naturalised playgrounds of early childhood settings.

Background to the Ethical Research Involving Children Project

The ERIC project was an international collaboration that emerged in response to the aforementioned concerns that the burgeoning field of research involving children, rich in methodological creativity, needed to simultaneously be accompanied by a more critical and ethical approach. The aim was to explore how to best support researchers and other key stakeholders to strengthen ethical practice at every stage of the research process. The project began with an online survey, responded to by 257 researchers involved in child research across 46 countries (Powell, Graham, Taylor, Newell, & Fitzgerald, 2011), and an extensive literature review (Powell, Fitzgerald, Taylor, & Graham, 2012). This was followed by formation of an Advisory Group, comprising leading international researchers, and an extensive consultation process, undertaken with nearly 400 researchers and other stakeholders, on ethical considerations and existing resources to support ethical research. The project culminated in the development of a suite of resources, freely accessible on-line and downloadable in six languages (Graham, Powell, Taylor, Anderson, & Fitzgerald, 2013).

As the ERIC project evolved, it became apparent that a more explicit understanding of how ethics was being conceptualised by childhood scholars was an important foundation for improving ethical research practice. It was evident that fields, such as health care, nursing and anthropology, had much stronger traditions in theorising ethics (see, for example, Bergum, 1992; Meloni, Vanthuyne, & Rousseau, 2015;

Noddings, 1984). When ethical dilemmas arise in participatory research with children (as in educational practice), there is rarely a clear answer, and hence understandings of ethical theory may assist in working through ethical decisions. Correspondingly, we begin with a very brief overview of relevant ethical theory informing the ERIC project that culminated in the framework of Three Rs.

Understanding Ethics in Research with Children

Ethics has its roots in moral philosophy, with notions of right and wrong conceived from a justice or legal standpoint and aligning with notions of human rights (Fisher, 2006; Herring, 2013; Noddings, 1984). As such, rights are one of the key, traditional, approaches for theorising ethics. This tradition was largely maintained in participatory research with children (Beazley, Bessell, Ennew, & Waterson, 2011; Hammersley, 2015; Lundy & McEvoy, 2012; Lundy, McEvoy & Byrne, 2011), because of the foundational influence of the United Nations Convention on the Rights of Child (UNCRC) (United Nations, 1989). Although the UNCRC does not specifically refer to research, participatory researchers have aligned themselves with the rights afforded to children in Articles 12 or 13 (respect for the views of the child, and freedom of expression, respectively). This allegiance makes sense because Article 12 is one of the four overarching general principles of the UNCRC, and positioned as important to the interpretation and implementation of all other rights.

A number of scholars have engaged more deeply with the Convention in an effort to provide guidance to researchers, with the work of Ennew (2009) particularly influential in this regard. Ennew has drawn upon four UNCRC Articles (Articles 3.3, 12.1, 13.1 and 36) to argue for children's 'right to be properly researched'. In addition to Articles 12 and 13 mentioned above, Article 3 foregrounds children's best interests, which Ennew connects to the exercise of high professional standards when working with children, and Article 36 encompasses children's protection from any form of exploitation. Through the concept of the 'right to be properly researched,' rights-based research practice, as extended by Ennew and colleagues, aims to ensure 'that both the process of research *and* the results are ethical, scientifically robust and respectful of children' (Beazley et al., 2011, p. 159). Lundy and McEvoy (2012) have argued for a similar idea, combining Article 5 (parental guidance and the evolving capacities of the child), which they extend to researchers, with Articles 12, 13 and 17 (right to information). In doing so, they place emphasis upon *facilitating* children's competence and rights within the research process through assisting children to engage with, and develop informed views, on the issues under investigation.

The work of the above scholars in drawing on the UNCRC provided a substantial impetus for the ERIC project. Yet, it was apparent through the survey, consultation and literature reviews undertaken early in the project, that ethical dilemmas arise in the relational space between researchers and the multiple others involved in the research process. As researchers gave consideration to matters of harm and benefit, informed consent, payment, privacy and confidentiality, the inherently relational nature of ethical decision-making was evident across different research sectors, disciplines and contexts (Powell et al., 2012). Therefore, early in the ERIC project, relational ethics (Bergum & Dossetor, 2005; Noddings, 1984) emerged as a key area of theoretical interest, alongside rights-based understandings of ethics.

Relational ethics has been most influential within the healthcare field where there has been long-standing recognition that justice-oriented, rights-based ethics did not always reflect practitioners' experiences of ethics as care (Bergum & Dossetor, 2005; Fisher, 2006; Noddings, 1984). Rather than considering ethics as objective and rational moral reasoning, a relational approach sets ethics within the web of interconnected relationships that comprise human life (Herring, 2013). Corresponding, relational ethicists take the view that objective rules can rarely advise on the 'right' way to proceed – what is 'right' depends upon the circumstances (Noddings, 1984) and will be *generated* within relationship (Bergum & Dossetor, 2005). Hence, relational ethics positions research ethics as an on-going social practice, with emphasis placed upon mutual respect, engagement, embodied knowledge, attention to the interdependent environment and uncertainty.

The importance of both rights-based and relational understandings of ethics to the work of child scholars created a level of tension that we had to reconcile during the ERIC project, because relational and rights-based approaches are commonly at odds in the *theorisation* of ethics (Bergum, 1992; Herring, 2013). Herring (2013) has elucidated the four key points of tensions. First, he suggests that rights tend to focus on a particular point in time, whereas relationships are constantly evolving. Second, focusing on the rights of each party assumes they exist in isolation, rather than recognising their messy interconnectivity. Next, a focus on rights places real world lives into a legal framework, potentially objectifying or marginalising lived experiences. Lastly, privileging rights downplays the extent of responsibility inherent in relationships. Despite this, a relational ethics approach need not diminish the importance of human rights and associated core principles such as justice and beneficence – this would, of course, be untenable. While relational ethics is necessarily situated within relationships, this does not need to be at the expense of an emphasis on rights (Herring, 2013). Instead, relational ethics invites closer consideration of the relational contexts in which children's rights are applied.

A Framework of Three Rs – Rights, Relationships and *Reflexivity*

In line with the above, we adopted a relational, rights-informed approach to engaging with ethics to underpin the ERIC initiative, making explicit the standpoint from which many childhood scholars were implicitly working. We then had to consider how to *operationalise* this approach to ethics – to move beyond understanding ethics to consider how to enact a relational, rights-informed approach in practice. Relational ethics, with its situated nature of right and wrong, highlighted the need to move beyond a prescribed set of rules or code of conduct. While such codes play an important role, in and of themselves they do not facilitate the kind of critical engagement that many ethical issues warrant. Hence, in line with increasing calls from the literature, it was clear that we needed to provoke *reflexivity* (Bourdieu & Wacquant, 1992) in practice.

Reflexivity in research refers to consideration of the impact of the research 'on participants and their communities, on researchers themselves, and on the body of knowledge under investigation' (Graham et al., 2013, p. 176). It should act to provoke critical engagement with the power dynamics between adults and children inherent to 'in-situ' ethical decision-making, as well as encourage researchers to challenge their assumptions and beliefs about childhood and about the role and place of children in society (Elwick, Bradley, & Sumsion, 2014; Powell, Graham, & Truscott, 2016). Therefore, reflexivity differs from reflection in that it is a pre-emptive and ongoing process, important throughout the research process.

Correspondingly, the ERIC project drew together children's *rights*, research *relationships* and researcher *reflexivity* (the 'Three Rs') to form the aspirational cornerstones underpinning ethical research involving children (Graham et al., 2016; Powell et al., 2016). Below we map out what this approach signals at key stages of the research process: during the research design process, when recruiting child participants and seeking informed consent, when working in the field, and when analysing and disseminating the research findings. As indicated earlier, we illustrate this with examples from a case study research project on young children's nature-based play.

Background to the Nature-Based Play Study

The case study examples included throughout this chapter are drawn from a study by one of the authors (Truscott), undertaken through the Centre for Children and Young People at Southern Cross University at the time of the ERIC project. The study sought to explore children's nature-based play in two Australian early childhood settings – a long daycare and a community pre-school – both of which had been inspired by the nature-based play movement to increase the natural features in their outdoor playgrounds. The overarching method for the study was the Mosaic approach (Clark & Moss, 2001), which encourages a collaborative, participatory methodology characterised by a mix of creative methods. A brief overview of how this was adopted is provided below, with research design and methods unpacked and discussed in more detail throughout the following sections.

Twelve children aged 3–5 years participated in the study, six from each setting. Four educators also participated in the study, two from each setting. The fieldwork was undertaken several times per week over a 2 month period in late autumn 2013. The study began with an initial period of participant observation during which the researcher interacted with the children primarily at their request or initiation. After 2 weeks of observation, the research process moved into a more participatory phase, involving child-led tours of the playground, child-framed photography and the creation of collage-style maps of the playground. These activities were undertaken in small, child-nominated groups of three, and involved the aid of a handmade fictional puppet called Wattle-Pottle (as described further below).

Ethical Research Design

Central to ethical research design is the imperative to protect children from harm and, beyond this, to endeavour to offer an experience of participation that is authentic. The work of childhood scholars may not equate to the potential harms of clinical studies, yet 'the hazards…are more varied and problematic than is commonly supposed' (Homan, 2001, p. 333). Such hazards may include, for example, distress and embarrassment caused by researchers' intrusion into children's lives (Alderson & Morrow, 2011) and inauthentic or potentially damaging representation of children's voices, interests and lives (Spyrou, 2016). While the ethical principles of beneficence and non-maleficence should inform researchers' obligations to balance the protection of children with the perceived benefits of the study (Powell et al., 2011), the assessment of potential harms and benefits is unique to each research context. Further, as relational ethics underlines, different stakeholders may hold divergent views about what constitutes harm and benefit, as well as acceptable levels of risk. Correspondingly, the ERIC framework of 'Three R's' is intended as a tool for ethical decision-making, encouraging researchers and other stakeholders to reflexively consider both children's rights and the relational context in an effort to identify the '*best* right choice' – that likely to cause least harm.

In striving to offer children a genuine experience of participation, attention to notions of power is critical. While participatory approaches aim to diminish adult–child power imbalances, such dynamics can still cause harm if children's 'voices' or perspectives are rendered inauthentic as a result of implicit relational tensions, unacknowledged personal assumptions, or inherent uncertainties in interpreting observational data (Elwick et al., 2014; Lundy et al., 2011; Spyrou, 2016; Willumsen, Hugaas & Studsrød, 2014). Gallacher and Gallagher (2008) have criticised the inference that child-friendly methods are required to empower children and facilitate their participation, suggesting that this contradicts the very notion of children's agency. On the other hand, Bae (2010) has advocated for a connection between children's right to play (UNCRC Article 31) and their rights to participation (Articles 12 and 13), suggesting that play provides the primary vehicle through which children enact their agency and self-expression. The UNCRC Committee's General Comment No. 12 (2009) also enshrines this idea, requiring 'respect for non-verbal forms of communication including play…through which very young children demonstrate understanding, choices and preference' (p. 9).

In the Nature-Based Play Study

Early in the research design process, the researcher met informally with the children and their educators, helping to lay the relational foundations for an ethical research encounter. For the children, this involved seeking to situate the role of a researcher within their existing experiences, and they asked, "Are you someone's mum?" "Are you a teacher?" as they sought to understand how they might be expected to behave. Adopting a reflexive mindset, the researcher decided to incorporate a puppet into the research design to help situate the research within a more familiar, playful context.

The central potential 'harm' for the children involved in the nature-based play study was an inauthentic experience of participation. One of the ethical complexities of working as an external researcher is that, unlike early childhood practice, it is more difficult to wait for an opportune, child-led moment to initiate collaborative exploration. The research topic and activities may not be aligned with the children's play interests at the time of the fieldwork, potentially impacting upon subjective experiences of participation. On the other hand, tension exists around retaining research rigour and gathering useful, comparable data (Beazley et al., 2011). In an effort to find a balance, the research aim and guiding research questions were framed in a broad and open-ended way to allow the children (and educators) to have some influence over the emphasis and direction of the research.

Research Aim: to explore nature-based play in the naturalised playgrounds of Australian early childhood settings.

Research Questions
1. How do pre-school children experience nature-based play within the naturalised playgrounds of early childhood settings?
2. How do pre-school children and their educators perceive the risks of nature-based play within the Australian early childhood context?

In addition to the framing of the research aim and questions, the researcher decided that incorporating a puppet into the research design (after the participant observation stage) would help to facilitate the children's interest in the research topic and support their subjective experiences of participation. She relied on a reflexive process to identify an appropriate puppet and create an introductory script, developing several iterations. She initially considered a badger puppet and developed a script explaining that the badger had stowed away in her suitcase (when she arrived from Scotland) and was looking for somewhere to live in Australia. The early versions of the scripts centred around encouraging the children to share any ideas about where the badger could live and making connections between these ideas and the natural spaces within their playground as a way of helping to instigate the child-led tours.

She thought a badger would be unfamiliar enough to the children to avoid evoking 'right' answers or have prior preconceptions attached. However, after further consideration and consultation she decided that making a fictional creature might be a better option for avoiding those concerns and created this from a combination of materials (colourful faux fur, scaly-looking material and feathers), with the aim of evoking connections to the many environmental spaces in the playgrounds (sandpits, 'dry creek beds', muddy hollows, trees etc.). In seeking a gender-neutral name for the creature, the researcher decided to begin with a native Australian tree to make the connection to nature, and then create a rhyming component to embody playfulness, settling on the name Wattle-Pottle.

Child-framed 'selfie' photograph of research tool, Wattle-Pottle.

The reflexivity involved in the above process led the researcher to question the validity of her initial script. She wondered if it might create the false expectation that Wattle-Pottle would come to live at the children's pre-school. Additionally, she questioned whether the storyline was entirely respectful of the children. She realised she was attempting to engage and facilitate the children's participation to such a degree that she was entirely shielding the subject of the research from them. This would potentially have breached their right to information (UNCRC Article 17). In addition, being unclear about the purpose of the playground 'tour' may have led to potential avenues for discussion being missed and curtailed the children's participation in the direction and journey of the research. This could have diminished their right to freedom of expression (UNCRC Article 13) and the ethical obligation upon researchers (in both relational and rights-based understandings of ethics (Fisher, 2006; Lundy & McEvoy, 2012)) to facilitate children's competence to fully engage with, and express informed views on, the research topic.

As a result of such reflexive engagement, the researcher decided to use Wattle-Pottle as a tool to more openly convey her research aim to the children, and more closely engage them in the joint meaning-making advocated by the Mosaic approach. The final script positioned Watte-Pottle as a creature who was intrigued by what the children were doing outdoors and wanted to learn more about nature-based play. In this playful narrative, the researcher was Wattle-Pottle's note-taker and translator, helping to ensure he remembered and understood the children's contributions. By placing Wattle-Pottle at the centre of the research journey, the researcher aimed for the children to have greater scope to be playful and agentic and to test out different ideas or modes of relating to the researcher and the research topic than might be possible in many adult-child research relationships. Following the first child-led tours, Wattle-Pottle accompanied the researcher and the children throughout the remainder of the research process.

An additional potential (study-specific) harm was the discussion of natural risks with the children. The researcher was strongly committed to ensuring that participation in the research did not heighten the children's fears of such risks, and she gave careful consideration to the wording of discussion questions. Wattle-Pottle was again useful in this endeavour. For instance, rather than talking about *danger*, the researcher asked the children whether there was anything in the playground that Wattle-Pottle needed to be *careful of*, and then how Wattle-Pottle could best remember to be careful of the things they mentioned.

Ethical Recruitment and Informed Consent

Ethical practices in recruiting children and gaining informed consent for their participation are underpinned by the principles of justice (ensuring children are treated equally in relation to inclusion and exclusion) and autonomy (Graham et al., 2013). It seeking a sample of young children for research, researchers frequently engage with pre-existing groups or organisations (daycare centres, mother and toddler groups, nursery schools or family support services etc.), which may not be socio-economically diverse. Beyond this, organisational staff play a 'gatekeeping' role in allowing researchers access, and this can lead to the exclusion of children who may not be deemed 'appropriate' for participation. Therefore, in line with relational ethics, the research literature highlights the importance of researchers taking the time to establish sound relationships with adult gatekeepers (Coyne, 2010; Sparrman, 2014).

Beyond gatekeeping, a core element of ethical research is ensuring participation is voluntary and not coerced. This requires participants to be able to make an informed choice about whether or not to participate (Graham et al., 2013). Early childhood researchers have played a key role in promoting the importance of children's consent (alongside that of their parents), often promoting notions of 'informed assent' to avoid legal confusion (Brown, Harvey, Griffith, Arnold, & Halgin, 2017; Dockett, Perry, et al., 2012). Innovative approaches to the consent process with children, such as pictorial consent forms, come with some caution, though, as the novel and appealing nature of these may prove to distract children from making an informed choice (Dockett, Perry, et al., 2012). In addition, as relational ethics signals, consent processes need to be considered in the broader social context – children's relationships with peers, parents and educators may influence their decisions about research participation (Ericsson & Boyd, 2017). Importantly, consent has become recognised as an ongoing process with many early childhood researchers highlighting that it must be open to renegotiation, allowing children to cease (and perhaps recommence) their participation should they wish to do so (Dockett, Einarsdóttir, & Perry, 2012). Sometimes referred to as 'process consent, this can require close attention to the non-verbal cues and expressions of young children, in an attempt to ascertain their on-going willingness to be involved or to have their play activities observed (Bitou & Waller, 2017; Brown et al., 2017; Dockett, Einarsdóttir, et al., 2012; Salamon, 2015).

In the Nature-Based Play Study

Educators at both sites were asked to identify potential children for involvement in the study, based on current play interests, compatible friendship groups and attendance patterns. At the daycare the researcher and the educators worked spontaneously together to identify potential children during the early informal visits (described above). A list of children was drawn up, comprising those who showed a particular interest in interacting with the researcher, and others who were observed autonomously engaging with nature, such as collecting lizards or frogs. This collaborative process helped to reduce the potential silencing of some children that can occur if relying solely on educator selection. For instance, when the researcher enquired whether it would be suitable to invite a particularly energetic child who had shown a substantial interest in talking with her, the educator was clearly surprised, but clarified that she was sure his '*mum would definitely say yes.*' With hindsight, it would have offered greater ethical validity to have made this collaborative recruitment process a key aim of the relationship-building period, and followed the same process at both settings.

In line with current ethical practice, children's informed consent was sought alongside that of their parents. A child-friendly information sheet with pictures was enclosed with the invitation and parental consent form, and parents were asked to discuss it with their child at home. The researcher then discussed the information sheet with the children at the start of the study. She also explained at the start of the observation phase, and before each of the participatory activities, that involvement was voluntary – 'they didn't have to take part if they didn't want to' – and monitored the children for physical signs of dissent throughout. Therefore, although parental consent was received on behalf of the children, minute-by-minute dissent from the child could over-ride this at any time. The Mosaic approach was useful in this endeavour, offering individual children choice over which activities they participated in, whilst allowing the overall research journey to continue. Some children chose to briefly stop and restart their involvement (saying that they wanted to go and do another activity instead, and then later coming back) and the youngest child chose (with a shake of her head) not to participate in the final collage-making.

Ethical Research Practice in the Field

Even with careful, reflexive attention to ethics during the research design process, ethical tensions will still likely arise as the research process unfolds. As mentioned earlier, terms such as 'in-situ ethics', 'situated ethics' and 'ethics in practice' have become popular to distinguish the on-going navigation of ethics in the field from one-off compliance with procedural ethics requirements (see, for example, Bitou & Waller, 2017; Ebrahim, 2010). Through this growing body of work, it is now better understood that situational ethical dilemmas are going to exist – arising in relationships, through the negotiation of power dynamics, at the junctures of assent and dissent, on the boundaries of privacy and confidentiality, and in relation to the context and focus of the research (Elwick et al., 2014; Pálmadóttir & Einarsdóttir, 2016; Salamon, 2015; Sumsion et al., 2014). It is also better recognised that the identification and discussion of in-situ ethical moments are critically important to the on-going evolution of ethical research practice with children, helping to illuminate and challenge assumptions and beliefs about childhood and the role and place of children in society (Graham et al., 2016; Powell et al., 2016). As Lahman (2008) has advocated: 'It may well be that the moment we feel our research has captured an understanding of childhood we are on the shakiest ground' (p. 283). In practice then, as the ERIC framework of 'Three R's' signals, what is important is the ability to identify tensions and respond to unanticipated events in a reflexive way.

In the Nature-Based Play Study

Despite careful attention to detail at the research design stage, not everything went according to plan in the field. However, the children were proactive in using Wattle-Pottle as a medium, and in this way he worked more powerfully than expected as a research tool for navigating 'in-situ' ethical issues. For example, during a discussion of natural risks, one child suggested, *'Wattle-Pottle might be getting a bit scared now'*. The researcher interpreted this as a veiled expression of the child's feelings, and redirected the conversation back to less frightening subjects, wondering whether the child would have felt so able to voice her concerns without Wattle-Pottle as a conduit.

The children also used Wattle-Pottle to steer the direction of conversations or activities and negotiate power dynamics. For instance, towards the end of one of the child-led tours at the community pre-school, one child said, *'I think Wattle-Pottle would like to paint now'*. The researcher was unsure whether this was a cryptic dissent request, and it may have been. However, in conversing through Wattle-Pottle to seek clarification, the children asked the researcher to bring Wattle-Pottle to the easels on the verandah to watch them paint. At the easels, the shift in power was palpable and this impromptu, child-initiated activity generated some of the study's richest inter-child dialogue regarding nature and nature-based play. While this data benefited the study, the researcher was left wondering about the children's subjective sense of agency and participation at other times during the study.

On a different occasion, the same group of children were collecting natural materials to add to the collage when two of the children picked up large pebbles from the playground and began gleefully throwing them over the pre-school fence into a ditch beyond. While the researcher tried to redirect the children involved, the remaining child became increasingly worried, repeating, *'Wattle-Pottle has to be very careful…if he throws a rock and it hits some people…'*. This was an explicit incident requiring the researcher to suspend the child-led play element and adopt a 'teacher persona' to maintain safety and regain boundaries. Indeed, in many respects, the key ethical challenges during the fieldwork were also methodological ones – finding a positive balance between play, power and data validity by guarding against playfulness that might be risky or too 'silly' to generate relevant and insightful data or offer a meaningful experience of participation.

Data Analysis and Dissemination

The ethical obligation to ensure that children are not harmed extends to the analysis and dissemination of the research findings. Ethical research requires researchers to strive to ensure that research is reported accurately, fairly and in ways that are not discriminating or misrepresentative of children's voice, experiences and circumstances (Graham et al., 2013). While notions of 'voice' and power dynamics influence the *generation* of research data, it is primarily during the data analysis process when children's perspectives, whether gathered via participatory means or not, are interpreted and represented. Thus, it has been argued that the involvement of children in this process is critical to the construction of knowledge about their lives (Clark & Moss, 2001; Coad & Evans, 2008).

In line with the above, the idea of 'co-researching' with children has gained methodological traction. A recent literature summary indicates that the term 'co-researcher' is applied broadly, sometimes referring to children who play an active role in collecting data (e.g. through participatory techniques such as child-framed photography), through to those who collaborate with adult researchers throughout the whole process (as peer-researchers engaged in gathering data from other children, as part of an advisory team, or as participant-researchers) (Spriggs & Gillam, 2017). It may be justifiably argued that the latter of these (children engaged collaboratively as participant-researchers throughout the whole process) should be synonymous with research endeavouring to be genuinely 'participatory' (Clark & Moss, 2001; Coad & Evans, 2008; Lundy et al., 2011).

At the analysis stage, collaborating with older children often involves the explicit development of children's skills such that they can co-analyse data using similar techniques to that of an adult researcher. Clearly, this is not possible with babies or young children with limited literacy and numeracy skills. However, the process can be adapted for young children (see Lundy et al., 2011), and as advocated in the Mosaic approach, young children can be involved in an organic, cyclical process of interpretation and data generation (Clark & Moss, 2001). To date, though, much research using participatory data collection methods, does not involve children in the analysis of that data. As such, the evolution of the techniques for involving children in the analysis process specifically, and associated discussion of the ethical tensions, has remained limited (Spriggs & Gillam, 2017).

The sidelining of children's involvement in analysis misses the potential to further dissolve the adult 'filter' and push the boundaries of knowledge, such as insider knowledge on children's lives as well as technical, methodological and ethical knowledge to further research practice (Bradbury-Jones & Taylor, 2015; Lundy et al., 2011). On the other hand, there is a risk that the research process turns from one aimed at knowledge generation, and perhaps social change, to an educational exercise, in which the facilitation of children's analytical skills and ethical thinking become necessary outcomes (potentially at the expense of ethical or data robustness lest the process become too protracted or 'boring') (Bradbury-Jones & Taylor, 2015; Graham, Simmons & Truscott, 2017; Willumsen et al., 2014). Authors have also highlighted that there may be a limit to the extent to which children want to be involved in the analysis process (Lundy et al., 2011; Spriggs & Gillam, 2017). At present then, while the extent to which children's lives and perspectives can be authentically represented by adults is a matter for debate (Elwick et al., 2014; Lahman, 2008; Spyrou, 2016; von Benzon, 2013), and perhaps particularly so without full subscription to a collaborative approach (Coad & Evans, 2008; Clark & Moss, 2001), the representation of children and their views can, at least, be ethical and appropriate, or conversely conform to stereotypes, be unrealistic and/or potentially harmful. In this way, a reflexive approach is no less important when researchers return from the field.

Following analysis, a key ethical consideration is ensuring the privacy of research participants. It is usual practice to afford participants anonymity in the publication and dissemination of findings. Typical strategies include removing identifying information from reports, changing the name of communities, omitting participants' names, and using pseudonyms. However, some researchers have found that young children can want to have their contributions identified, and that repeatedly trying to explain anonymity to them can foster the belief that participating in the research is 'dangerous' (Dockett, Einarsdóttir, et al., 2012). An additional dilemma that can arise in research involving young children is the anonymity or confidentiality of children's data amongst adult stakeholders in the study. Young children have greater reliance upon adults and are subject to more prevalent supervision, and as such their privacy and confidentiality may not be considered with the same respect as that of older research participants. Parents or educators, in particular, may feel they have a right to see data, whether this is to screen it, to satisfy curiosity or to offer context and insight.

In the Nature-Based Play Study

At the outset of the study, the children were invited to make up their own pseudonyms. This offered the children an opportunity to identify their contributions in research publications, while still allowing for the anonymity usually afforded to research participants. The researcher wrote their chosen pseudonyms onto wooden necklaces, like the one she had worn as a name badge when first attending the settings, and which many of the children had admired. The necklaces helped to avoid the complex, potentially anxiety-inducing conversations that other researchers have reported when seeking to explain anonymity to young children (Dockett, Einarsdóttir, et al., 2012). Instead, the process of choosing a pseudonym felt playful and the children were thrilled to have their own necklace. The researcher and the children wore these when they were 'doing' their research and the children took them home at the end of the study as a small keepsake of their participation.

In line with the Mosaic approach, the researcher sought to involve the children in the data analysis process. After each visit, she coded her observations and the children and educators' contributions in a thematic way. She then adopted an evolving analytic process, in which she revisited emerging ideas and themes with the children and educators, with this a particular focus during the final activity (the collage-making). In preparation for this activity, the researcher typed up anonymised soundbites from the children's contributions throughout the previous visits, including graphics to aid the children's understanding of the text. The children loved seeing their stories in print and featuring them on the relevant areas of the collage-style map of their playground. The process offered an opportunity to revisit any areas of potential misinterpretation and seek further detail as well as to explore analytical connections from the children's perspectives. In this way, children played a small role in reflecting upon their research contributions. Further, this concluding activity served an important purpose of conveying to each child that their perspectives had been 'heard'. On reflection, though, the researcher felt the children's involvement in the analysis was largely limited to verifying and expanding upon her own analysis, and she identified this as an area for future reflexive engagement.

The participatory nature of the research process also raised 'in-situ' ethical dilemmas in relation to data confidentiality. The playful research context, and possibly the children's sense of empowerment within this, led to some quite fantastical research contributions. In line with ideas proposed by von Benzon (2013), the researcher perceived it unethical to completely dismiss these, and sought to identify potential meanings where possible. However, distinguishing fact from fiction was not always easy. For instance, Dr.K., explained that she did not like to get muddy at pre-school because she attended a ballet class afterwards. This seemed plausible, although she was one of the children who was observed as particularly immersed in the natural environment – being recorded knee-deep in sand or leaning back to let her hair trail through puddles from the swing. When, in an interview, one of the educators described an anecdote in which Dr.K. had requested help to set up a kitchen right in the centre of the mud pit, the researcher mentioned Dr.K.'s comment about the ballet class. The educator was surprised and she later enquired about the class with Dr.K.'s parents. It transpired that Dr.K. didn't attend ballet at all. The experience left the researcher questioning if she had acted in the 'right' way by mentioning it, whether from an ethical perspective, confidentiality should have overridden data validity, and whether there may have been unintended repercussions for Dr.K – such as her parents reprimanding her for 'lying'. Notwithstanding such ethical angst, the incident had a positive dimension in that it provoked deeper conversations between the researcher and educators in this setting, particularly concerning children's perceptions of the social acceptance of nature-based play and children's understandings of socially desirable responses.

The overarching finding from the nature-based play study was that pedagogy is critical to children's nature-based play experiences. For children to have the *opportunity* to become fully immersed in nature-based play, environmental changes to the playground must be accompanied by an explicit commitment to shifting beliefs about children and to working with intention to foster children's autonomous collaborative play skills (Truscott, 2018). At the end of the study, in addition to more formal research outputs, plain-text summaries of the anonymised findings were prepared for the educators and parents, along with a child-friendly version (with pictures). This helped to close the research loop by creating potential for the findings to inform changes at the settings involved, thus directly benefiting the children involved.

Conclusion

The ethical challenges identified in the above case study were inextricably bound up with the nuanced relational and methodological dimensions of the research context. The examples highlight that, while the ERIC framework of 'Three R's' cannot offer definitive answers to the diverse dilemmas arising in research involving children, the tripartite concept nevertheless offers a useful tool for navigating ethical dilemmas throughout the research process, from research design, through a breadth of 'in-situ' ethical issues, to analysis and dissemination of the findings. The overviews and examples shared here are intended to provide insight, rather than firm direction – to shed light on the kind of evolving ethical thinking and practice that potentially takes place during the period of any social research endeavour involving younger children. Through reflexive questioning and concurrent attention to children's rights and relationships, understandings of ethics surrounding childhood research will continue to evolve, pushing the boundaries of current research cultures, thinking and practice.

Questions for Reflection

- How might you recruit children for a participatory study in an authentically ethical way? What are the pluses and minuses of an approach like the one taken in this case study?
- How might you go beyond the case study example shared here and better involve young children in the *planning and design* of your research?
- How will you balance playfulness with children's research participation? What tools, strategies or approaches will you employ?
- How could you build upon the case study shared here to better involve young children in analysing and interpreting the data gathered during the research? What support will they require and what strategies could you use?

References

Alderson, P., & Morrow, V. (2011). *The ethics of research with children and young people*. London, UK: Sage Publications.

Bae, B. (2010). Realizing children's right to participation in early childhood settings: Some critical issues in a Norwegian context. *Early Years: Journal of International Research & Development, 30*(3), 205–218. https://doi.org/10.1080/09575146.2010.506598

Beazley, H., Bessell, S., Ennew, J., & Waterson, R. (2011). How are the human rights of children related to research methodology? In A. Invernizzi & J. Williams (Eds.), *The human rights of children: From visions to implementation* (pp. 159–179). Oxon, UK: Routledge.

Bergum, V. (1992). Beyond rights: The ethical challenge. *Phenomenology and Pedagogy, 10*, 75–84.

Bergum, V., & Dossetor, J. B. (2005). *Relational ethics: The full meaning of respect*. Hagerstown, MD: University Publishing Group.

Bitou, A., & Waller, T. (2017). Participatory research with very young children. In T. Waller, E. Ärlemalm-Hagsér, E. Sandseter, B. Hansen, L. Lee-Hammond, K. Lekies, & S. Wyver (Eds.), *The SAGE handbook of outdoor play and learning* (pp. 431–445). London, UK: Sage.

Bourdieu, P., & Wacquant, L. J. D. (1992). *An invitation to reflexive society*. Chicago, IL: University of Chicago Press.

Bradbury-Jones, C., & Taylor, J. (2015). Engaging with children as co-researchers: Challenges, counter-challenges and solutions. *International Journal of Social Research Methodology, 18*(2), 161–173.

Brown, H. R., Harvey, E. A., Griffith, S. F., Arnold, D. H., & Halgin, R. P. (2017). Assent and dissent: Ethical considerations in research with toddlers. *Ethics & Behavior*. Published on-line ahead of print. https://doi.org/10.1080/10508422.2016.1277356

Clark, A., & Moss, P. (2001). *Listening to young children: The Mosaic approach*. London, UK: National Children's Bureau.

Coad, J., & Evans, R. (2008). Reflecting on practical approaches to involving children and young people in the data analysis process. *Children & Society, 22*, 41–52.

Coyne, I. (2010). Accessing children as research participants: Examining the role of gatekeepers. *Child: Care, Health and Development, 36*(4), 452–454. https://doi.org/10.1111/j.1365-2214.2009.01012.x

Dockett, S., Einarsdóttir, J., & Perry, B. (2012). Young children's decisions about research participation: Opting out. *International Journal of Early Years Education, 20*(3), 244–256. https://doi.org/10.1080/09669760.2012.715405

Dockett, S., Perry, B., & Kearney, E. (2012). Promoting children's informed assent in research participation. *International Journal of Qualitative Studies in Education, 26*(7), 802–828. https://doi.org/10.1080/09518398.2012.666289

Ebrahim, H. B. (2010). Situated ethics: Possibilities for young children as research participants in the South African context. *Early Child Development and Care, 180*(3), 289–298. https://doi.org/10.1080/03004430701822958

Elwick, S., Bradley, B., & Sumsion, J. (2014). Infants as others: Uncertainties, difficulties and (im)possibilities in researching infants' lives. *International Journal of Qualitative Studies in Education, 27*(2), 196–213. https://doi.org/10.1080/09518398.2012.737043

Ennew, J. (Ed.). (2009). *The right to be properly researched. How to do rights-based, scientific research with children: A set of ten manuals for field researchers*. Bangkok, Thailand: Black on White Publications, Knowing Children.

Ericsson, S., & Boyd, S. (2017). Children's ongoing and relational negotiation of informed assent in child–researcher, child–child and child–parent interaction. *Childhood, 24*(3), 300–315. https://doi.org/10.1177/0907568216688246

Fisher, C. B. (2006). Paper Three: Relational ethics and research with vulernable populations. *Commissioned Papers*. Retrieved 4th November 2015, from http://onlineethics.org/cms/9004.aspx

Gallacher, L.-A., & Gallagher, M. (2008). Methodological immaturity in childhood research? Thinking through participatory methods. *Childhood, 15*(4), 499–516. https://doi.org/10.1177/0907568208091672

Graham, A., Powell, M., & Truscott, J. (2016). Exploring the nexus between participatory methods and ethics in early childhood research. *Australasian Journal of Early Childhood, 41*(1), 82–89.

Graham, A., Powell, M. A., Taylor, N., Anderson, D., & Fitzgerald, R. (2013). *Ethical research involving children*. Florence, Italy: UNICEF Office of Research – Innocenti. Retrieved from http://www.childethics.com

Graham, A., Simmons, C., & Truscott, J. (2017). 'I'm more confident now, I was really quiet': Exploring the potential benefits of child-led research. *International Journal of Qualitative Studies in Education, 30*(2), 190–205.

Hammersley, M. (2015). Research ethics and the concept of children's rights. *Children & Society, 29*(6), 569–582. https://doi.org/10.1111/chso.12077

Herring, J. (2013). Forging a relational approach: Best interests or human rights? *Medical Law International, 13*(1), 32–54. https://doi.org/10.1177/0968533213486542

Holland, S., Renold, E., Ross, N. J., & Hillman, A. (2010). Power, agency and participatory agendas: A critical exploration of young people's engagement in participative qualitative research. *Childhood, 17*(3), 360–375. https://doi.org/10.1177/0907568210369310

Homan, R. (2001). The principle of assumed consent: The ethics of gatekeeping. *Journal of Philosophy of Education, 35*(3), 329–343. https://doi.org/10.1111/1467-9752.00230

Horgan, D. (2017). Child participatory research methods: Attempts to go 'deeper'. *Childhood, 24*(2), 245–259. https://doi.org/10.1177/0907568216647787

Lahman, M. K. E. (2008). Always othered: Ethical research with children. *Journal of Early Childhood Research, 6*(3), 281–300. https://doi.org/10.1177/1476718x08094451

Lundy, L., & McEvoy, L. (2012). Children's rights and research processes: Assisting children to (in)formed views. *Childhood, 19*(1), 129–144. https://doi.org/10.1177/0907568211409078

Lundy, L., McEvoy, L., & Byrne, B. (2011). Working with young children as co-researchers: An approach informed by the United Nations Convention on the Rights of the Child. *Early Education and Development, 22*(5), 714–736.

Meloni, F., Vanthuyne, K., & Rousseau, C. (2015). Towards a relational ethics: Rethinking ethics, agency and dependency in research with children and youth. *Anthropological Theory, 15*(1), 106–123. https://doi.org/10.1177/1463499614565945

Noddings, N. (1984). *Caring: A feminine approach to ethics and moral education*. Berkeley, CA: University of California Press.

Palaiologou, I. (2014). 'Do we hear what children want to say?' Ethical praxis when choosing research tools with children under five. *Early Child Development and Care, 184*(5), 689–705. https://doi.org/10.1080/03004430.2013.809341

Pálmadóttir, H., & Einarsdóttir, J. (2016). Video observations of children's perspectives on their lived experiences: Challenges in the relations between the researcher and children. *European Early Childhood Education Research Journal, 24*(5), 721–733. https://doi.org/10.1080/13502 93X.2015.1062662

Powell, M. A., Fitzgerald, R., Taylor, N., & Graham, A. (2012). *International literature review: Ethical issues in undertaking research with children and young people.* Lismore, Australia/ Dunedin, New Zealand: Southern Cross University, Centre for Children and Young People/ University of Otago, Centre for Research on Children and Families. Retrieved from http:// epubs.scu.edu.au/ccyp_pubs/40/

Powell, M. A., Graham, A., Taylor, N., Newell, S., & Fitzgerald, R. (2011). *Building capacity for ethical research with children and young people: An international research project to examine the ethical issues and challenges in undertaking research with and for children in different majority and minority world contexts.* Dunedin, New Zealand/Lismore, Australia: University of Otago, Centre for Research on Children and Families/Southern Cross University, Centre for Children and Young People. Retrieved from http://www.childwatch.uio.no

Powell, M. A., Graham, A., & Truscott, J. (2016). Ethical research involving children: Facilitating reflexive engagement. *Qualitative Research Journal, 16*(2), 197–208. https://doi.org/10.1108/ QRJ-07-2015-0056

Robson, S. (2011). Producing and using video data in the early years: Ethical questions and practical consequences in research with young children. *Children & Society, 25*(3), 179–189. https:// doi.org/10.1111/j.1099-0860.2009.00267.x

Salamon, A. (2015). Ethical symmetry in participatory research with infants. *Early Child Development and Care, 185*(6), 1016–1030. https://doi.org/10.1080/03004430.2014.975224

Sparrman, A. (2014). Access and gatekeeping in researching children's sexuality: Mess in ethics and methods. *Sexuality and Culture, 18*(2), 291–309. https://doi.org/10.1007/ s12119-013-9198-x

Spriggs, M., & Gillam, L. (2017). Ethical complexities in child co-research. *Research Ethics.* Published on-line ahead of print. https://doi.org/10.1177/1747016117750207

Spyrou, S. (2016). Troubling children's voices in research. In F. Esser, M. S. Baader, T. Betz, & B. Hungerland (Eds.), *Reconceptualising agency and childhood: New perspectives in childhood studies* (pp. 105–118). Oxon, UK: Routledge.

Sumsion, J., Bradley, B., Stratigos, T., & Elwick, S. (2014). 'Baby cam' and participatory research with infants: A case study of critical reflexivity. In M. Fleer & A. Ridgway (Eds.), *Visual methodologies and digital tools for researching with young children* (Vol. 10, pp. 169–191). Cham, Switzerland: Springer.

Truscott, J. (2018). Toward a pedagogy for nature-based play in early childhood settings. In A. Cutter-MacKenzie et al. (Eds.), *Research handbook on childhood nature.* Cham, Switzerland: Springer. https://doi.org/10.1007/978-3-319-51949-4_82-1

United Nations. (1989). *Convention on the rights of the child.* Geneva, Switzerland: Office of the High Commissioner for Human Rights.

United Nations (UN) Committee on the Rights of the Child (CRC). (2009). The Right of the Child to be Heard: General comment No.12: United Nations.

von Benzon, N. (2013). 'I fell out of a tree and broke my neck': Acknowledging fantasy in children's research contributions. *Children's Geographies, 13*(3), 330–342. https://doi.org/10.108 0/14733285.2013.829662

Willumsen, E., Hugaas, J. V., & Studsrød, I. (2014). The child as co-researcher: Moral and epistemological issues in childhood research. *Ethics and Social Welfare, 8*(4), 332–349.

Chapter 3
"You Have to Sign Here:" A Hermeneutic Reading of Young Children's Politeness Play

Francesca Pase

Introduction

As part of a larger research project on cultural variations in young children's under-standings of politeness, I conducted a pilot study with two young American chil-dren. I visited their home to observe the presence or absence of politeness as the children and their family went through their daily routines. When I entered their home, before beginning my observations, I went through the informed assent proto-col required by my university's institutional review board. When I designed this study, I saw the Institutional Review Board (IRB) protocol as something inconse-quential to "get out of the way." However, the process of negotiating this assent turned out to provide a richer case of children's engagement with politeness than my observations that followed. When the children engaged with the IRB they approached it as both a serious document and a vehicle for play. According to Gadamer (1960/1989), "play has a special relation to what is serious… the player himself knows that play is only play and that it exists in a world determined by the serious-ness of purposes. But he does not know this in such a way that, as a player, he actu-ally intends this relation to seriousness" (p. 106). In this paper I use an analysis of this assent play to open a wider discussion into ethical, epistemological, and practi-cal considerations of conducting qualitative studies with young children.

F. Pase (✉)
University of Georgia, Athens, GA, USA
e-mail: francesca.pase@uga.edu

© Springer Nature Switzerland AG 2019
A. Eckhoff (ed.), *Participatory Research with Young Children*, Educating the Young Child 17, https://doi.org/10.1007/978-3-030-19365-2_3

The Visit

I arrived at the children's house with the children's parents, Nate and Shelby. When we pulled into the driveway, the children, Rebekah (age 6) and Dixon (age 4), were getting out of the car of their grandmother, who had driven them home from school. The six of us entered the house together, the children bubbling over with stories of their day as their parents asked questions about school. As the household settled, I put my bags down in the kitchen and shuffled my IRB paperwork.

Shelby sat down at the kitchen table and I began the informed consent process with her. This included handing her a stack of documents as well as reading her a recruitment script approved by my university's institutional review board:

> If you are interested in participating in this research project, I will observe interactions between you and your child(ren) both in and outside of your home. This research project requires four observations each lasting no more than three hours each and three interviews with your child(ren). I will photograph and video-record your interactions with your children, your spouse, or others. I will allow you to view all video and photographic records before they are presented. Any video or photographic data that you do not want included in the final project will be destroyed within 30 days of your initial access. I will also provide snacks for you and your family during observations. I request a list of potential allergens before you or your child(ren) enter my home and before I enter your home with any food items. I will also provide a list of ingredients for your approval before I bring food into your home or you and/or your children enter my home.

The children stood quietly next to their mother as I read. Because the children were too young for a written assent form, I received permission from the IRB to do a verbal assent. I read the approved assent script to the children:

> We are doing a research study to find out how children think about politeness. We are asking you to be in the study because you are a child between the age of 2 and 10. If you agree to be in the study, you will be asked to draw pictures, plan a party for your parents, and answer questions about politeness. You will also allow me to take your picture and make videos of you and your family talking and playing. I will also ask if I can have any pictures you draw and I will audio record our talking. Being in this study will help grown-ups understand how kids think about politeness.

As I read, Rebekah stood still with her head cocked up toward me while Dixon jumped up and down behind her saying "Yes! Yes! Yes!" As soon as I finished the last line, Rebekah began to jump up and down too and said, "Yes! I know what politeness is. It means being nice!" Dixon agreed. If my goal was to learn how these children define politeness, I could have packed up my equipment and gone home. I had an answer: Politeness is niceness. But I did not pack up and go home.

As I was setting up my camera Dixon, the 4-year-old, came over to me and said, "Do you want to come in my hidee space?" (an area behind their loft beds). I said yes, and he showed me a piece of paper and replied, "You have to sign this first. Or you have to pay a dollar." I signed. He then crossed my name out, telling me, "You didn't do it right. But that's OK. I'll do it for you." He then scribbled a signature on the paper, and then continued to go around the room, asking his parents and older sister to also sign.

As I was setting up my camera and microphone, Dixon came over back to me and directed me to sign again. My hands full of equipment, I said, "Sorry. I forgot how to sign my own name." Dixon nodded understandingly and told me that I could use a check instead of a signature, as he drew a line through my name on his permission sheet. Dixon carried this "informed consent" form with him for the majority of the evening, periodically asking each of us for signatures. At one point there was a discussion about whether or not the dog should be allowed to sign the form to which Dixon replied "No." Rebekah said the dog wasn't allowed in the hidee space because the dog breaks things. This led into a family conversation about space and who can be in what spaces in what contexts, and with whose permission and consent.

I had anticipated to lead the children through a series of tasks and questions that would elucidate their understanding of the concept of politeness. But as it turned out, throughout the evening, beginning with Dixon's asking me to sign his permission document, the children were less passive research subjects than co-constructors of the research process.

The Institutional Review Board

When I designed this study, I did not consider the potential impact the IRB process would have on my data generation. The dialogic relationship between myself, the children, their parents, my academic institution, and our shared conceptions of research were joined together by Dixon's playful version of the research consent process. In this moment of play a bureaucratic document was transformed into a meaningful tool for discussions of consent and more generally of ethics and politeness.

The IRB process was founded on the goal of protecting vulnerable populations from being harmed by research and based on the principles of respect, beneficence, nonmaleficence, and justice. This is similar to research ethics protocols worldwide. IRBs follow the ethical guidelines established in the Belmont report, whose key principles are to "Treat individuals as autonomous agents," "Protect persons with diminished autonomy," "Do unto others as you would have them do unto you," and "Distribute the risks and potential benefits of research equally among those who may benefit from the research (Amdur & Bankert, 2010, p. 19).The most important consideration for researchers when planning a study is: Can what I'm doing harm my participants? How can I reasonably mitigate this harm?

Harm is not always physical. Kellett (2010) asks researchers to consider the unique position of children in the process of informed consent. Informed consent must be an ongoing process, but children may not be in the position to consider future implications of their participation in research. This is particularly true if photographic or video data are generated by the study. For example, a 4-year-old child may find it exciting to watch a video of himself singing a song about potty training. That same child 10 years later might feel humiliated to have others view this video. In order to mitigate some of the possible complications of informed consent that arise with children, I felt it was important to be as clear as possible with the children in my study. This meant including in the assent instructions that the focus of my study was politeness.

Participatory Research

"Participant observation" is a term ethnographers use to describe their involvement in the lives of their informants. In addition to observing and asking questions, ethnographers participate in activities with their informants. These activities could be something as formal as a sacred ritual, or as informal as preparing the day's meals. Because I was visiting the children's home at the end of their school day, I understood that I would be participating in this family's informal ritual of coming home from school.

Participatory research differs from participant observation in significant ways. Participants in a participatory research study are often considered to be co-researchers; they may assist in the development of research questions, methods, analysis, and sometimes even in the final write-up and dissemination of a study (Cohen, Manion, & Morrison, 2011). The participatory research approach acknowledges and then seeks in various ways to ameliorate power differences between the researcher and the researched. Children usually have little control over major life decisions such as where they live, with whom they associate, how and where they spend their days. Their voices are often not heard; their behaviors are rarely understood on their own terms. They must follow sometimes seemingly arbitrary rules to which many adults do not adhere. In the schools, which are their places of work, they have little to say about policies or what they will be doing. Participatory research is a valuable tool for facilitating an environment where children become agents of change within the context of their own communities.

Participatory research with children problematizes the power adults wield over children and deficit views of children. It emphasizes research *with* children instead of research *on* or *for* children (Kellett, 2010).

My study was not a traditional participatory research project in that it did not begin with my reaching an agreement with the children to study a problem of concern to them, or with a goal of changing something about their lives. And yet this when this is study approached hermeneutically it incorporates aspects of traditional participatory research. Dixon's IRB play shifted the focus of my analysis away from "appropriate behaviour" as a general topic to discussions of consent and permission to access space.

Hermeneutics in Research

Hermeneutics is an approach to understanding that emphasizes human experience and relationships. Hermeneutics, much like traditional participatory research, is founded on the idea that we are all co-participants in any endeavor that seeks understanding. However, unlike most forms of participatory research, hermeneutics does not prescribe a method that seeks definitive conclusions or that leads directly to addressing a problem. Instead, hermeneutics emphasizes the complexity of human experience and beseeches us to continue to seek understanding despite the possible futility of our endeavor.

Gadamer's work emphasizes the dialogical nature of interpretation, with attention to historical and linguistic modes of understanding. Although Gadamer's project was focused on the dialogical nature of interpretation, this does not preclude attention to gestures and embodied communication. His project emphasizes a necessity for openness to all discourse, be it written, spoken, sensory, or visual (Moules, McCaffrey, & Laing, 2015; Vilhauer, 2010). Human experience is not limited to the linguistic, as all pathways to understanding require negotiation.

Gadamer made clear that he did not want his work to be thought of as a *method* of interpretation:

> My revival of the expression hermeneutics, with its long tradition, has apparently led to some misunderstandings. I did not intend to produce a manual for guiding understanding …. I did not wish to elaborate a system of rules to describe, let alone direct, the methodical procedure of the human sciences. Nor was it my aim to investigate the theoretical foundation of work in these fields in order to put my findings to practical ends. If there is any practical consequence of the present investigation, it certainly has nothing to do with an unscientific "commitment"; instead, it is concerned with the "scientific" integrity of acknowledging the commitment involved in all understanding. (Gadamer, 1960/1989, p. xxv).

Gadamer was interested in a quest for truth. Truth itself is not attached to a particular method. The process of searching for truth, rather than truth itself is emphasized in hermeneutics (Van Manen, 2016). Gadamerian hermeneutics is interested in the process of interpretation, not in the outcomes.

A hermeneutic approach to the informed consent and assent process would begin with an understanding that the rules of consent emerge out of the relationships we have with each other, within the context of particular social conventions and discourses. The hermeneutic circle refers to the ongoing interaction between subject and object, past and present. Gadamer explains this relationship as the I/Thou relationship. When two people are in dialog they bring with themselves not only their own interpretations of a particular phenomenon, but their knowledge of past experiences with the phenomena. This is their subjective relationship with tradition. As one person (the I) interacts with another (the Thou), they mutually influence one another. In order to understand the "I/Thou" relationship we need to acknowledge the history and tradition that each interlocutor brings with them in to the act of interpretation.[1] As Gadamer writes: "What is… understood is not the Thou but the truth of what the Thou says to us. I mean specifically the truth that becomes visible to me only through the Thou, and only by my letting myself be told something by it" (Gadamer, 1960/1989, p. xxxii).

Personal histories are written in relation to experience, and then constantly altered through the reflective process. In the context of this study, my past experiences with and understandings of politeness entered into a hermeneutic circle with the children's experiences and understandings. Dixon and Rebekah came to the study with their own understandings of politeness, understandings that informed how they should behave toward me in a study. They also had preconceived ideas about what it means to be in a study, and how they should behave with an adult. And then, as they interacted with me and the informed consent process, their understandings of research, consent, and politeness met mine and in the process were changed, as were mine.

Hermeneutics is inherently pedagogical because it recognizes the constant learning and reflection that arises out of human experience. It requires an openness to the other, a willingness to accept the affects others have on ourselves. As we engaged together in this research project, the children and I were both teaching and learning about politeness, consent, and research. The findings from this study emerged from this hermeneutic engagement.

According to Gadamer (1960/1989), thinking hermeneutically "will make conscious the prejudices governing our own understanding" (p. 309). Prejudices are neither good nor bad, but essentially neutral. They are neutral because they are an intrinsic component of human experience. Prejudice is a form of pre-understanding; prejudices are not a threat to validity, but instead the position we occupy as we enter the hermeneutic circle. Prejudices are what make us different from one another. According to Moules et al. (2015), "the main point (of dialog) is the creative interaction from difference" (p. 13). In this study I needed to attend to the moments of difference, where my foreknowledge of politeness appeared to be different than the children's.

---

[1] A special thank you to Steven Binnig for providing the design for the hermenutic circle on pg. 43

Research Design

I was trained in anthropology, specifically ethnography. Ethnographic research is primarily focused on people of non-Western backgrounds. Children are rarely described as primary sources in ethnographic research, although much ethnographic research has focused on modes of child rearing and enculturation (LeVine, 2007). I find a research approach that focuses on children without including children's voices and acknowledging their role as co-producers of knowledge problematic because children are part of culture and socialization is not a unidirectional experience. Adults do not unilaterally experience and transmit culture onto children. Socialization and enculturation is a reciprocal process that occurs between children and adults.

I view children's culture as distinct from, but not outside of adult culture. From an ethnographic perspective, as an adult, I view myself as a "cultural outsider" so I approached the design of the study as an ethnographer would: I positioned the children as "informants." I would be the patient listener who would make space for children to tell me their experiences with and understandings of politeness. I would do this without directly asking them questions about "politeness," and instead by creating an environment that would require them to behave in polite ways. I saw my role in the study as a kind of translator or mediator between children's and adults' worlds of meaning.

Phenomenology and ethnography are often used in conjunction to explore complex cultural constructs (Geertz, 1973). According to Good (2012), the blending of ethnography and the phenomenological tradition is useful for "demonstrating the power of this rich, largely philosophical body of writing to frame ethnographic explorations of the lived, local worlds, cultivated perspectives, and modes of embodiment that form the basis for knowing and acting in distinctive cultural settings" (p. 25). Phenomenology along with traditional ethnographic methods adapted for research with children helped provide insights into children's lived experiences within their cultural world.

I constructed the interviews for my study using what Seidman (2013) refers to as the three stage phenomenological interview. "The method combines life-history interviewing … and focused, in-depth interviewing informed by assumptions drawn from phenomenology" (Seidman, 2013, p. 12). This interview method emphasizes open-ended questions that are provided in three separate stages, each interview is conducted 2–3 weeks apart. The first interview is primarily reflective and establishes the context of the informant's lived experience. The second interview protocol was written after I generated data from the first interview. The purpose of the second interview is to explore specific experiences related to the phenomena that were addressed in the first interview. The third interview protocol is reflective, asking participants to address those experiences described in the second interview to the contexts provided in the first interview. I adapted the standard protocol by borrowing from "the mosaic" approach as described by Clark and Moss (2011). My goal was to combine visual and verbal prompts and responses so that the children could communicate in a variety of symbolic ways. The following is my interview protocol for the first interview:

Interview Protocol #1
1. Show the children a photograph of a child receiving a gift and ask them: What is happening here? Have you ever gotten a gift? What did you do when you got the gift?
2. Show the child a photograph of a child sitting in front of a broken vase and a baseball and ask the child open ended questions about the photo such as: What just happened here? Have you ever broken anything/seen someone break something accidentally? What happened next?
3. Ask: Have you ever been to a party where you had to dress up special? Will you draw a picture of yourself at that party? Can you tell me about this drawing?

My goal with this protocol was to illicit responses about polite behavior in a variety of contexts. The drawings and questions were intended to invite reflections on contexts that elicit polite behavior. The final two questions were designed to be jumping off points where the children could tell me about polite behaviors that are employed in social settings.

In this design I adhered to the Husseralian approach of "bracketing." Bracketing is an approach used in phenomenology to decenter the researcher's assumptions: Husserl used bracketing as a way to approach phenomena without imposing theoretical assumptions. Qualitative researchers apply bracketing at various stages of data collection and generation and analysis. Though it may not apply in all contexts, the strength in bracketing is in that it allows researchers "to reveal ourselves as our own best critic" (Vagle, Hughes, & Durbin, 2009, p. 348) because it forces the researcher to narrow their scope and focus on the experience of conducting research with others instead of jumping to explanations.

"Phenomenological inquiry begins with silence" (Psathas, 1973). However, the informed consent process did not allow for me to be silent. When I read the informed assent protocol to the children, which included the explanation that this was a study of politeness, my chance to be silent on the topic of politeness was shattered. This explanation positioned me as "the politeness lady", an expert on politeness who was there to test them. I attempted to bracket my understandings of politeness, but the children were watching me and taking cues about polite behavior from me.

And yet, when viewed hermeneutically, this is not necessarily a problem. Gadamer argues that all processes of interpretation are a negotiation between "I" and "Thou." There is no distinction between the subject and the object, because understanding is a bidirectional process where individuals are simultaneously acting on and being acted on by one another (Gadamer, 1960/1989). Though it wasn't intended as such, the IRB protocol became a way for the children and me to play at being polite and in the process to change our understandings.

For example, here is an excerpt from Rebekah's answer to the first prompt on the protocol, a photograph of a child receiving a gift:

F: So when you get a gift, what do you do?

R: You usually smile and you're kind of excited about what it's going to be.

F: What is the best gift you've ever gotten?

R: Probably my whole kit of art. I can show you where it is, it's inside. So once you do (conduct your interview with) Dixon I can show you it's in my room. I might not be able to find it, because I have this humungous container with all of my stuff. It's still, it still has stuff that needs to go and it's already almost overflowing.

F: Oh my gosh! I like art.

R: I hardly every do it because of TV and Ipad but.. .

F: Who gave you that gift?

R: It was my Mimi. So I had my sixth birthday and she gave that kit to me. And it even has a little notebook that goes with it.

F: Neat, I would love to see that. After you got it, did you do anything else?

R: I said "Thank you."

On the surface this structured this line of questioning seems not to have provided me with any rich insights into Rebekah's understandings of politeness. From showing her a picture of a gift, I learned she is excited by gifts and she believes she should say thank you when she receives a gift.

However, from a hermeneutic perspective, viewing Rebekah as a knowing participant in a study about politeness, we can see deeper meanings in these data. Rebekah took my prompt as an invitation to playing at politeness. When she talked about showing me her art supplies, she was inviting me into her room. Much like Dixon's IRB play, Rebekah graciously granted me access to her private space, something I officiously requested via the informed consent and assent processes.

Although hermeneutics is inherently pedagogical and can be therapeutic, there is no distinction between subject and object and participants meet on an equal plane. Neither participant is teacher or therapist. Gadamerian Hermeneutics emphasizes the importance of decentering the power between interlocutors (Moules et al., 2015). In this interview, both Rebekah and I were playing at politeness even though we were not directly addressing politeness.

In order to decenter the power, all voices must be heard. I spoke through the IRB, and I told the children that their understanding of politeness might be different than mine. They heard. This provided a space for them to help us both understand similarities and differences in our understandings of politeness. They participated in my inquiry and I participated in theirs. Aware that I was interested in their understanding of politeness, Rebekah did less *telling* me about politeness, than enacting it. Just as I was attempting to facilitate data generation with her, she was guiding me with her words and her behavior to understand what she understands it means to be polite.

Approaching Dixon's IRB Play Hermeneutically

I am guided as a researcher by the assumption that "kids are smart, they make sense, and they want to have a good life" (Graue & Walsh, 1998, p. 57), but I no longer consider myself their interpreters. In this study of politeness, we were co-interpreters. When Dixon approached me with his paper and his crayons and asked me to sign my name to get access to his "hidee space," he was playing at politeness.

According to Vilhauer (2010), "Gadamer's concept of play carries with it an implicit attack on the traditional conception of the human being as the independent 'subject' who observes and knows (by making properly corresponding pictures or representations of them in his mind) the alien "objects" of the world" (p. 26). When Dixon witnessed and participated in the process of informed consent he became engaged with the IRB and its formal protocols. Dixon's play here suggests that he understood that seeking and granting permission for access are aspects of politeness. It is possible that his sister had become angry with him for entering her space without his permission. He may have carried with him this idea that it is not nice, and therefore not polite, to acquire access without consent. When we were engaged in the process of informed consent, Dixon learned a new way to request and provide access to space.

However, in the process of informed consent I entered his house with a sense of power and authority. I carried with me official documents that his mother carefully read over and signed. As much as the informed consent documents are designed to protect the rights of participants, they also are designed to protect the researcher and the sponsoring institutions. They also function as a kind of contract: If I follow the terms of the contract and yet harm were to come to the children as a result of their participation, my sponsoring institution and I would be protected from potential litigation. The children's mother, Shelby, who is familiar with human subjects research protocols in the medical field, was aware of the litigious implications of the IRB process. The seriousness with which I requested and Shelby gave her permission by signing the form was communicated through our gestures, gaze, and tone of voice.

This interaction had an impact on Dixon's understanding of politeness. Usually when a guest, such as a friend of his parents enters his home, they do not bring with them documents and begin the social interaction with a somber signing ceremony. The verbal assent process then made Dixon aware that I was there not for a social call, but to learn about his and his sister's understandings of politeness. His subsequent IRB play was his response to these issues of politeness and power, a response which disrupted and, in the end, enriched my understanding.

When I reviewed my field notes and videos from that day I was particularly drawn to the moment when Dixon crosses out of my signature. He asked for my signature twice, both times indicating that I could not sign my own name. This behavior is not congruent with the understanding of politeness I had when I began this study. Nor is it congruent with previous research on politeness: crossing out my name and telling me that I was not doing it correctly was what Brown and Levinson

(1987) would describe as a "face threatening act." It highlighted my incompetence at a task expected from every adult.

However, I do not read this moment as Dixon highlighting my incompetence. Rather, I think he was creating a problem (my incorrect signature) that provided him with the opportunity to step in and be kind to me by assisting me with the process of signing. In order for Dixon to be polite/kind there had to be some sort of problem that he could help me with. In his play he created that problem so he could demonstrate his knowledge of politeness. It then became my job to be receptive to this way of conceptualizing politeness, as a way of being helpful and considerate. This reinforces some prior research on politeness, mainly that it is a collective or team performance (Goffman, 1959), with the added component of play as understanding (Vilhauer, 2010).

If, following Goffman, we were to view Dixon and his family as a team, we can interpret Dixon's act of kindness as him taking responsibility for his family's hospitality to a guest. My entering this frame by holding out an officious document introduced a level of bureaucratic formality that caused what Goffman would call a social breach. Dylan repaired this breach by asking me to sign his form, and in this way incorporating my performance of official researcher into a family game.

After I expressed my inability to sign my name, Dixon saved face by suggesting I put a check instead of writing my name. My saying "I forgot how to sign my own name" was read by Dixon as a request for assistance. Whether he took my words at face value believing I was having trouble, or as a playful performance of inability, he responded by performing a polite act. He was being kind to me when he offered an alternative to a signature and corrected my mistake.

Although Dixon may not have had an existing framework for conceptualizing the roles, rights, and responsibilities of "researcher" and "research subject," the IRB interactions at the beginning of my visit introduced a level of formality that he may have seen as inappropriate for an introduction between hosts and a guest. We can interpret his IRB play as a kind of good-hearted parody of my IRB protocol, a parody which eased the tension while at the same time engaging sincerely with my request to understand his understanding of what it means to act politely. By playfully taking on my role of the form-toting research, Dylan took the pressure off of me, allowing me to relax and to exchange my formal role as researcher for becoming part of the team.

Approaching Dixon's actions hermeneutically, I understand our interaction as our participating in the process of understanding politeness together, each of us bringing our past understandings of politeness to our interact. According to Schwandt (2015) hermeneutics "aims to explicate a way of understanding (or a mode of experience in which we understand) through which truth is disclosed and communicated... understanding is an event or process that one participates in" (p. 144).

These are a few of many possible interpretations of Dixon's IRB play. It is a fusion of what was produced when my foreknowledge about politeness and childhood met Dixon's foreknowledge about politeness and adults in a moment of data generation. Critics of Gadamer claim that "fusion amounts to the projection of one's own meaning or interpretation onto that of the Other, which results in the inter-preter's ethically suspect denial of the other's difference, and a failure to recognize the true uniqueness of the Other's point of view that is central to his individuality and personhood" (Vilhauer, 2010, p. xiii). However, according to Gadamerian hermeneutics, we are all trying to make sense of a world that was already consti-tuted and interpreted for us before we begin our inquiries. Within this paradigm, our job as researchers is not to claim to be developing new knowledge but instead to unveil what already exists at a given moment in time. This can only be done through interaction, with the points of view of researcher and researched equally important in this process. We, as researchers can choose to acknowledge that children we study are equal participants in meaning making, or we can close ourselves off to new understandings.

Participatory Aspects of Assent and Consent

Informed assent is vital in our work with children. However, the bureaucratic pro-cesses of informed consent and assent are designed by adults, in the world of adults, for adults. The IRB process requires researchers to use "age appropriate" language, but without adequate attention to what it would take to make the research process meaningful to a young child.

It is our job as researchers to ensure that consent is an ongoing process between researcher and participant. However, the IRB informed consent process was not designed for children. Children have elaborate systems of meaning, just like adults. The informed consent process is not inherently meaningful for children. Consent must be addressed in a way that is meaningful to our participants. My assent script was not written in a way to be meaningful to Dixon, and yet his subsequent IRB play was his attempt to make the IRB process meaningful. If the purpose of informed assent is to help children understand what it means to agree to be part of a research project, we need to do view the process not as a negotiation to be completed before the research begins, but instead as an ongoing engagement, in which the children have a perspective and a voice. The informed assent process can be viewed as a legalistic ritual, as something to "get out of the way," or it can be reimagined as a meaningful tool to open conversations with children about asking and giving con-sent, and other performances of ritualized behavior that facilitate social interactions.

Questions for Reflection
- How can one approach an informed assent document hermeneutically?
- What are some ways that Gadamerian hermeneutics can help us think about the IRB protocol in relation to young deaf and preverbal children?
- What are some ethical considerations of purposefully incorporating play in the informed assent process?

- Many of the children we do research with are members of minoritized or culturally and linguistically marginalized populations. Many of the theories that inform our practice as researchers, including hermeneutics, are grounded in or responses to Western philosophy. How do Western concepts of "ethics" and "self/other" inform our practice as researchers when we work with children?

References

Amdur, R. J., & Bankert, E. A. (2010). *Institutional review board: Member handbook*. Burlington, MA: Jones & Bartlett Publishers.

Brown, P., & Levinson, S. C. (1987). *Politeness: Some universals in language usage* (Vol. 4, 2nd ed.). Cambridge, UK: Cambridge University Press.

Clark, A., & Moss, P. (2011). *Listening to young children: The mosaic approach*. London, UK: Jessica Kingsley Publishers.

Cohen, L., Manion, L., & Morrison, K. (2011). *Research methods in education* (7th ed.). London, UK/New York, NY: Routledge.

Gadamer, H.-G. (1960/1989). *Truth and method* (J. Weinsheimer & D. Marshall, Trans.). London, UK: Bloomsbury.

Geertz, C. (1973). *The interpretation of cultures: Selected essays*. New York, NY: Basic books.

Goffman, E. (1959). *The presentation of self in everyday life*. New York, NY: Doubleday.

Good, B. J. (2012). Phenomenology, psychoanalysis, and subjectivity in Java. *Ethos, 40*(1), 24–36.

Graue, M. E., & Walsh, D. J. (1998). *Studying children in context: Theories, methods, and ethics*. Thousand Oaks, CA: Sage Publications.

Kellett, M. (2010). *Rethinking children and research: Attitudes in contemporary society*. London, UK: Bloomsbury Publishing.

LeVine, R. A. (2007). Ethnographic studies of childhood: A historical overview. *American Anthropologist, 109*(2), 247–260.

Moules, N., McCaffrey, G., & Laing, C. (2015). *Conducting hermeneutic research: From philosophy to practice* (Vol. 19). New York, NY: Peter Lang Publishing.

Psathas, G. (1973). *Phenomenological sociology: Issues and applications*. New York, NY: Wiley.

Schwandt, T. A. (2015). *The Sage dictionary of qualitative inquiry* (2nd ed.). Thousand Oaks, CA: Sage Publications.

Seidman, I. (2013). *Interviewing as qualitative research: A guide for researchers in education and the social sciences*. New York, NY: Teachers College Press.

Vagle, M. D., Hughes, H. E., & Durbin, D. J. (2009). Remaining skeptical: Bridling for and with one another. *Field Methods, 21*(4), 347–367.

Van Manen, M. (2016). *Phenomenology of practice: Meaning-giving methods in phenomenological research and writing*. Abingdon, UK: Routledge.

Vilhauer, M. (2010). *Gadamer's ethics of play: Hermeneutics and the other*. Lanham, MD: Lexington Books.

Part II
Exploring Children's Agency Through Engagement in Participatory Research Practices

Chapter 4
Participatory Research Interviewing Practices with Children

Krista M. Griffin

Introduction

As Robbie left his third-grade elementary classroom and walked toward the office, he knew he was going to talk to someone about reading. Reading was not really his thing. He wondered why anyone wanted to talk to him about it. As a striving reader, Robbie's desire to talk about reading with a researcher was not high on his "this is going to be fun" list. It sounded like something he was required to do because the adults told him to. As his teacher walked him down to the student support services room where I was, a room that was familiar to him, I was sitting on the floor, preparing to conduct research with Robbie and other students on their use of reading strategies. The moment he opened the office door and saw me sitting relaxed on the floor, his resistance and reserve seemed to melt away. Using a goofy, friendly voice, introductions were made, and Robbie did not hesitate to sit right next to me— shoulder-to-shoulder. A delightful conversation followed where Robbie shared his love of all things dragon, even dragon books. Despite reading below grade-level expectations, Robbie shared with me how he constructed meaning from complex texts that included specialized vocabulary. He shared how he was the dragon expert in his class. That conversation generated rich data that helped answer my literacy research question while the participant engaged in a mutually respectful conversation situated within a natural environment. Robbie, with his advanced knowledge of dragons, had expert power in the conversation. His expert power equalized some of my positional power as the adult in the conversation. His engagement in the research process demonstrates how children have valuable experiences and perspectives that equip them to be active participants in the qualitative research process.

Research *with* children requires an ideological and methodological shift from research *on* children. Children have the language skills to actively participate in the

K. M. Griffin (✉)
Metropolitan State University- Denver, Denver, CO, USA
e-mail: kfiedle3@msudenver.edu

© Springer Nature Switzerland AG 2019
A. Eckhoff (ed.), *Participatory Research with Young Children*, Educating
the Young Child 17, https://doi.org/10.1007/978-3-030-19365-2_4

data generation of qualitative research, but researchers may need to listen differently, negotiate power respectfully, and structure the interview and the data-generation environment strategically. They need to consider the theory(ies) behind their research decisions, and the ethical considerations of researching with children. In the following chapter, I lay out how these considerations are the forces behind different participatory methods that support research with children and the power of the shoulder-to-shoulder and walk-around interviewing methods. The vignettes and data research referenced in this chapter are based on five participatory studies that I have conducted exploring various aspects of early literacy, identity, and motivation.

Theoretical Beliefs

All research decisions are grounded in the researchers' conscious or unconscious theoretical beliefs and values. Constructionist researchers believe "all knowledge, and therefore all meaningful reality as such is contingent upon human practices, being constructed in and out of interaction between human beings and their world, and developed and transmitted within an essentially social context" (Crotty, 2008, p. 42). The key concept here is that data generation requires an interaction between the researcher and the child participant in their world. The question becomes what kinds of interactions and practices are best suited for developing knowledge with young participants. Creswell (2007) believes the purpose of the researcher is to understand or interpret the meanings others have about the world. Constructionist researchers posit that we generate our own knowledge and meaning from our experiences. Hence, constructionism clearly supports my beliefs on how best to conduct meaningful research with children.

Research *with* children requires an ideological and methodological shift from research *on* children. As we consider the history of child research, it was common practice for children were tested and observed in laboratory conditions. The perspective of the day was that children were "unable to understand or describe their world and life experiences due to developmental immaturity" (Coyne, 1998, p. 410). Only those considered "experts" (e.g. doctors, teachers, psychologists) and more recently, parents, were interviewed, and they were considered proxies for the children. This substitution of the adult view of the child's world for the child's view was accepted as close enough to the child's actual view. Although perhaps cynical, researching children seems reminiscent of animal observational research. Greene and Hill (2005) support this idea by stating, "It is evident that the predominant emphasis has been on children as the objects of research rather than children as subjects, on child-related outcomes rather than child-related processes and on child variables rather than children as persons" (p. 1). This view of children as objects came from the idea that through scientific research, researchers could expect to know the child through "rigorous examination of its properties under controlled circumstances" (Hogan, 2005, p. 25).

This important shift in the role of children in research aligns with the shift they have experienced in society and should not be minimized (Pillay, 2014; Pufall & Unsworth, 2004; Shriberg, Wynne, Briggs, Bartucci, & Lombardo, 2011; Smith, 2002; Stainton Rogers, 2004). This concept was affirmed by the United Nations Convention on the Rights of the Child in 1989; basic rights for children were acknowledged and this generated discourse applying child rights to research. Research concerning all facets of children's lives is essential. "We need to understand our children-their lives, their circumstances, their needs and the services and supports required to meet their needs" (Dublin Department of Children and Youth Affairs, 2012).

As qualitative researchers, we are inviting researchers to take the next step forward in honoring children's experiences and move again from children as subjects, to children as participants. We want to move far beyond Bronfenbrenner's famous quotation, "the present development psychology to a large extent seems to be the science of strange behavior of children in strange situations with strange adults, analyzed within time periods as short as possible" (1979, p. 33).

When we consider the role children can play in the research process, we can easily understand why contemporary researchers reject the idea that it is methodologically appropriate for adults to speak for children. Alderson (1992) agrees, saying that theories put forth by adults are mere attempts to describe something close to the child's actual world, while Clark (2011) descriptively labeled this "ventriloquizing" children. Mahon Glendinning, Clarke and Craig (1996) stated that "On the contrary, children's views can and ought to be taken seriously" (p. 146). We want to ethically co-construct understanding of behavior of children in their authentic environments as inquiring adults knowing that this will require strategic time investments.

Children have the expressive language skills to actively participate in data generation of qualitative research. They are skillful communicators and can employ a broad range of visual and verbal ways to communicate. Adults serve as facilitators, providing different opportunities for children to express themselves. 8. Children not only have the abilities to communicate with adults but they also **want** to communicate with adults. As any observer of children will tell you, children in classrooms where observations are happening continually seek to engage in conversations with the observer, and ask questions such as, "What are you doing? Who are you? What are you writing down?" When I review my observation transcriptions from research done with children from ages five to eighteen, I see repeated examples of these types of questions. "Are you a teacher?" many of them wonder. "Why do you want to watch us?" they ask. "Are you writing down **everything** we say and do?" they inquire, bemusedly.

Graue and Walsh (1998) describe the unique relationship between the reflexive researcher and the child as one that is upside down because the child research participant is being asked to teach the adult researcher. In this realm, it is understood that "young children are experts in their own lives" (Langsted, 1994, p. 22).

Although all adults were once children, this does not mean they share the experiences and perspectives of all children, and because they are no longer children, cannot adequately analyze or write about the thoughts, motives, or experiences that comprise the child's lived experiences especially if they do not try to access and capture the child participant's own words. For example, when researching what motivates children to read, it was not enough for me to watch children's reading practices, but it was essential for me to ask children why they read or why they didn't read. I had to put aside my own adult researcher assumptions and ask the children the questions and truly listen to their answers.

An example of this was when a student told me he didn't like to read if he had to do book reports afterward (Motivation Study, 2015). I immediately projected my own thoughts about how book reports are often unmeaningful busy work and replied: "Yeah, book reports are the worst." The student looked at me strangely and replied: "No, it isn't that I don't like book reports. It is that when we have to do book reports, the teacher writes down the page numbers we have to read at home that night. I don't like being told how many pages we have to read, and she only does that when we do book reports." Instead of projecting my feelings about book reports, a better response would have been for me to ask a follow-up question, like "Why do book reports affect how you feel about reading?"

As I ask questions, listen intently to the answers of the children I research with, and ask follow-up questions to make sure I understand their words, it is important that I also value their experiences and perspectives. Graue and Walsh (1998) believe that researchers should operate from three assumptions when engaging in research with children and believing in their competence. The first is that children are smart. The second assumption is that children make sense. The third is that they want to lead a good life. I can not have a dismissive attitude during data generation. I have to believe that even if a child's reading skills are below abstract grade-level expectations, they are smart. I have to believe that even if I don't understand what they are saying as they describe their reading experiences, that their description is accurate, I just may need to ask follow-up questions and listen for the meaning of what was being shared in different ways than I am used to, to more fully understand the phenomenon they are sharing. And above all, I have to remember that if they don't believe in the value of reading, it is not because they don't want to lead a good life. My stance as a researcher is essential to the construction of shared knowledge.

Ethical Values

Understanding my theoretical beliefs is a good starting point, but I must also consider the ethics around research with children. Lahman (2018) thinks about research ethics this way: "If ethics is the study of how humans decide what is good and bad behavior then research ethics clearly must be the study of how researchers and the research community decide what is good and bad research behavior" (p. 3). In current qualitative research practices, it has become an ethical requirement for qualitative researchers to intentionally reflect and study data generation methods developed for and used with children. We can no longer blindly apply methods that were originally used exclusively for adults. Because of the growing research base that exists on conducting research with children, there is no excuse for researchers to use antiquated methods. An example of ethical, or "good research behavior" would be staying informed of this current practice before planning data generation methods. Once research with children has been carried out, reflecting on the research process as well as the knowledge generated is critical. Children are considered vulnerable in research, and ethics require us to protect them as we plan and carry out our research with them. It is important to remember that vulnerable does not mean incompetent or unable to contribute to research. Lahman (2018) coins the phrase "capable and competent yet vulnerable" (p. 13) when describing children and other "othered" participants.

There is also the ethical need for researchers of young children to be reflexive. Finlay and Gough (2003) tell us that the root of the word reflexive is to bend back upon itself. This can be interpreted in research with children to mean thoughtfully and critically analyzing the dynamics between the researcher and the child, especially around issues of power, and to continually monitor and contemplate the research process to ensure best research practices throughout the study, not just when the study is over. One tool I use to attempt to be reflexive is the researcher journal. The following is an excerpt from my researcher journal when I was piloting a research method I termed "shoulder-to-shoulder" while I generate reading identity data.

> *I went to second grade to begin the shoulder-to-shoulder interviews today. I started with Z. I asked him if we could sit on the ground against a wall. I deliberately chose this so that I wouldn't be tempted to turn around and look at him* [The shoulder-to-shoulder interview is based on the fact that the researcher and the child are sitting side by side, usually on the floor, in an attempt to make students more comfortable without direct eye contact]. *Z. spoke easily and seemed very comfortable as we conversed. However, because it seemed more conversational, I tended to talk much more than I normally would in an interview, adding information and sometimes almost interrupting him. I am dreading transcribing because of this, and I'll need to make sure I don't repeat this behavior on my part the next time I'm there for research. I worked with M right after Z. She was very verbose and had a twinkle in her eye. She seemed to want eye contact, however, and twisted her body to try to face me. That was not a problem for Z, who was happy to look straight ahead. I guess what it shows is that children have different needs for this, and I'll just start out shoulder to shoulder, but adapt like I did today with M. Using the books between us as a springboard for conversation was very successful and I will do that again.* (Research Journal, 2011).

I reflect on my own researcher behavior, and also on student responses, and what I might need to change based on what I notice. Generally, I can implement the changes I've determined need to be made by the next day I research, instead of reflecting after the project is over.

Research Practices

When field observation is the only method of research used, researchers must rely heavily on other adult interpretations of the behavior observed. Additionally, research is limited to those things likely to occur in the environment one is researching. Observation does not provide the opportunity for deeper exploration of the thoughts and perspectives of children. Interviews with children, however, allow researchers to explore topics that are important to children, ones that may not often be talked about or occur too infrequently to be studied by observation alone. Typical interviews with children are permeated with power dynamics (i.e. the adult perceived by the child as having power over them), so they may answer in a way they feel the researcher wants them to. Children are familiar with the IRF classroom discourse pattern, which is described as the teacher initiating a discussion with a question (I), the response of the child (R), and the feedback provided by the teacher (F) (Westcott & Littleton, 2005). Because they are well trained in the use of this pattern, they often predict that the adult in power expects them to follow this norm in the interview setting. To counteract this, researchers such as Eder and Fingerson (2002) have recommended conducting interviews in natural contexts and embedding interviews into everyday routines when at all possible. Interviewing children in pairs or groups also helps to offset the perceived power of the adult. An example of this comes from noted researcher Maria Lahman, who conducted what she termed "naturally occurring focus groups" during children's snack times. She spent considerable time at the children's snack table for weeks before introducing topics she was interested in, in order to gain insight into the ways the children naturally conversed (Rodriguez, Schwarz, Lahman, & Geist, 2011).

Even when approaching the research with the right stance and value of children's voices, specific methodological considerations need to be planned for. We understand that research cannot be scripted. There are no magical methods that work best for all children in all contexts (Dokett & Perry, 2005), but there are some strategies for creating spaces where children's voices and experiences can best be captured and understood. Asking "What is it I want to know?" begins the process of discerning what methods of research might be employed. Once the initial decisions about the study have been made, the following four suggestions can be considered: create a safe, interactive interview environment, minimize the power differential, use engagement to ensure involvement of participants, and use the most appropriate data-generating methods, such as the shoulder-to-shoulder and the walk-around interview methods.

Strategically Create a Safe, Interactive Interview Environment

The focus of qualitative research with children is to form deep understandings, to interpret and contextualize experiences (Glesne, 1999). The interview continues to be a primary method for data generation that captures young participants' perspectives. However, it is important that the young participants feel comfortable throughout the interaction. In this section, I share six basic ways a researcher can strategically create a safe, interactive interview environment and share examples of how I have tried to do this in my own research, followed by two innovative interview strategies I designed based on these guiding principles.

Situate the Interview in a Place That Is Familiar to the Children Although John Dewey (1902) was advocating for investigation done in the child's natural context as early as the turn of the century, research was mainly done in laboratories for much of the twentieth century. Vygotsky (1978) and Bonfenbrenner (1979) argued for the observation of children in real life settings, doing routine activities, beginning the shift from child as object to child as subject. Therefore, the first strategic step to create a safe, interactive environment is to situate the interview in a place that is familiar to the children such as the school library or classroom. The setting should be a place where children are familiar with the established routines and purposes of the setting. This enables them to feel comfortable, not let their curiosity of the setting distract them from the intent of the conversation, and to utilize the natural speech patterns that they practice in the common setting. Along with selecting a natural setting for the child participant, it is important that the setting be conducive to facilitating and potentially recording the conversation. Specific considerations should include evaluating the temperature, light, space, visual stimulus, and noise and activity levels. If it is appropriate and available, offering children the choice between two interview settings helps them determine where they are more comfortable. When I interviewed students in my Peer Recommendation study, I allowed them to choose between interviewing at a table in the library or at stations in the computer lab, both places they visited often with their class, and both met the considerations mentioned above.

Give the Child Initial Control of the Interview Through Small Talk The second strategic step is to intentionally ease into the interview, giving the child initial control of the interview through small talk. Coyne (1998) describes how "allowing children the freedom to talk about their lives and views helped them relax and enabled the interviews to proceed smoothly" when she engaged in research with children (p. 413). Because I often observe students for one or more days before I attempt to engage in interviews, this aids with the "easing in" process. Students have seen me before, and we most likely have engaged in friendly ways with small talk before the day of the interview. The following example from my Peer Recommendation Research study shows how a 10-year-old student and I eased into an interview by laughing about her pseudonym choice.

Krista: [Beginning recording] *I'm sitting here with.....what was your fake name choice?*
Arya: *Arya*
K: *Arya. That's right because Brittany wanted to use that fake name.*
A: *She did?*

K: *She did.*
A: *That's funny.*
K: *Yeah, and she said: "Oh, I knew she would take that name!"*
A and K: [laughing together]

I also often walk with students from their classroom to the interview site, and I take advantage of that time to ask how their day has been, or what they think about the local athletic team, or whatever topic seems appropriate.

Build Upon The Child's Responses by Sharing Personal Information in Response The third strategic step is to build upon the child's responses by sharing personal information in response. This can be done more naturally when you know something about the child's experiences in the context of the research environment. The goal is to create a natural conversational transaction. I do this by sharing information about my children, if appropriate, and by creating situations in which we can laugh together, as seen in the transcription table from an interview from a motivation research study I conducted with young readers.

13	Krista	And have you read other Captain Underpants books before?
14	Arnold	Noooo
15	Krista	So this is your first one? Do you think you'll read more?
16	Arnold	Um probably
17	Krista	Yeah, my son likes those. So what made you want to read this book originally?
18	Arnold	Just the cover of the book, it made me think it was going to be funny
19	Krista	(laughing) It would be funny if that book was serious, wouldn't it? We'd be very fooled because it has a man with underpants and a toilet on it. (We laugh together) What makes you want to keep reading it? So you started reading it. And what makes you want to keep reading it?
20	Arnold	The adventures the two kids have and what Captain Underpants does, and all that

Discuss the Purpose of the Research The fourth strategic step is to clearly discuss the purpose of the research so that the children understand that they are the experts who have the knowledge and experience the researcher needs to answer his or her important questions. Children can tell when their input is valued, so make it clear from the beginning that they have information that you don't have. When I have students fill out the assent form, I go over what I am researching, and how they can help me. I stress that I cannot do it without them, and I use child-friendly words and phrases like "what I am wondering about" instead of "my research question is." After sharing the purpose of the research, it is essential to stress at the beginning and throughout the interview that there are no right or wrong answers to the open-ended questions being asked. Children also need to understand that it's okay to not have an answer to a particular question. As the adult in the language exchange, it is also important to not lead their answers, shut their answers down, or misunderstand.

Strive to Maintain Meaning This leads to the fifth step, which is striving to maintain meaning. Working to ensure that meaning is maintained during research is imperative. This emphasis on meaning is a two-way street. Researchers need the participants to understand what they are being asked, but they also want to understand what the children are saying in response to their questions or prompts. Kortesluoma, Hentinen, and Nikkonen (2003) state that children actively attempt to understand the questions they are asked, and work hard to give the questions a context. Their interpretations of the questions are not always accurate, however, so researchers must work strategically to prevent as many misunderstandings as possible. Tailoring language to the child's developmental level is the first step. Sticking with concrete vocabulary, as I suggested above, is one way to do this, as abstract concepts are often hard to translate into 'kid language.' Researchers can also listen to the child's own language use and adjust their own language to fit the child's. During my reading strategy research project, I was talking with a first grader about a decoding strategy I noticed her using. I originally referred to it as a "chunking words strategy," but quickly adjusted my language when she referred to it as the "chunky monkey" strategy she learned about in her class. They can work to ask the types of questions that help children open up honestly and expressively. Coyne (1998) recommends asking 'here and now' type of questions and soliciting stories about recent experiences to get meaningful responses.

The researcher can repeat back participant answers to ensure that they are understanding the child, paraphrasing and exploring their answers. Asking simple questions like "Am I getting what you are trying to say?" is also very appropriate to ensure meaning is maintained. Once the interviews have been transcribed, the researcher could member check with the participants, reading them to them and asking something like "Did I capture what you meant to say?" Not only is this ensuring that meaning is maintained, but the message is sent to students that not only is meaning important, but *their* meaning is important.

Frame Nonverbal Cues The sixth strategic step is to intentionally frame all nonverbal cues shared with the participants. "The interest an interviewer shows by use of facial expression and body language determines the impression more effectively than does verbal behavior" (Coyne, 1998, p. 414). As a teacher of young children, I am very familiar with how important using nonverbal cues like an open body position, smiling, a friendly tone of voice, and nodding are to encouraging participation with students in the classroom, so this was a natural leap for me when researching. Potentially even more important is attending to the nonverbal clues the child is giving you. Watching for outward signs of stress or fatigue such as change in voice tone, increased difficulty in concentrating, posture changes, pulling away from the interview reduced eye contact or the like can help the researcher know when to keep going and when to end the interview. The optimal time limit around interviewing depends on the age and engagement level of the child, but I have found anything over 10 min can start to be too much for some children. Making it as engaging and lighthearted as possible can reduce the stress and enhance endurance for a longer interview.

Negotiate Power Respectfully

A key component of a safe, engaging research environment is to negotiate power respectfully. When researchers are aware of the power imbalance that is both implicit and explicit in the adult child interaction, they can address it in different ways while working with children, working to ensure the data being collected is a good reflection of the child's understandings and beliefs.

The above strategies work to accomplish this key objective. Research with children highlights the shift from the adult researcher as all-knowing and all-powerful expert to a more balanced power distribution. Although there is no way to totally eliminate the power differential between the adult and the child (Lahman, 2008), the key is to allow the participants to have some control over the situation and distribute the power (Nutbrown, 2011; Mahon et al., 1996).

Student Assent While parental consent is always required prior to research with minors, assent from participants is equally important. When possible, Coyne (1998) recommends conducting observation periods where the researcher chats informally with the children before assent is asked for. This allows the researcher to become somewhat familiar with the children and gives the opportunity for informal assessment of communication skills. In all of my research studies, I begin by setting up two observation periods of at least an hour on two different days, focusing on the students that will be in my study. Sometimes I will just watch, but often I will interact with students and try to make connections. An example of this can be found from an entry in my participant observation notes from my motivation research investigation.

> 9:44 a.m. Eduardo and Devyn are at the back table, near me. The other students in the class are wondering who in the world I am and look at me strangely. Devyn smiles at me, and I talk briefly with him, explaining that I am here today to write down. what I see in the classroom so I will know more about the class and the students when I talk with them. He seems to want to continue interacting and tells me he sits by himself because he has trouble in school. I say "Oh, it is easier when there aren't distractions!" He nods, and I tell him I do better my myself, too. He smiles and goes back to working with Eduardo. I want to go look so I can see exactly what they are working on, but I don't because I feel it would be disruptive.

Coyne also suggests giving children time to decide if they would like to be in the study by conducting interviews on a different day than assent is requested. I honor this in my own research because it not only gives children time to decide, but it also gives me one more opportunity to interact less formally with them before the interview. Further recommendations are to request assent privately, have children sign their own assent forms, and to check the body language of the participant to ensure it matches the verbal or written assent being given. At the time assent is requested, a thorough and developmentally appropriate description of the study is recommended. The researcher could take the time to go through it orally or could present a visually engaging, colorful handout or brochure about the study that is written in kid terms. Mahon et al. (1996) argue that children are capable of deciding if they want to be interviewed, especially if it is made clear that participation is not expected. Asking for cooperation in respectful and sensitive ways sets the tone for a child-centered study.

Pseudonym Selection Selecting their own pseudonyms is another way to shift power to children. I agree with Hurst (2008) who speaks to her concerns about the power in naming by stating, "I am concerned about the power of the researcher to rename his or her respondents. Personal names do matter" (p. 345). As children I am researching with are filling out the assent form, I tell them that we use fake names in research studies, so they need to think about a name they would like to use to represent themselves. After having to transcribe names like "Eunice Laquisha Lafonda Myrtle the Fourth" and "Homer Simpson" in my peer recommendation study, I soon added the caveat that it needed to be a one-word first name. The transcript below from my motivation study shows how I explain this to one of the third grade participants, and how he responds.

Krista	Now when we do this research, you get to pick a fake name. This is because I'm not going to use your real name when I write about you in a paper. But the fake name has to sound like a real name. It couldn't be something like Batman, because that would sound weird in my paper. So can you think of a fake first name that I could use for you? What pretend name would you like to be known as?
Richard	Richard! (said with a giggle)
Krista	Richard! Awesome! Alright. You are now Richard. I'm going to put that right down in my fake name notebook.
Richard	(laughs)

Two Specific Methods of Data Generation

Because the acquisition of data is an active and sometimes unpredictable process requiring action on the part of the researcher, Graue and Walsh (1998) argue that "data-generating methods" is a more accurate description of the process compared to "data-collection methods." Regardless of word choice, the key is that participants with their unique individuality are more important than the planned data-generation method. As you plan the research process, researching what methods work well for different developmental age groups is important, as is returning to the goals of the study to ensure the method aligns with the objectives. Methods should not be selected for their novelty. Remember, all children may not wish to draw create a mosaic or dance with you. At times, a good conversational interview may suffice. This chapter highlights the shoulder-to-shoulder and walk-around interview as not only data generation methods, but strategic ways to engage participants. The keys are intentionality, preparedness, and flexibility.

Shoulder-to-Shoulder Research The term "shoulder-to-shoulder" comes from a pedagogical idea that is found in the field of reading instruction. Paired, partner, buddy, or shoulder reading is a classroom strategy often used by teachers to facilitate the development of reading fluency (Meisinger, Schwanenflugel, & Bradley, 2004). It is sometimes called "EEKK," or elbow to elbow, knee to knee. Meisinger et al. call this form of reading with a partner a "cooperative interaction" (p. 117). In the classroom, shoulder reading begins when partners or buddies sit next to each other, shoulder-to-shoulder, and share a book. The shoulder-to-shoulder interview I developed in researching children is similar, with the interviewer and interviewee sitting side by side, often on the floor, looking together at a book or other artifacts, or sometimes just sitting and talking. When there is something to look at together, it becomes a natural focus. This idea to transfer the idea of partner reading into the research arena began when I was speaking with my research partner, Maria Lahman, about how my 9-year-old son seemed more willing to share things with me at night, at bedtime after prayers, when the lights were off. She shared that she had similar experiences when she was in the car with her children. She noticed they seemed to share more when they driving somewhere and they were sitting in the back seat. We realized that the common denominator seemed to be lack of direct eye contact, either because the lights were off or because the parent was driving and looking at the road and not the children. This seemed to create a level of comfort for the child not found when we attempted conversations where direct eye contact was maintained. Additionally, I wondered if having a book or something else to focus on would take pressure off of the child being interviewed. After this discussion, I searched to see if other researchers reflected on any similar techniques. Since I could not find anything after researching it, I decided to pilot this methodological idea with the research I was currently conducting on reading identity, and have used it in four other research studies since then. Below I share what it looked like with four students who were my collaborators in a reading identity research investigation.

After I obtained parental consent and student assent, I interviewed four 7- and 8-year-old students individually in a classroom adjacent to the library. I told the students that because I used to be a kindergarten teacher, I was most comfortable sitting on the floor, and asked them if it was ok if we sat on the floor for the interview, or if they preferred sitting at a table. They all chose the floor, so we sat with our backs against the wall, shoulder-to-shoulder, looking at the books I had asked them to bring with them. I began each interview by asking them about the book they brought as we looked at it together. From there, our conversations evolved naturally into questions about reading and identity. Eye contact was the exception, not the rule, and the recorder was unobtrusively on the ground between us.

When I compare the data I received before using this method, I found that the richest data seemed to come from this methodology. While I can't discount other elements that certainly influence the richness of data, such as how old participants are, or their natural personalities, I believe that the success of this project was strongly due to the nature of the shoulder-to-shoulder method itself. As I repeatedly and closely reviewed these transcripts, I found that I was less conscious of myself as "the researcher," and avoided putting the children in situations Graue and Walsh (1998) have characterized with the question "Would you rather stay here and answer my clumsy questions or go have fun with your friends?" (p. 112). We often joked together and made additional connections to our lives that were outside of the interview topic. The following transcript of my interview with Andrew, an 8-year-old boy, (Griffin, Lahman, & Opitz, 2016) illustrates this as he tells me about how he approached reading a book.

Andrew: *I was reading the Hardy Boys. It had such big words, but … was kind of easy. I just sounded them out and … and if you couldn't sound it out, I was kind of just guessing, but trying to get close to the word.*
Krista: *And did it still make sense?*
A: *Yeah.*
K: *Do you know what else is true about Hardy Boys and Nancy Drew? They use words we don't use anymore.*
A: *Yeah, oh yeah, there's just this one word, and I asked my mom what does that mean and she says I don't know what that means.*
K: (laughing) *Those books were written … in*
A: (interrupting) *I think it was like 1946?*
K: *I think it was the 40's and the 50's because I'm 41, and when I was little, I read those books.*
A: *My mom's like 48 and she read them when she was little.*
K: *When my daughter Julia read Nancy Drew there were tons of words she didn't know. One of them was icebox and that was for refrigerator.* (pg. 20).

When I read this transcript, it reads more as a conversation and less as the stereotypical interview. I believe the conversational flow of this interview was influenced by the reduction in eye contact, and the focus on the topic at hand. I suspect the lack of eye contact, the focus on something between us to look at, such as a book, and the natural safety of sitting side by side with someone allows for this type of positive transaction. Upon further reflection, it appears that the focus of a book to look at creates object mediated space that adds to the level of comfort of the child.

Walk-Around

A second interviewing method I have in my method tool box is the walk-around interview. Most interviews are generally "a-mobile" or sedentary in nature (Brown & Durrheim, 2009, p. 915). Traditionally, we haven't envisioned interviews as anything other than the researcher and the participant sitting down and facing one another, with the recorder right in front of the participant. The dialogue was always the primary focus, with the context becoming something we might include in our field notes or something we would want to manage only if it was less than ideal. We would pull the child out of their natural environment into a place we chose that was usually foreign to him or her, one that we generally controlled highly. Even if we did not intend to highlight the unequal distribution of power, it was obvious nonetheless.

Advocating for mobility in research is a current movement that attempts to take advantage of the natural movement of people as they interact with their environment. This also coincides with the increased ability of the researcher to move around because of more flexible technology. No longer are we told to avoid recording in noisy rooms and spaces where there are lots of people.

A new mobile method of interviewing, one that has been called a "go-along" interview (Carpiano, 2009; Kusenbach, 2003) or a roving interview (Propst, McDonough, Vogt, & Pynnonen-Valdez, 2008) in addition to the walk-around, gives researchers a way to increase their ability to interview children in a more natural, authentic way. In such mobile interviews, the researchers move along with the child in their natural environments and daily activities. This offers "researchers a hybrid of observation and interviewing that provides a more thorough look into participants' lived experiences than can be garnered from the interview data, alone" (Kusenbach, 2003).

There is not a lot to draw on when researching this type of mobile researching method. One example found in the literature is the neighborhood walks that Bryant (1985) wrote about.

Although Brown and Durrheim (2009) were not referring to researching with children when they describe the "alongside" (p. 917) nature of a mobile interview, it is worth applying to research with children because of the possibility of deemphasizing the power imbalance between adults and children in research.

I was very interested in this methodology, and after consulting with experts decided to try it with 4th-grade students in during a reader identity research project. I interviewed five 9- and 10-year-old children using the walk-around interview over a 2-week period. As the walk-around interview is described as the researcher moving with the child as the child follows their normal routine, I did exactly that with fourth graders in the library, during their regular class library time. Many selected books and then checked them out, while others already had a book and spent their time reading at a table. I started the interview wherever the child in my study happened to be. If they got up to go find a book, I followed them and continued the interview during that process. Of the five students I was researching with, one was reading a book at a table, two were selecting books in different places around the library, and two were in line to check out books. I did have a set of questions ready, but I followed the natural direction their activities took my questions, asking things like "What kind of books do you like?" as they walked around the library during the book selection process. When they weren't doing anything that I could specifically tie my interview questions to, I chose to ask more general questions, but still walked around with them. I recorded these interactions with a hand-held recording device, and the average length of each interview was about 10 min.

Before I attempted this type of interview, I admit to having concerns about it. I was worried that it would seem unnatural for me to chase students around bookshelves while trying to interview them, and I was unsure how the librarian would feel about the noise level. I was surprised at how natural and authentic the walk around turned out to be. I also hadn't predicted how much more social it was than the traditional interview. As we walked around talking, other children would join in from time to time, adding comments to the questions I was asking the participants. Somehow this was not distracting, and they never monopolized the conversation. As far as the participants themselves, they freely shared where they found the books they enjoyed in the library, and it all felt very natural. As I reflected on this type of mobile interview, I realized that it mirrors my own discussions with my children in the normal flow of life. Conversations often take place in the car, on walks, in grocery stores, and in other on-the-go moments.

As I reviewed the transcripts of these interviews, I found rich information gathered fairly quickly. An example of this is a walk around interview I had with a third-grade girl named Casey, where she has just described to me how much she likes funny books (Griffin et al., 2016).

Krista: *I read books because they are funny too! So let's look around here. Where do you normally pick your books from?*

Casey: *Sometimes I pick the Warriors books. And then I usually look around here for this book (points to bottom shelf) and all the way over here …* (takes me across library).

K: *What's over here?*

C: *I get the Franny K. Steins or the How I Survived Middle School books.*

K: *Oh, cool. And what do you like about those kinds of books?*

C: *How I Survived Middle School, well, for one thing, it's kind of funny …*

K: *I'm sensing a theme!*

C: *Yes. And then … it's also kind of like reality, so I kind of like that idea. And with the Franny K. Stein, well, that's funny and it's about a mad scientist girl. She has bats, and she has a dog named Igor. She says he's like dog and half weasel.*

K: (Laughing) *Weasel!!*

C: (Laughing) *Yes!* (p. 22).

During this interview, the participant could walk to wherever he or she wanted, and do whatever he or she felt like doing, and my job was just to follow. Besides of obvious shift of power from the interviewer to the participant, another strength is the natural environment in which it takes place. I was surprised by how much I enjoyed this type of interviewing, and the children seemed to enjoy it as well.

Conclusion

Research *with* children requires an ideological and methodological shift from research *on* children. This shift has many facets. In this chapter, I spoke to what this shift has looked like for me in my research, and the tenets that have been helpful so that children can actively participate in the data generation of qualitative research. It is important for all participatory researchers to consider the theory behind their individual research decisions and the ethical considerations of researching with children in order become a reflexive researcher and practice listening differently. It will be important for early childhood researchers to attempt to negotiate power respectfully and to structure the data-generation environment strategically.

Questions for Reflection
- Because data generation requires an interaction between the research and the child participant, what strategies will you use to honor your participant's world?
- In what ways can the use of a Researcher Journal enhance ethical data collect when researching with children?
- What are some strategies you can use to diffuse the power differential as an adult researcher when researching with children?
- What do you view as the participatory affordances of shoulder to shoulder and the walk around interviewing techniques?

References

Alderson, J. (1992). In the genes or in the stars? Children's competence to consent. *Journal of Medical Ethics, 18*(3), 119–124.

Bronfenbrenner, U. (1979). *The ecology of development: Experiments by nature and design.* Cambridge, MA: Harvard University Press.

Brown, L., & Durrheim, K. (2009). Different kinds of knowing: Generating qualitative data through mobile interviewing. *Qualitative Inquiry, 15*(5), 911–930.

Bryant, B. (1985). The neighborhood walk: Sources of support in middle childhood. *Monographs of the Society for Research in Child Development* 50 (3, serial no. 210).

Carpiano, R. M. (2009). Come take a walk with me: The "go-along" interview as a novel method for studying the implications of place for health and well-being. *Health & Place, 15*(1), 263–272.

Childers, S. (2008). Methodology, praxis, and autoethnography: A review of getting lost. *Educational Researcher, 37*(5), 298–301.

Clark, C. D. (2011). *In a younger voice: Doing child-centered qualitative research.* New York, NY: Oxford University Press.

Coyne, I. (1998). Researching children: Some methodological and ethical considerations. *Journal of Clinical Nursing, 7*(5), 409–416.

Creswell, J. (2007). *Qualitative inquiry and research design: Choosing among five traditions* (2nd ed.). Thousand Oaks, CA: SAGE.

Crotty, M. (2008). *The foundations of social research: Meaning and perspective in the research process.* Thousand Oaks, CA: SAGE.

Dewey, J. (1902). *The child and the curriculum.* Ithaca, NY: Cornell University Library.

Dockett, S., & Perry, B. (2005). Researching with children: Insights from the starting school research project. *Early Childhood Development and Care, 175*(6), 507–521.

Dublin Department of Children and Youth Affairs. (2012). *Guidance for developing ethical research projects involving children.* Dublin, Ireland: Ministry of Children and Youth Affairs.

Eder, D., & Fingerson, L. (2002). Interviewing children and adolescents. In J. F. Gubrium & J. A. Holstein (Eds.), *Handbook of interview research: Context and method* (pp. 181–201). Thousand Oaks, CA: SAGE.

Finlay, L., & Gough, B. (Eds.). (2003). *Reflexivity: A practical guide for researchers in health and social sciences.* Oxford, UK: Blackwell.

Glesne, C. (1999). *Becoming qualitative researchers: An introduction* (2nd ed.). Don Mills, ON, Canada: Longman.

Graue, M. E., & Walsh, D. J. (1998). *Studying children in context: Theories, methods, and ethics.* Thousand Oaks, CA: SAGE.

Greene, S., & Hill, M. (2005). Researching children's experiences: Methods and methodological issues. In S. Greene & D. Hogan (Eds.), *Researching children's experience: Approaches and methods* (pp. 1–21). London, UK: SAGE.

Griffin, K. M., Lahman, M. K. E., & Opitz, M. F. (2016). Shoulder-to-shoulder research with children: Methodological and ethical considerations. *Journal of Early Childhood Research, 14*(1), 18–27.

Hogan, D. (2005). Researching "the child" in developmental psychology. In S. Greene & D. Hogan (Eds.), *Researching children's experience: Approaches and methods* (pp. 22–41). Thousand Oaks, CA: SAGE.

Hurst, A. L. (2008). A healing echo: Methodological reflections of a working class researcher on class. *Qualitative Report, 13*(3), 334–352.

Kortesluoma, R. L., Hentinen, M., & Nikkonen, M. (2003). Conducting a qualitative child interview: Methodological considerations. *Journal of Advanced Nursing, 42*(5), 434–441.

Kusenbach, M. (2003). Street phenomenology: The go-along as ethnographic research tool. *Ethnography, 4*(3), 455–485.

Lahman, M. K. E. (2008). Always Othered: Ethical research with children. *Journal of Early Childhood Research, 6*(3), 281–300.

Lahman, M. K. E. (2018). *Ethics in social science research.* Thousand Oaks, CA: Sage.

Langsted, O. (1994). Looking at quality from the child's perspective. In P. Moss & A. Pence (Eds.), *Valuing quality in early childhood services: New approaches to defining quality* (pp. 28–42). London, UK: Sage Publications Ltd..

Mahon, A., Glendinning, C., Clarke, K., & Craig, G. (1996). Researching children: Methods and ethics. *Children & Society, 10*(2), 145–154.

Meisinger, E. B., Schwanenflugel, P. J., & Bradley, B. A. (2004). Interaction quality during partner reading. *Journal of Literacy Research, 36*(2), 111–140.

Nutbrown, C. (2011). Naked by the pool? Blurring the image? Ethical issues in the portrayal of young children in arts-based educational research. *Qualitative Inquiry, 17*(1), 3–14.

Pillay, J. (2014). Advancement of children's rights in Africa: A social justice framework for school psychologists. *School Psychology International, 35*(3), 225–240.

Propst, D. B., McDonough, M. H., Vogt, C. A., & Pynnonen-Valdez, D. M. (2008). Roving focus groups: Collecting perpetual landscape data in situ. *International Journal of Qualitative Methods, 7*(3), 1–14.

Pufall, P. B., & Unsworth, R. P. (2004). The imperative and the process of rethinking childhood. In P. B. Pufall & R. P. Unsworth (Eds.), *Rethinking childhood* (pp. 1–21). New Brunswick, NB: Rutgers University Press.

Rodriguez, K. L., Schwarz, J., Lahman, M. K. E., & Geist, M. R. (2011). Culturally responsive focus groups: Reframing the research experience to focus on participants. *International Journal of Qualitative Methods, 10*(4), 400–417.

Shriberg, D., Wynne, M. E., Briggs, A., Bartucci, G., & Lombardo, A. C. (2011). School psychologist's perspectives on social justice. *School Psychology Forum, 5,* 37–53.

Smith, A. B. (2002). Interpreting and supporting participation rights: Contributions from sociocultural theory. *International Journal of Children's Rights, 10*(1), 73–88.

Stainton Rogers, W. (2004). Promoting better childhoods: Constructions of child concern. In M. J. Kehily (Ed.), *An introduction to childhood studies* (pp. 125–144). Maidenhead, UK: Open University Press.

Vygotsky, L. (1978). *Mind and society.* Cambridge, MA: Harvard University Press.

Westcott, H. & Littleton, K. (2005). Exploring meaning through interviews with children. In Greene & Hogan (Eds.), *Researching children's experience: Approaches and methods* (pp. 141–157). London, UK. Sage Publications.

Chapter 5
When Students Generate Questions: Participatory-Based Reading Instruction in Elementary Classrooms

Molly Ness

Introduction

Walk into any elementary language arts classroom and you are likely to see teachers posing questions to children. Open up the teacher's manual to any core reading program, and you'll find a series of questions that teachers are meant to pose to children. The ubiquity of teacher-generated questions has been well documented in research, perhaps most famously by Delores Durkin (1978–79) in her landmark observational study of fourth-grade classroom instruction. In observing over 3000 min, she noted that over 12% of instructional time was allotted for teacher-generated questions. Though teachers were likely to use questions as a means to assess students' comprehension, they almost never provided explicit instruction to facilitate comprehension (Durkin, 1978–79; Ness, 2008).

The trend of teacher-generated questions continues today. In the vast majority of classrooms, the responsibility for generating questions belongs to the teacher. In fact, the typical teacher asks 300–400 questions a day (Cazden, 2001; Leven & Long, 1981). That figure translates into up to two questions every minute, around 70,000 a year, or two to three million in the course of a career. In her 2001 book, Courtney Cazden studied the use of teachers' language in classrooms. She found that teachers most naturally relied on a language pattern known as "Initiate, Respond, and Evaluate" (IRE). In the three-step IRE process, the teacher initiates classroom talk by posting a question to students. Next students respond to the question, and finally the teacher evaluates the correctness or appropriateness of their responses. Furthermore, the majority of these questions are low-level questions that focus on lower cognitive skills, such as memorization and factual recall (Wilhelm, 2007). Richard Allington (2014), a distinguished literacy scholar, called the "interminable number of low-level literal questions" a "misguided but common instruc-

M. Ness (✉)
Fordham University, New York, NY, USA
e-mail: mness@fordham.edu

© Springer Nature Switzerland AG 2019
A. Eckhoff (ed.), *Participatory Research with Young Children*, Educating the Young Child 17, https://doi.org/10.1007/978-3-030-19365-2_5

tional move" (p. 18). A common instructional approach, teacher-generated questions seem to allow little room for deep interaction, involvement, and engagement of young children.

When we shift the responsibility for asking questions away from teachers and towards students, we transform research and practice into participatory acts. We honor knowledge, skills, and experiences that children bring to the classroom. By validating children's innate curiosity, we reposition the role of children in education. This chapter draws from my research with K-5 elementary English Language Arts classrooms where teachers adopted a participatory approach that aimed to share responsibility for question posing between teachers and students. In this chapter, I highlight the instances in which I observed teachers working alongside children to explore the power of student-generated questions as both participatory pedagogy and research. In my role as a researcher sharing the participatory space opened to me by both the teachers and students, I was responsible for the careful observation and documentation practices that appropriately reflected the meaning and value of the shared voice within the classroom settings.

Shifting Question Generation to Students: Participatory Research

My interest in participatory designs began at home, as I experienced the power of student-generated questions as a parent of a young child. When my daughter was 4 years old, each day began with her rapid-fire questioning.

> Mama, can ants swim? Why do worms come out of the ground when it rains? If there is a Big Dipper and a Little Dipper, why isn't there a medium Dipper?

During her particularly inquisitive phase, I tried my best to indulge her questioning. I'd pat myself on the back for giving eloquent answers or for finding an appropriate book which answered her question. Sometimes, my patience wore thin, and I found reassurance in knowing that I was not alone. Willingham (2015) noted that "even the most responsive parents don't answer something like 25 percent of the time" (p. 45).

In my dual role as a parent and teacher educator, I knew that his 'why' phase is a normal developmental phase for young children. These questions are the signs of our children being naturally curious about the world around them. As children perseverate with the seemingly endless 'whys', they are trying to make sense of the world around them. The magnitude of questions generated by young children is impressive. On the average day, mothers typically are asked an average of 288 questions a day by their children aged 2–10 (Frazier, Gelman, & Wellman, 2009). Parents field one question every 2 min and 36 s. Within 1 year, children have posed 105,120 questions. Chouinard and colleagues (2007) revealed that children ask between 400 and 12,000 questions each week.

As a teacher educator, however, I noticed a stark contrast between the frequency of children's questions at home and their questions at school. Why did children ask so many questions in their home environments, yet so few in formal educational settings? What happens in classrooms that carve out instructional time and space for student-generated questions? When questioning moves away from teachers and towards students, what is the impact? With these question in mind, I set out on a participatory study in which I explored the role of student-generated questions in reading instruction. Using purposeful sampling, I reached out through my professional network of current and former graduate students, teachers, and school leaders to situate myself in classrooms taught by teachers who valued inquiry-based classrooms and student-generated questions and who designed instruction around these questions. Over a 4-month period, I worked alongside teachers and children in a participatory design to highlight the value of inquiry-driven classrooms. The vignettes below come from a variety of classrooms, where I acted as a non-participant observer and documented classroom discourse through audiotaping and field notes. In many cases, I followed up my observations with teacher interviews and member checking, in which I debriefed with the teacher to have them explain and make sense of the classroom observations.

Understanding the Research Base of Student-Generated Questions

The most commonly accepted definition of question generation comes from the National Reading Panel (2000), which defined question generation as a type of instruction where readers ask themselves questions about various aspects of the text. Taboada and Guthrie (2006) defined student questioning as self-generated requests for information within a topic or domain. The student or reader, not the teacher, asks the questions. Student-generated questions help to focus readers and promotes better reading comprehension or understanding of the written text (Chin, Brown, & Bruce, 2002).

Recently, neuroscientists have used magnetic resonance imaging (MRI) to understand blood flow activity in the brain when asking questions. A 2014 research team from University of California Davis (see Singh, 2014) monitored brain activity to measure how engaged learners were in reading questions and their answers. When learners' curiosity is piqued by questions and their answers, the parts of the brain associated with pleasure, reward, and creation of memory underwent an increase in activity. These findings indicate that curious brains are better at learning tasks, leading researchers to conclude that, "Curiosity really is one of the very intense and very basic impulses in humans. We should base education on this behavior." These benefits of student-generated questions are explained in detail below:

Asking Questions Motivate Students

When children ask questions, they demonstrate intellectual curiosity. As curious children ask the whats, whys, and wherefores, they build internal motivation for learning and attach personal relevance to what they learn. Researcher Lillian Katz

(2010) posited that intellectual curiosity is innate and inborn, and that educators must nurture that quality in children. Questions show our children as engaged and inquisitive. As children generate questions, they learn to not accept information at its face value, but instead to extend their learning in a self-directed manner. As Postman and Weingartner (1971) wrote, "Once you have learned how to ask relevant and appropriate questions, you have learned how to learn and no one can keep you from learning whatever you want or need to know."

Additionally, questioning activities promote a positive attitude towards reading and literacy. Yopp and Dreher (1994) randomly assigned sixth-grade students to two different treatment groups: (a) teacher-generated questioning and (b) student-generated questions. The students who received instruction on how to generate their own questions were more engaged in literacy instruction, assigned texts, and classroom discourse. Simply put, students are motivated by questioning and finding the answers to their questions (Singer & Donlan, 1989).

Asking Questions Promotes Academic Achievement

The learning benefits of children posing questions are profound. As children pose questions, they engage their higher-level thinking skills. Question generation aids students with memory, recall, and identification and integration of main ideas through summarization. Students who generate their own questions show improvement in reading comprehension scores; in their meta-analysis of question generation, Therrien and Hughes (2008) reported significant findings for the use of question generation as a way to improve students' comprehension. Harvard-based reading researcher Catherine Snow (2002) wrote that, "teaching students in grades 3-9 to self-question while reading text enhances their understanding of the text used in the instruction and improves their comprehension" (p. 33). Janssen (2002) noted that, "self-questioning leads to increased comprehension and more and more high-level questions" (p. 98). Furthermore, question generation holds the reader accountable for "deeper interactions with text" (Tabaoda & Guthrie, 2006, p. 4). When students generate questions they performed better on tests examining knowledge of story structure than those who did not receive such training (Nolte & Singer, 1985).

Asking Questions Promotes Comprehension

An additional benefit of student-generated questions is a deep engagement and involvement with text. By posing and answering their own questions, students become more involved with their reading. A wealth of research demonstrates the effectiveness of question generation, leading the National Reading Panel (2000) to conclude that, "the strongest scientific evidence for the effectiveness of a text comprehension intervention was found for the instructional technique of question generation (pp. 4–45)". Grasesser, McMahen, and Johnson (1994) described an active learner as one who shows that inquisitiveness and curiosity. When students pose questions about text, they are "actively involved in reading and...motivated by his or her queries rather than those of the teacher" (National Reading Panel, 2000, pp. 4–110). This active involvement gives students an initiating role in their learning (Taboada & Guthrie, 2006).

When Kindergartners Ask Questions

My observations took me to Amelie Anderson's Kindergarten classroom; Amelie Andersen is a veteran Kindergarten teacher, who attended a professional development workshop that I facilitated. Self-described as a "play-based, constructivist-oriented early childhood educator", she explained her logical inclusion of questions in her classroom:

> My kids love to ask questions. It comes naturally and easily to them, and so I want to honor their innate curiosity. In my classroom, they know that their questions matter and that their juicy questions will often take our learning in new and different directions.

I observed Ms. Andersen encourage student questioning through text images. Prior to this lesson, the Kindergarteners had rudimentary understandings of essential elements of fiction text, including characters, setting, and sequencing. To encourage text-based predictions, she selected the children's picture book, *My Friend Rabbit* by Eric Rohmann (2007). Written for beginning readers, the book tells the story of mischievous Rabbit, who gets Mouse's brand new airplane stuck in a tree. In an effort to dislodge the airplane, Rabbit tugs, drags, carries, and cajoles a wide variety of animals to stand one on top of another under the offending tree. Mouse just reaches the wing of his plane when the entire group comes crashing to the ground. The text of *My Friend Rabbit* is simple:

> *My friend Rabbit means well. But whatever he does, wherever he goes /trouble follows. "Not to worry Mouse! I've got an idea!" / The plane was just out of reach. Rabbit said, "Not to worry Mouse. I've got an idea!" /So Rabbit held Squirrel, and Squirrel held me, but then.../The animals were not happy. /But Rabbit means well. And he is my friend. /Even if, whatever he does, wherever he goes, trouble follows.*

After gathering a small group of children on the rug before her, she held up the cover of *My Friend Rabbit*. Ms. Andersen explained, "This story is about a mouse that is friends with a rabbit. Somehow this rabbit always gets into trouble. Today is a special day because before we even read the book, you get the chance to ask any question you'd like." She pointed to sentence strips in a pocket chart, displaying the question prompts "How? Who? Why? What? Where? When?" She continued, "Remember that good questions start with these words. I'm going to give you a silent minute to think of some questions, and then I'd like you to turn and talk to your neighbor to share some of the questions that you'd like to ask just by looking at the picture on the cover."

After brief silence, students murmured their questions while she circulated to eavesdrop on their conversations. When students called out their questions, she acted as a scribe to write each one on the board. As students were quite familiar with making predictions, they initially resorted to their comfort zone and offered predictions based on the cover art. She adeptly modeled converting one child's statement of "I think that the mouse is driving the plane" to the question "Who is driving the plane?" When a boy stated, "I think the bunny is the main character because he's much bigger than the mouse," Ms. Andersen, "How could we rewrite that prediction into a question that we hope the text answers for us?" She reported, "What I hear you asking is, 'Who is the main character?' The following questions were generated from these Kindergartners:

- Who is driving the plane?
- Where is the plane going?
- What is the name of the bunny?
- What is the name of the mouse?
- What is going to happen in the story?
- What happens in the beginning, middle, and end?
- What is the setting of the story?
- Is this story nonfiction or fiction?
- How is the bunny feeling in the picture?
- Why is the mouse sitting in the plane?
- Who is the main character?

Satisfied with the quantity and quality of queries generated from the cover illustration, Ms. Andersen showed the rest of the illustrations – page by page. From a picture depicting the rabbit holding up an airplane, a student asked, "How much does an airplane weigh?" Another picture showed a rabbit lifting an alligator, a goose, and a bear, prompting a student to ask, "Are rabbits really strong?" When the illustration's orientation changes – forcing the reader to change the book from horizontal to vertical – a student posed, "Why did they draw the picture like that?"

Having generated these questions, students began the book eager to search for the answers.

Through this simple activity, Ms. Andersen shows the power of student voice and inquiry; she demonstrates that readers ask questions prior to reading and during reading, and that these questions sometimes go unanswered in the text itself. With a simplistic text, she provides the academic language of question generation to students so that they successfully apply questioning to support their comprehension.

When First Graders Ask Questions

Young children often start their questions with wondering statements, or what Barell (2008) calls *wonder talk*. Judith Lindfors (1999) identified some of the common wondering statements that young children shared in informal discussions:

- There's a part I wanted to ask about…
- I'm trying to figure out…
- This is what I don't get…
- I thought it was…
- I wonder why….
- Maybe….perhaps….

'I Wonder' journals are adapted from Barell's (2008) use of inquiry journals, who noted that "one of the best ways I know of to become aware of my own inquisitiveness has been to keep my own journals." An 'I Wonder' journal is a log of readers' wonderings, inquiries, and observations that lead to question generation. Though often used for higher-level, more metacognitive students, the following evidence from Ethan Byrne's classroom highlights how the strategy can be modified for first graders.

Mr. Byrne followed a scripted basal curriculum. His charter school was housed in New York City's East Harlem neighborhood, with high numbers of students qualifying for free and reduced lunches. Nearly 70% of his students spoke a language other than English at home. A second-year teacher, Mr. Byrne came to the classroom through an alternative certification route while also pursuing graduate-level coursework.

Mr. Byrne incorporated 'I Wonder' journals during his poetry unit. Already familiar with the basic conventions of poetry, he selected the poem "Honey, I Love" by Eloise Greenfield. Published in 1978, this poem was written from the viewpoint of a young narrator. The narrator loves visits from her cousin, with his Southern accent, his whistling habit, and his swagger. She loves hot summer days when her neighbor Mr. Davis cools off children with a hose. She loves laughing at her paper doll creations with her friend. She loves car rides to the country in her uncle's crowded car. She loves church picnics with delicious food. She loves kisses from her mother. Of all the things in her life, the only thing the young girl does not love is going to bed. The crux of the poem is the simple things that mean the most, like sharing laughter with a friend, taking family rides in the country, and kissing her mama's arm. The poem reminds readers that love can be found just about anywhere.

Before Mr. Byrne read the poem aloud, he encouraged students to listen for its rhythm. He distributed their 'I Wonder' journals – simple folders with blank pages with the sentence starter "I Wonder" and a graphic of a thought bubble. He used the title to think aloud as a means to showcase his thought processes.

> The title of this poem makes me think all about love. But I wonder if it is a love letter from someone to the person that they love. What do they love? Who do they love? All of these questions belong in my 'I Wonder' journal.

As some of his young students were not yet independently writing, he allowed them to express their questions in illustrations. A student drew a picture of a young girl. The teacher stooped next to her and whispered, "Tell me about this picture. How does it show your question?" The child reported that the picture is the speaker in the poem, and told the teacher she wanted to know what the character looked like, particularly what color her skin was. Acting as her scribe, Mr. Byrne used a blank "I Wonder" page and wrote, "What does the girl look like? What color is her skin?

The teacher read each stanza of the poem aloud, making sure to stop and to allow children to note their questions in their 'I Wonder' journals. He used a variety of approaches to encourage these questions; sometimes students turn and talk to a neighbor about their questions, sometimes he called on the whole group to share out their questions, and he also left independent time for them to write on their own. At the conclusion of the poem, he scanned their journals and jotted juicy questions down on the whiteboard:

- How old is the cousin? What do they like to do on his visit? How long does he visit for?
- What does it mean when it says "words just kind of slide right out of his mouth?"
- Can you really tell where someone is from by how they talk?
- Why is the word 'love' in all capital letters in the middle of the poem?
- How do you learn how to whistle?
- Why does she love the way her cousin walks? Does he walk funny?
- Can the sun really 'stick to her skin"? Does that just mean she's hot?
- Who is Mr. Davis?
- Does this take place in the summer?
- Where does this girl live?
- Why does Mr. Davis turn on the hose? Is there a fire? Is he watering plants in the garden?
- Does it feel good when the 'water stings her stomach' or does it hurt?
- What is a flying pool?
- Who is Renee? Is Renee a boy or a girl? How old is Renee?
- Why does Renee's doll not have a dress? Does she not have money to buy clothes for her doll?
- How does she make a dress out of paper?
- Does it hurt Renee's feeling when the narrator laughs at her doll?
- Why do they laugh so hard?
- How many people are in her uncle's crowded car?
- Where is the car going? Where is she sitting?
- Why do the church folks like to meet in the country? What do they do there?
- Who are the church folks?
- How does her mama feel when the girl kisses her arm?
- Why does the girl trying not to cry? What does she want to cry about?
- Who is this girl speaking too? Who is the 'you' in the final line?

These questions prompted a rich conversation, as some of their questions were addressed by the text and others prompted talk where students attempted to answer questions with their personal and real world knowledge. When one student questioned, "Where does this girl live?", her classmate purported that "I think she lives in the city, because it sounds like all the church folks meet in the vacation as a little vacation."

For the remainder of the school year, students returned to their 'I Wonder' journals as they approach other text genres. They added questions to their 'I Wonder' journals during science class and on their field trip to a farm. One student wrote the following questions in his 'I Wonder' journal:

- Why do trees and plants grow?
- When was the earth made?
- Why do we walk on two legs?"

For any unanswered question, Mr. Byrne directed them, "Go jot that down in your 'I Wonder' journal."

In these I Wonder journals, Mr. Byrne demonstrated the omnipresence of questions: a space to house the curiousity sparked by poetry, everyday observations, and daily interactions. By creating a space in which students frequently visit to generate questions, they are more likely to continue their questions.

When Second Graders Ask Questions

Erin Gilson was a midcareer second-grade teacher in the South Bronx. Her school structured its literacy block in a reading and writing workshop model, which allowed her "to highlight the wealth of fabulous authentic children's literature." Her students – most of whom qualify for free and reduced lunches – wer "sometimes limited by their lack of life experiences, so I read aloud frequently to build their background knowledge." She explained that their limited life experiences often was a detriment to their comprehension:

> In particular, they struggle with nonfiction text – because they don't have firsthand experience with dolphins, or exhibits at museums, or the countryside, or whatever is the topic of our text. I try to use images and Internet resources to build their background knowledge and pique their curiosity so that they are more motivated to approach a text.

A tried-but-true question generation strategy, Ms. Gilson incorporated the KWL graphic organizer with the following structure:

- K (What I Know): Where students activate their background knowledge before reading a text
- W (What I Want to Know): Where students set a purpose for reading – by asking questions or listing what they hope they gain from text
- L (What I Learned): Where students reflect – after reading – on the knowledge they gained from the text

Ms. Gilson began a small-group social studies lesson about Gandi with an essential question. On the classroom computer, she projected two pictures: one of Mahatma Gandi and the second a map of India. The following conversation unfolded:

> This man was a leader of India, where people who were not white were treated unfairly in the 1940s. He used nonviolence to work peacefully to get fairer treatment for everyone.

Now I'm sure that these pictures and our essential question make you think of some questions that you'd like answered in our reading, so let's use a KWL chart to jot some of those wonderings down.

Students shared out the following five questions:

- I want to know why he didn't do violence?
- I want to know how he died.
- Did he have a family?
- Why didn't he want to fight?
- When he was first born, was he treated unfairly like others?

After recording their questions on the whiteboard, Ms. Gilson praised their efforts and handed out individual copies of the KWLS chart.

KWLS Chart

Before Reading		After Reading	
K	W	L	S
What do I know?	What do I want to know?	What did I learn?	What do I still want to know?

The traditional KWL chart has three columns; this chart divided questions into those generated *before* reading and those generated *after* reading. To highlight the notion that texts do not answer all of students' questions, the chart also included a fourth addition: the S column, to hold the place for questions that students *still* wanted to address.

Since students were loosely familiar with both Gandhi and the KWL chart, they set to work individually on the K portions of their charts, recording the following background knowledge about Gandi. The majority of their background information came from Ms. Gilson's quick frontloading instruction, with the essential question and the visual references. Any misinformation in the K column reflected the authenticity of student work.

- He saved India.
- He died.
- He is black.
- He is a leader in India.
- Gandi wanted to help the others in India so it is a better place.

- Gandi was born in India.
- He didn't want to fight.
- He was treated unfairly.
- He went to school.

After praising them for thinking about what they already knew, Ms. Gilson pushed students to generate questions about what they hoped the text will answer.

> Next, let's take some time to think of questions that we hope the text will tell us. Some of your questions might piggyback off of what you wrote in the K column. Some might be about the photos I showed you and our essential question. This is the chance to think of as many questions about Gandhi, about India, about nonviolence, and about this time in history as you can.

Students set to work writing their own questions, as the teacher circulated to provide support. For students struggling with the academic language of question generation, she pointed to the "Wonder Wall", a bulletin board with questions starters (e.g. "Who", "What" "How" "When) to jumpstart their thinking. Table 5.1 lists of the comprehensive questions generated by individual students.

The remainder of the lesson was spent reading a leveled biography of Gandi. Students were directed to use a sticky note to flag pages that answered the questions

Table 5.1 Before reading questions: "What do I want to Know?"

Name of student	Questions generated
Anya	Was Gandi the first Indian to make people nice? When was Gandi born? Where did he go to school at?
Fadima	When did he die? When was he born? Did he have a family? Why didn't he fight? Why didn't he do violence? Where was he living?
Samantha	I want to know if Gandi is old. I want to know if Gandi wears different clothing. Did he go to school?
Leighton	I want to know if he died. I want to know if he knows karate. I want to know if he's joyful. I want to know if he's relaxed and magical.
Yumaris	How did he die? How did he make India fair? Why didn't he want to fight? Has he ever been to jail?
Oumar	Why is he dead? What did he speak? What was his favorite color? Did he have a family? Did he get married?

in their "What do I want to know?" columns. After reading, they refered directly to the text to share out their findings.

With the objective of showing students that one text cannot address all of their questions, Ms. Gilson directed students to the column titled, "What do I still want to know?"

> Let's look across our W and L columns. We've come a long way in answering some of the questions that you first asked. But some of your questions might linger – that means, you still might want to know their answers. The text might also have made you think of new questions. Good readers know that one book can't answer everything, and good readers are always asking all sorts of questions. So now, let's add to the "What do I still want to know column?" For example, I have a question that this book made me think of. We learned that Gandi stopped wearing Western clothes and instead wore robes and sandals. I want to know more about this, so I'm going to record this question in my S column: Why did Gandi only wear sandals and robes? Let's hear some of your S questions.

> S1: Why did he fast? What made him think a fast would work?
> S2: How long did he stay in jail for?
> S3: How long can someone fast for before dying?
> S4: Did Gandi ever meet Martin Luther King?
> S5: Did he have a family? Any kids?
> S1: Are things in India fair now?
> S3: Why is he bald in all the pictures? Did his hair fall out or did he shave his head?

This teacher adapted one of the most commonly used reading strategies to place more instructional focus on question generation. KWL was originally designed to be a pre-reading activity which encouraged students to activate their background knowledge, to set a purpose for reading, and to monitor their learning from a text. The simple addition of the S column pushed students to generate more questions, either the nagging questions unanswered in the scope of one text or the questions that inevitably arise as learners become more familiar with a topic.

In subsequent lessons, Ms. Gilson might bring in supplementary texts which address their unanswered queries or incorporate ways to have students conduct outside research. The power of the "What do I still want to know" column is clear. Not only do the questions in the S column outnumber the questions in the W column, but these fourth-grade students were better able to address the teacher's initial essential question.

When Third Graders Generate Questions

"Why do roller coasters make me barf?"
"When you lose weight, where does it go?"
"Can hair really grow as long as Rapunzel's?"

These questions, scribbled in student handwriting on colorful sticky notes, covered an enormous poster, titled "Parking Lot", hanging in a fourth-grade classroom. For this fourth-grade teacher, the parking lot was as an ongoing log of children's unanswered questions. A former student in my literacy methods classes, Mr. Dewitt taught in his fourth-grade classroom for 8 years. He explained:

> When kids have a question – one I can't answer or one that is off topic – I tell them to jot it down and put it in the parking lot. When we've got a couple extra minutes of time, I pull things from the parking lot and try to answer them.

The parking lot was the home for questions that a teacher prefered to momentarily leave unanswered. When a student asked a seemingly off topic question or a question that could not immediately be answered, the teacher acted as a scribe and records it on the parking lot – be it a classroom poster or a section of a white board. Harmin and Toth (2006) explained that the parking lot "reminds us to handle such deferred questions, assures students that their questions will not be forgotten, and, of course, helps us to keep our lessons flowing with active involvement" (p. 219).

In our interview, Mr. Dewitt admitted that time has prevented him from fully addressing the questions in the parking lot, noting that, "the parking lot is the place where my students' questions have gone to die." As he aimed to bring life back to their unanswered questions, he uses an inquiry-based model that is student-centered, collaborative, and motivating for young readers. Mr. Dewitt created student-centered small-group sessions, in which students determined the origin of their parking lot inquiries and purposefully used informational text to address their questions. The list below shows the questions that emerged within the first week of creating the parking lot:

- Why do our hands get wrinkled after we take a bath?
- Why can't penguins fly?
- Why are apples different colors?
- Why don't snakes have feet?
- What are our belly buttons for?
- Why do we drink milk from cows?

Next, Mr. Dewitt modeled how to tackle the parking lot question "Can hippopotamuses swim?" The question originated from the children's picture book *The Circus Ship* by Chris Van Dusen (2009), which shows a shipwrecked hippopotamus swimming to shore. Using a digital document camera to project an informational text, he overviewed the headings, tables of contents, maps, graphs, charts, and indexes. Students directed him to turn to two chapters "Staying Cool" and "River Horses". In a "eureka!" moment, the teacher read aloud a paragraph explaining that though they spend the majority of their lives submerged in water, hippopotamuses cannot swim nor float.

In their leveled guided reading groups, students were matched to appropriately leveled text to tackle their parking lot questions; a higher-level group tackled a complex text *Grossology* to answer the question "Why do I burp?" For groups that needed additional support, sticky notes direct students to the relevant pages.

Mr. Dewitt explained that the parking lot quickly became the hottest location in this classroom. Instead of emptying of questions, the sticky notes in the parking lot increased in number. As students saw authentic purposes for their questions and informational text, they actively generated questions. Not only did students' questions increase in quantity, they also increased in quality. Initially students posed literal and basic questions (e.g. "What do hippopotamuses eat?"). Subsequently, students posed questions that are more analytical, evaluative, and interpretive (e.g. "Where did the myth that elephants are afraid of mice come from?").

Concluding Thoughts

In these inquiry-based classrooms, we see teachers who shy away from traditional approaches to reading instruction. In the traditional approach to reading, the teacher is viewed as the purveyor of information; in the classrooms I observed through a participatory design, students had powerful contributing roles to knowledge. They participated in the co-construction of learning, guided by the questions that they generated. These children – as young as 5 years old – determined the direction of their learning, simply through the questions that they posed. For this to happen, their teachers gave up some of their control and took the lead from their students. These teachers offer evidence of the connection between participatory research design and participatory classroom practices.

These classrooms value the notion that the question often has more power than the answer. In early childhood classrooms where teachers embrace the questions that children ask, their voices are the steering wheel of reading instruction. When teachers recognize that the most powerful questions come not from a teachers' manual, but from children themselves, young children are more engaged in discussion and more purposeful in their reading.

Questions for Reflection
- In what ways do you honor the questions that students bring to your work?
- Which of these approaches or vignettes most closely resonates with you? How might you adapt one of the ideas to your research practices?
- How would you describe a balance approach between adult-generated questioning with student-generated questions?
- Do schools today honor or discourage student-generated questions? How can your research serve to support student questioning and honor their ways of knowing?

References

Allington, R. (2014). Reading moves: What not to do. *Educational Leadership, 72*(2), 16–21.
Barell, J. (2008). *Why are school buses yellow? Teaching for inquiry PreK – 5*. Thousand Oaks, CA: Corwin Press.
Cazden, C. (2001). *Classroom discourse: The language of teaching and learning*. Portsmouth, NH: Heinemann.

Chin, C., Brown, D., & Bruce, B. (2002). Student-generated questions: A meaningful aspect of learning in science. *International Journal of Science Education, 24*(5), 521–549.

Chouniard, M. M., Harris, P. L., & Maratsos, M. P. (2007). Children's questions: A mechanism for cognitive development. *Monographs of the Society for Research in Child Development, 72*, 1), 1–1)129.

Frazier, B. N., Gelman, S., & Wellman, H. M. (2009). Preschoolers' search for explanatory information within adult-child conversation. *Child Development, 80*(6), 15–92. https://doi.org/10.1111/j.1467-8624.2009.01356x

Grasesser, A. C., McMahen, C. L., & Johnson, B. (1994). Question asking and answering. In M. A. Gernsbacher (Ed.), *Handbook of psycholinguistics*. San Diego, CA: Academic.

Harmin, M., & Toth, M. (2006). *Inspiring active learning: A complete handbook for today's teachers*. Washington, D.C: Association for supervision & Curriculum Development.

Janssen, T. (2002). Instruction in self-questioning as a literary reading strategy: An exploration of empirical research. *Educational Studies in Language and Literature, 2*(2), 95–120. https://doi.org/10.1023/A:1020855401075

Katz, L. (2010). Knowledge, understanding, and the disposition to seek both. *Exchange, 32*(6), 46–47.

Leven, T., & Long, R. (1981). *Effective instruction*. Washington DC: Association for Supervision and Curriculum Development.

Lindfors, J. (1999). *Children's inquiry: Using language to make sense of the world*. New York, NY: Teachers College Press.

National Reading Panel. (2000). *Teaching children to read: An evidence-based assessment of the scientific research literature on reading and its implication for reading instruction*. Washington, DC: National Institute of Child Health and Human Development.

Ness, M. (2008). Supporting struggling readers: When teachers provide the 'what,' not the 'how. *American Secondary Education, 37*(1), 80–95.

Nolte, R. Y., & Singer, H. (1985). Active comprehension: Teaching a process of reading comprehension and its effects on reading achievement. *The Reading Teacher, 39*, 24–31.

Postman, N., & Weingarten, C. (1971). *Teaching as a subversive activity*. New York, NY: Dell Publishing.

Singer, H., & Donlan, D. (1989). *Reading and learning from text*. Hillsdale, NJ: Erlbaum.

Singh, M. (2014). What's going on inside the brain of a curious child? *National Public Radio*. Retrieved from http://blogs.kqed.org/mindshift/2014/10/whats-going-on-inside-the-brain-of-a-curious-child/

Snow, C. (2002). *Reading for understanding: Toward a R & D program in readingcomprehension*. Washington, DC: RAND Reading Study Group. Retrieved from http://www.rand.org/pubs/monograph_reports/MR1465/MR1464/pdf

Taboada, A., & Guthrie, J. T. (2006). Contributions of student questioning and prior knowledgeto construction of knowledge from reading information text. *Journal of Literacy Research, 38*(1), 1–35. https://doi.org/10.1207/s15548430jlr3801_1

Therrien, W. J., & Hughes, C. (2008). Comparison of repeated reading and question generation on students' reading fluency and comprehension. *Learning Disabilities: A Contemporary Journal, 6*(1), 1–16.

Wilhelm, J. (2007). *Engaging readers and writers with inquiry*. New York, NY: Scholastic Press.

Willingham, D. (2015). *Raising kids who read: What parents and teachers can do*. San Francisco, CA: Jossey-Bass.

Yopp, R. H., & Dreher, M. J. (1994). Effects of active comprehension instruction on attitudes and motivation in reading. *Reading Horizons, 34*(4), 288–302.

Chapter 6
"My Mom Said You Can't Use My Face, But My Voice Is Alright": Children As Active Agents in Research Utilizing Video Data

Nicholas E. Husbye

Introduction

The art room is already buzzing as children filter into the space on the second day of *Lights, Camera, Action*, locating both their friends as well as seats, readying themselves for the work to be done in the next 45 min. They are here for an elective filmmaking class, a four-week-long experience in which students will be drafting stories, creating costumes, and, ultimately, filming their stories for the culminating Film Festival on the last day of class. As a researcher, I am interested in the media production practices of children particularly the ways in which students take up the practices of filmmakers and the multiple pathways they might take to produce a final product.

As this is a study and my second session of inquiry, several students are already returning the permission forms I distributed the previous day. A standard form vetted by my institutional review board, they ask for permission to analyze the video data from the various cameras within the room, asking the data about its insights about children's decision making as filmmakers. The children treat these forms, which I anxiously count as students deposit them in a wire basket in the back of the room, nonchalantly. Just another adult piece of paper; here, it's signed. Can I use that camera yet?

Cameron, seven-years-old and one of the last children to enter into the art room, hovers around the wire basket, shifting from one foot to the other, his form grasped tightly in his hand. "Nick," he shouts urgently, beckoning me from the front of the classroom, where I'm preparing to launch the day's production meeting. I make my way across the room. "This," Cameron thrusts the permission form up in the air, "is signed. My mom said you can't use my face, but my voice is alright." He pauses before he adds, "Is that okay?" I do my best to assure him that even if he chose not

N. E. Husbye (✉)
University of Wisconsin – Milwaukee, Milwaukee, WI, USA

© Springer Nature Switzerland AG 2019
A. Eckhoff (ed.), *Participatory Research with Young Children*, Educating the Young Child 17, https://doi.org/10.1007/978-3-030-19365-2_6

to hand in his form, his participation in the class would be completely fine. "No, no, I'll hand it in. You're going to want me for your paper."

Context

This chapter draws upon data from a larger case study of elementary students, grades kindergarten through eight, engaged in the production of original film. Working in a public charter school in a mid-sized midwestern college town serving students in kindergarten through grade eight, I utilized a daily elective class to create a course for students called *Lights, Camera, Action* (LCA). In LCA, students planned for, filmed, and shared movies of their own design, working individually or on self-selected teams. The elective course was open to all students enrolled at the school and was but one option on a larger menu of elective offerings. LCA was offered for three cycles lasting four-to-six weeks each during the 2011–2012 school year, with anywhere from eight to twenty-four children participating the class within each cycle.

Within each of the cycles, students had opportunities to utilize a wide variety of technology to support the development of their films, including FlipCams, iPods, digital cameras for capturing still images, and MacBook computers for editing. All students, regardless of age, had access to these materials.

As a researcher, I came to this project curious about the ways elementary students were making decisions that impacted their films, particularly in the ways students were networking modes together as they created film. To this end, I collected copious amounts of data, including video data from research cameras within the classroom, raw footage from participants' filmmaking process, artifacts created for use within individual films, and daily field notes detailing our work together in addition to the final versions of the films.

Beyond my role as a researcher, I was also an instructor supporting the students in creating their films. Both roles of researcher and instructor are laden with power. My approach to working with children in Lights, Camera, Action sought to negotiate power discrepancies. I already benefited from a teacher-but-not-Teacher status in the school, having served, for a short time, as a literacy tutor for multiple students at the school as well as a literacy interventionist working with kindergarten and first grade students. While many other elective courses were taught by community members whose presence in the school was restricted to the courses themselves, I was afforded some level of familiarity and comfort by students by my historical presence in the building. This, I hypothesize, allowed me some fluidity in my relationships with the students in the class as they knew of me even if they didn't know me personally. Furthermore, within the class itself, students self-selected their film projects, set their own production schedules, and, being aware of how the social construction of data would be captured by the research cameras in the classroom, actively engaged in the collection of video data around their production processes.

Early in the project, I explained to students that, as they were making films of their own, I was making a documentary about their process, a behind-the-scenes film about children making film. It was an analogy that was particularly fitting given the work we were engaged in. Students, having some familiarity with the genre, citing the special features often found on DVDs of their favorite movies, began to conceive of ways they might reconfigure their relationship to the research camera. In treating the research video camera as an active agent in the classroom, and something they could negotiate rather than as an all-seeing and fixed being, students were able to participate in the research process in ways that "remixed" the ways power played out in the research space (Gallagher, 2008).

Negotiating Power

Within the LCA space, I was careful to design my role in such a way that would provide students with access to as much power around the creation of their films and the ways in which their process was documented. I was the adult of record, responsible for the wellbeing of the students within my care, articulating the most basic boundaries of my role within LCA. Given my interest in the choices these young filmmakers would make throughout their experiences, I wanted to maintain as many opportunities for the students to engage in decision-making as possible. There was no specific kind of film I wanted students to make within LCA, rather leaving as many options as possible.

These decisions included the use of technology; aside from a dedicated video camera for each group, the young filmmakers also had access to a variety of other technology, including additional video cameras, still image digital cameras, and laptops. Access to these devices was unfettered after all the devices were introduced and their functions demonstrated at the beginning of LCA. While technology was of import, the materials the young filmmakers utilized within their films became equally important. While we did not have access to all the materials requested, I sought to collaborate with the young filmmakers to think through alternative materials we did have or could gain access to easily. I sought to be upfront about our resources, and worked diligently to follow up any "no" with a "but" as an invitation to think together about other materials that we could use to the same cinematic effect. The economics of the project became an interesting thread as students began to inquire about obtaining materials, demonstrated in this interchange between Garrison, Walter, and myself:

Walter:	Nick! We need more Legos! Can we buy more Legos?
Garrison:	What do you mean we? He's [Nick] spending all his money. Do you think, does he have money to buy more Legos?
Nick:	Might be a stretch, friends, depending on what you need.
Garrison:	We just need some, some more basic blocks to build the, um, setting, like the turret. I can bring those from home. Ignore him.

Just as Garrison brought materials into the LCA space, so did the other filmmakers, augmenting the resources I was able to provide, which also served to further the personal investment of these young filmmakers in their projects.

Video Data in Literacy Research

Technological innovations have created opportunities for education researchers to collect data in a multitude of ways and at detailed levels never before possible. Video, in particular, has become quotidian in education research as researchers utilize cameras that are becoming smaller and less expensive as well as software that allows for efficient analysis of the resulting video footage. Digital video, as a data source, is noted for its ability to "replicate what is set before them" (Prosser, 2000), as though the video camera and its digital eye is an all-seeing witness to human activity. Jewitt (2012), in writing about the potential of video data in social research, delineated three characteristics that "underpin its distinctive potential" (p. 4): video data possesses a real-time sequence, creates a fine-grained multimodal record, and is data that is durable, malleable, and shareable. These characteristics, and how they manifest in video data, are summarized in Table 6.1.

Video can provide with a record of educational practices that is complex and provides the opportunity for a researcher to "systematically look for patterns that would be impossible to observe directly *in situ*" (Blikstad-Balas, 2017, p. 511; emphasis in original). Given this advantage, it is relatively easy for researchers to assume video data is an authentic representation of educational activity, but such data really is representative of a social reality constructed and shared by both the researcher and the participants and is often spoken of as reactivity (Harper, 2001; Pink, 2003). While the presence of a camera certainly can influence the behaviors of individuals being recorded, some assert these concerns are exaggerated (Heath,

Table 6.1 Characteristics of video data in research

Characteristic	Operationalization	Implication in video
Real-time sequence	A video camera captures actions happening with its gaze, allowing for a record of activity that is external to an observer	Human activity is ephemeral; video data allows researchers to examine and re-examine human activity in ways articulated by the boundaries of the video itself
Fine-grained multimodal record	In addition to capturing talk, video data also captures a variety of other modes that may be of interest to a researcher	Multimodal analysis allows researchers to understand how particular ways of making meaning, including and in addition to language, are utilized within the given activity
Durable, malleable, & shareable	Video is able to be re-watched and shared with other researchers	Analysis of human activity can be collaborative and temporally displaced from the actual activity being studied

Adapted from Jewitt (2012)

Hindmarsh, & Luff, 2010; Blikstad-Ballas, 2017). Beyond concerns about how video cameras may influence behavior, there has been much perseveration about the ethical dimensions of collecting video data, particularly access, the reactivity described previously, and the potential for bias in the collection of video data (Luff & Heath, 2012), though such concerns do little to illuminate the challenges of video analysis (Blikstad-Ballas, 2017).

As a research tool, the video camera becomes an active agent in the research process, a co-conspirator of sorts, as researchers consider the position of cameras in the research space, the frames they will capture on their memory cards, all in an attempt to capture as much of the interaction as possible. As researchers, we often attempt to normalize the camera, pushing the presence of it to the very margins of the participants' minds and of the physical space itself. What happens, however, when the rethink the relationship researchers and research participants have with the research camera? What happens when the research camera, rather than being relegated to the very edges of activity and mind, is actively engaged?

Again, my project was most interested in the ways in which young filmmakers made decisions during the creative process, but I struggled with how I would collect data that would support my inquiry. Traditional approaches would involve a single or multiple cameras in the space, taking wide views of the activities of all the filmmakers. Such an approach would provide general perspectives but would do little to help me think about individual decisions that would only be hinted at in the data. Given I was not only a researcher in the space, but also the instructive adult in the space, I did not have the luxury of focusing my energy strictly on data collection. Given this was my third round of LCA, I made the decision to maintain one designated research camera, and created a collection of research cameras that LCA students were encouraged to access and use to document their own process.

For the remainder of this chapter, I take up questions about the co-construction of data collection, particularly when inquiring into process, in work with elementary-aged children engaged in making film, shifting notions of the research camera as passive documentarian of children to children as active agents in the co-construction of video data. It is a shift that, I will argue, strengthens literacy research.

Methods and Data Analysis

I approached this particular project with an interest in the ways children engaged in filmmaking practices; as such, I adopted an explanatory multiple case study methodology, with each of the production teams comprising a single case for a total of approximately 8 individual cases, three of which are addressed in this chapter. Multiple case studies allow the replication of procedures on multiple cases, enhancing both the validity and, to some extent, the generalizability of the findings (Galloway & Sheridan, 1994). Yin (2009) asserts cases should be viewed as independent from one another rather than a unit of a larger inquiry project; in this way, a multiple case study design can be viewed as having the same logic as a cross-experimental design (Yin, 1982, 2009).

My analysis began with building descriptions of how the filmmakers were or were not utilizing access to the research cameras. Working through the larger corpus of video data, this phase emphasized isolating footage originating from each of the designated research cameras, identifying whether that camera was stationary or utilized by students, and coding for positioning within the frames of the footage. In addition to creating descriptions of these interactions with the research cameras, this also supported developing the reliability of descriptions, whether the practices I was observing were habitual or were they interesting but isolated anomalies.

A second phase sought to shift to explanation and validity, with video data analyzed in ways that examined children's agency with relation to the research camera, aligning with Yin's (2009) notion of validity: that generalizability is analytical rather than statistical, generalizing to theory rather than population. Particular attention was paid to how engagement with the gaze of the research camera functioned for the young filmmakers; these emerging insights were triangulated (Huberman & Miles, 1994; Yin, 1982) with data from field notes and student-created artifacts, including notes students wrote to me during the class. As such, both phases of analysis, when taken together, sought to both describe patterns of participation with the research cameras while also building explanation why these patterns were enacted.

In this chapter, I have focused on three different teams or individuals who established very particular relationships with the research cameras in the space. These relations were, drawing upon de Certeau (1984), strategic in nature. Each of the teams engaged in "the calculation (or manipulation) of power relationships that become possible as soon as a subject can be isolated" (1984, pp. 35–36). By encouraging awareness of the research camera, the young filmmakers were able to strategize in regards to how they would represent their process with within the filmmaking process. I will argue that encouraging children, as participants in research, to engage in these strategies in regards to the research camera allowed for the researcher to have a deeper understanding of the childrens' literacy practices while engage in the process of making film. Analysis of the strategies students engaged in augmented and expanded the possibilities to understand students' perceptions and understandings of digital literacy practices. Within this project, students engaged in three specific strategies: camera ownership, selective positioning, and camera avoidance. Through the use of vignettes within the data, each of these strategies will be articulated as well as how they supported the larger research inquiry.

Camera Ownership

Second graders Walter, Garrison, and Otto huddle around a classroom table, shifting the stances of the Lego minifigures positioned throughout the landscape they have constructed from Legos, cardboard, and other sundries. The trio begins to argue about what needs to happen in the image they are about to create to make the sequence move seamlessly. A heated discussion erupts, adjustments are made, and

Garrison looks to the ceiling, shouting, "I hope you could hear that!" to a camera suspended from an overhead pipe stretching the length of the room.

Suspending the camera from said pipe was an idea conceived by Walter, who hypothesized the view from above the table upon which the trio of film producers was working would provide me with integral information about how they went about creating a stop motion animation film. Such an aerial set up, as seen in Fig. 6.1, permitted my analysis to map both their interpersonal interactions as they made decisions through their production process, but also allowed their interactions with the material objects of their stop motion animation film to be analyzed clearly. Walter, Garrison, and Otto clearly owned the research camera, to the extent they claimed a single research camera as their own and would often utilize additional research cameras, when available, to capture their interactions with one another.

Beyond simply claiming research cameras for themselves, the ability for active engagement with the tools of research permitted students to develop ways of thinking through what was particularly interesting about their own process. Garrison, for instance, ended a work session telling me: "wait until you see our [still] camera today! Walter did this really cool thing with Legos and we thought you'd want to see it because we were pretty boring today" (Field Notes, June 02, 2011). Garrison's seemingly flippant comment undergirds a sophisticated understanding of how he and his co-producers' work is represented in the video data. While the overhead camera captured the three boys huddled around a small collection of Lego pieces, it was unclear what they were attempting to accomplish until the still images taken that day were examined. During that particular work session, the trio was

Fig. 6.1 *Garrison, Walter, and Otto, from above.* A group of filmmakers who embraced the potential of the research camera to provide additional information about their filmmaking process, suspending the research camera from the ceiling to provide an overview of their activity was a strategy that originated from the filmmakers themselves

experimenting with the effect the still image camera's flash would have on translucent Lego pieces, attempting to create the effect of those pieces glowing. Forman (1999) experienced the same kind of higher-level thinking regarding children and the collection of video data, writing:

> Children would see me approach with my camera. Their knowledge that I was recording gave the children a reason to consider what in the classroom or their own play was interesting. It turns out that thinking about what is interesting requires rather high-level thinking (p. 5).

Beyond simply thinking about what was interesting about their own play, this trio of filmmakers was also thinking about which sources of data best conveyed what was interesting about their own work.

Selective Positioning

Cameron, whose eventful IRB consent form submission opened this chapter, was placed in a precarious position: he was charged by his mother to avoid showing his face on camera yet had a larger desire to participate and be recognized in the inquiry. Whereas Lucinda and Nancy wholly avoided the camera's view, explored in the next section, Cameron sought to engage the camera from the periphery, close enough to be noted, but far enough away to abide by the rules set forth for him. Cameron is an example of children's unique positioning within research, wherein children's "sociopolitical positioning means that adults must give permission. In considering access to children, adults give priority to the adult duty to protect children from outsiders; this tool precedence over children's right to participate in the decisions to [participate]" (Hood, Kelley, & Mayall, 1996, p. 126).

Cameron and his relationship with the camera highlights an ongoing tension within research utilizing video collection regarding anonymity and confidentiality. While the study described here was very explicit in not being able to ensure anonymity, measures were taken to address confidentiality. All students, for instance, were assigned pseudonyms within all coding and reporting of analysis and information about their specific contexts were masked as much as possible. Students were also informed of any and all reports of the research, including this chapter. This process is another way to recognize the "provisional" (Flewitt, 2006) nature of consent, particularly with young children, providing participants with yet another opportunity to provide feedback on the research report as well as withdraw their consent.

Highly cognizant of the tensions between anonymity and the threat digital video data presented to it, Cameron was conscious to always be aware of the sight lines of all the research cameras within the classroom space, positioning himself on the

Fig. 6.2 *Cameron positioned between two research cameras.* While Cameron never fully occupied a frame of any given research camera, he was careful to position himself in ways that allowed cameras to capture some elements of his work as a filmmaker

periphery of the camera's gaze in order to be part of the data set while also abiding by the charge his mother put forth. Figure 6.2, for instance, depicts how Cameron often positioned himself: between research cameras, never the focus, but still present as he was certain I would want to know about his process for my "paper," as he called it.

Like Lucinda and Nancy, Cameron's position in relation to the camera was a valuable analytical tool for myself as a researcher. He was making very specific decisions to provide data in regards to only certain elements of his production process. My charge as a researcher was to make sense of what Cameron believed was important about his process; analysis then began with what Cameron chose to share with the research camera, making sense of what he felt was important in his own work. Iterative review of the digital video established Cameron's focus and attention to the role of sound within his stop motion animation film, which challenged my assumptions that the focus of his time in production would be spent creating motion as he sequenced images. Rather, he sought to layer his voice onto the images he was creating and, while the film was not a particular exemplar in terms of stop motion animation, he did create a rich sonic landscape within his film. (For a more thorough and detailed analysis of Cameron's stop motion animation film, see Husbye & Rust, 2013).

Camera Avoidance

When considering the larger corpus of video data, Lucinda and Nancy, in grades five and three respectively, are remarkably absent from the majority of camera footage. Even when they are present within the data, they are only visible in quick glimpses and, in those instances, they are vocal regarding their dislike of being filmed. Oliver, a grade eight student, often enjoyed capturing the actions of his fellow students as we waiting for his own digital film to download from his home server, creating what he called "behind the scenes" footage for the culminating film festival. He would procure a research camera and check in with various production teams, asking them questions about their activity and filming their responses. This was a naturally-evolving role for Oliver and one that was readily recognized by other students in the class given Oliver's school-wide reputation as an accomplished filmmaker, having produced a documentary film about the school the previous year and whose screening was a school-wide event. These interviews were often places for students to talk about what was going well in their production while also engaging in trouble shooting the issues they were experiencing in their own filming; Oliver would offer suggestions he thought were appropriate responses to the issue and pass more complex problems onto me.

While the majority of the students in the elective film class welcomed Oliver's attention, Lucinda and Nancy actively avoided the gaze of any camera that was not their designated production camera, often going out of their way to avoid Oliver's questioning. The duo would collect all of their materials, which was a substantial amount given the scale of their musical film, and move to spaces beneath desks and tables, where Oliver was least likely to follow. This was not Oliver-specific behavior; rather, both Lucinda and Nancy sought to avoid all cameras in the classroom space, carefully selecting their working spaces as though the sight lines of the various cameras in the room were laser beams that would set off some distant alarm. During an early production session, Lucinda and Nancy began working in an area normally occupied by a team who were more welcoming of the camera's attention. As I captured in my field notes:

> Lucinda approached me today during work time and asked why there was a table aimed at the table she and Nancy were working at. I explained that it was a research camera and she and Nancy were sitting at the table Garrison, Walter, and Otto normally do and they wanted footage of them making their film. Lucinda then explained that Nancy didn't like the camera. A glance over to the corner of the room revealed Nancy crouched beneath the table, out of the gaze of the research camera mounted on the door handle. They were, Lucinda explained, afraid others would steal the ideas for their movie. Their movie, she told me, was top secret and that was why she carried the zippered envelope to and fro from *Lights, Camera, Action*, never leaving it out of her possession. They would move tables, she said, and both girls gathered their materials and moved to the table in the opposite corner. (Field Notes, May 24, 2011)

What is interesting in Lucinda's comment is how she is constructing their position as original and creative, placing their production process in danger of being mimicked by other, less-talented filmmakers in the space. Lucinda and Nancy isolated themselves for fear of the aesthetics of their film being replicated. This sense of self as creative genius (Banaji, 2009) is reified in the larger film, drawing upon classic tropes of both high culture and taste. In this way, their production process, and lack of presence in the larger video data around production, is representative of their final film product.

Discussion

There is a particular framing that tends to accompany participatory research, usually involving an adult researcher co-researching with children a single or common set of questions. *Lights, Camera, Action* is not an instance of such joint activity. Rather, individuals and teams were actively involved in the creation of film with an opportunity to participate in data collection. Participation was voluntary; just as this chapter delineated the ways in which children interfaced in specific ways with the various research cameras in the space, there were individual and groups of children who were indifferent. These children were less interested in their participation in the larger research project, giving all of their energy to the production of their own film. There was, however, significant energy exerted by both those who did and did not want to utilize research cameras and that energy went beyond the three groups described here, illuminating potential ways forward in helping researcher understand filmmaking process. While this volume, overall, wrestles with conducting research with children in early childhood, Lucinda and Nancy, as fourth graders, have transitioned out of the age range typically associated with early childhood. They have been included here to illustrate a range of responses within a project open to students across the elementary school spectrum. Their inclusion also hints at, though my analysis did not focus on, the developmental implications for participatory research researchers may face when moving from early childhood to general elementary contexts. That students were active in the development of the data set supports the analysis of that data, addressing common pitfalls that often befall researchers utilizing video data, particularly in the ways it suggests the articulation of boundaries of context and assists in navigating the seemingly overwhelming amount of video data (Blikstad-Balas, 2017).

Articulating the Boundaries of Context In exploring filmmaking as a literacy practice, I was interested in the ways the young filmmakers would make decisions regarding foregrounding and backgrounding particular modalities in their production process. While a research camera recorded the macro activity of the class, that data only provided hints at the production processes of individuals and teams. This overview of activity, however, makes that individual comprehensible, providing an external viewer with opportunities to understand how LCA was lived by the young filmmakers. As a researcher, these overviews also provided an opportunity to revisit the activity of the session, augmenting notes made in the moment; due to my dual status as both researcher and adult of record, much of my note taking during LCA reflected the present and anticipated needs of the young filmmakers. This wide-angle view of class activity allowed a second – and third and sometimes even fourth – opportunity to think about the activity as a researcher, making notes about larger patterns of production, building and testing hypotheses about the ways the young filmmakers were engaged in production, and recording questions I would ask of individuals and teams the next session.

Again, this wide view of activity was less helpful when considering the practices of individuals and teams; however, providing access to research cameras in addition to the stationary research camera illuminated individual practices. Garrison, Walter, and Otto, for instance, carefully documented their own process of production, making decisions about where to place a research camera to best represent the work they were doing on video. Students who chose to actively engage the research cameras were also articulating the boundaries of the context they were working within. Even Lucinda and Nancy, who are only seen in quick dashes across the screen, arms often filled with materials, are conveying much about the context within which they are working. This is not to say context is ever completely accounted for; rather, by attending to the ways these young filmmakers engaged the research camera, I was able to articulate the boundaries of context in ways I would not have been able to if there were only one primary research camera or only research cameras utilized by the students.

Navigating Video Data   Despite my habit of reviewing the stationary research camera every day during LCA, upon the close of the course, I faced a hard drive bursting with video data, a common occurrence for researchers working with video data (Barron, 2007). Partially due to the sheer amount of data generated, there is an ongoing threat of sampling bias wherein analysis of small chunks of video data fail to represent the larger patterns within that which is being observed (Lemke, 2007).

My interest as a researcher was in the ways that young filmmakers were making decisions as they were engaged in the processes of production; if I were relying on a research camera alone, decision-making, particularly individual decision making, would be markedly more difficult to identify in the dataset. By providing access to research cameras for the young filmmakers, I was afforded insights into their decision-making over the course of their filmmaking project. In this manner, I was able to avoid making claims on limited evidence or through overemphasizing an individual occurrence. Each of the strategies illustrated in this chapter were captured in the video data repeatedly and over the course of the project.

That these strategies were enacted time and time again within the data highlights the issue of representation and re-representation. The work in this chapter delineates my own particular analysis of the video data, particularly as I took a step back and began to look at children's patterns of participation in the creation of the larger corpus of data. Given the richness of video data, it is entirely possible that another researcher might look at the data set and come away with a different set of understandings. To this end, I have been careful in the ways in which I have represented the ways in the children oriented themselves to or controlled research cameras.

In some ways, providing young children with options in terms of their relationship to the camera allowed them to articulate some boundaries of how they want to be represented, though there is still a wide range of interpretations that could be made.

Conclusion: Participatory Research, Video Data and Literacy Learning

This book chapter concerns itself with three particular kinds of participation patterns in a literacy research project involving digital video data, suggesting that each type of interaction with the research camera has analytical value in light of lines of inquiry being pursued. Digital video itself provides a rich source of data for literacy researchers; this richness is multiplied as the participants with whom the researchers work engage in the construction of the data set. In this way, there is intentionality to the video data: an exploration of why participants engaged in particular kinds of representations within the video data collection, such as Lucinda and Nancy's near-complete absence from the video data, enhanced analysis of the literacy practices all students detailed in this chapter were engaged in.

In this way, the "innocent act" (Dahlberg, Moss, & Pence, 2013) of digital video research data is inverted: the data reveals itself as a coordinated attempt by both the researcher and the participants within the inquiry itself. This coordination, a form of participatory research, enables participants to construct narratives about their own work. When participants are actively involved in the construction of visual data, the degree to which analysis was be considered subjective and ambiguous is narrowed (Stasz, 1979). This is demonstrated in the work of Garrison, Walter, and Otto, whose awareness of how they were portrayed on the research camera while engaged in experimentation with the still camera flash prompted them to focus my attention on a particular kind of data. They wanted to ensure that I, as a researcher, understood how they were attempting to make meaning in their film that particular day.

This is not to say that participatory video data collection is not fraught with ethical and pragmatic considerations. There are issues of consent and assent to be attended to. As seen in Cameron's relationship with the video camera, participatory approaches can create possibilities for alternative pathways for engagement. Cameron, operating under the stringent directive from his mother, managed to negotiate active participation in the overall project while maintaining his anonymity. His negotiations, in combination with my efforts to engage in on-going consent processes after the project ended, have strengthened the research as my own thinking about their literacy practices have evolved through these conversations.

Such an approach redistributes the power dynamics between the researcher and the participant; rather than being cast as a passive subject, participants are actively designing how they will be represented in the larger data set. The responsibility of the researcher becomes to provide opportunities for this type of work within the larger inquiry. As demonstrated in this chapter, the ways participants engage in this can take a variety of forms, all valuable.

Questions for Reflection
- In this project, Nicholas sought to create opportunities for child participants to co-construct the corpus of video data with him. In your own project, how might you invite child participants to engage in similar collaboration?
- Relationships are crucially important in qualitative research work, particularly when video is involved. How were these relationships navigated? What is your plan in your own research to support relationship building with children?
- If we want to engage children in research, we need to position them in agentic ways. In order to do this, adults need to be willing to concede some power, both as researcher and instructive adult. How did you see this exchange in Nicholas's work with children? How might you negotiate this in your own work?

References

Banaji, S. (2009). Creativity: Exploring rhetorics and realities. In R. Willet, M. Robinson, & J. Marsh (Eds.), *Play creativity and digital cultures* (pp. 147–165). New York City, NY: Routledge.

Barron, B. (2007). Video as a tool to advance understanding of learning and development in peer, family, and other informal learning contexts. In B. Barron, R. Pea, R. Goldman-Segall, & S. J. Derry (Eds.), *Video research in the learning sciences* (pp. 159–187). New York City, NY: Routledge.

Blikstad-Balas, M. (2017). Key challenges of using video when investigating social practices in education: Contextualization, magnification, and representation. *International Journal of Research & Method in Education, 40*(5), 511–523. https://doi.org/10.1080/174372X.2016.1181162

de Certeau, M. (1984). *The practice of everyday life*. Berkeley, CA: University of California Press.

Dahlberg, G., Moss, P., & Pence, A. (2013). *Beyond quality in early childhood education*. New York City, NY: Routledge.

Flewitt, R. (2006). Using video to investigate preschool classroom interaction: Education research assumptions and methodological practices. *Visual Communication, 5*(1), 25–50. https://doi.org/10.1177/1470357206060917

Forman, G. (1999). Instant video revisiting: The video camera as "Tool of the mind" for young children. *Early Childhood Research and Practice, 1*(2), 1–7.

Gallagher, M. (2008). "Power is not an evil": Rethinking power in participatory methods. *Children's Geographies, 6*(2), 137–150. https://doi.org/10.1080/14733280801963045

Galloway, J., & Sheridan, S. M. (1994). Implementing scientific practices through case studies: Examples using home-school interventions and consultation. *Journal of School Psychology, 32*(4), 385–413.

Harper, D. (2001). Wednesday-night bowling: Reflections on cultures of a rural working class. In C. Knowles & P. Sweetman (Eds.), *Picturing the social landscape: Visual methods and the sociological imagination* (pp. 93–114). New York City, NY: Routledge.

Heath, C., Hindmarsh, J., & Luff, P. (2010). *Video in qualitative research: Analyzing social interaction in everyday life*. Thousand Oaks, CA: Sage.

Hood, S., Kelley, P., & Mayall, B. (1996). Children as research subjects. *Children and Society, 10*(2), 117–128.

Huberman, A. M., & Miles, M. B. (1994). Data management and analysis methods. In N. Denzin & Y. L. Guba (Eds.), *Handbook of qualitative research* (pp. 428–444). Thousand Oaks, CA: Sage.

Husbye, N. E., & Rust, J. (2013). Considering design: The challenges of assessing multimodal texts. In R. E. Ferdig & K. E. Pytash (Eds.), *Exploring multimodal composition and digital writing* (pp. 135–149). Hershey, PA: Information Science Reference.

Jewitt, C. (2012). *An introduction to using video for research* (NCRM working paper). National Center for Research Methods. Retrieved November 13, 2017, from http://eprints.ncrm.ac.uk/2259/

Lemke, J. (2007). Video epistemology in-and-outside the box: Traversing attentional spaces. In B. Barron, R. Pea, R. Goldman-Segall, & S. J. Derry (Eds.), *Video research in the learning sciences* (pp. 39–51). New York City, NY: Routledge.

Luff, P., & Heath, C. (2012). Some "Technical challenges" of video analysis: Social actions, objects, material realities and the problems of perspective. *Qualitative Research, 12*(3), 255–279.

Pink, S. (2003). Interdisciplinary agendas in visual research: Re-situating visual anthropology. *Visual Studies, 18*(2), 179–192. https://doi.org/10.1080/14725860310001632029

Prosser, J. (2000). The moral maze of image ethics. In H. Simons & R. Usher (Eds.), *Situated ethics in educational research* (pp. 116–132). London, UK: Routledge.

Stasz, C. (1979). The early history of visual sociology. In J. Wagner (Ed.), *Images of information: Still photography in the social sciences* (pp. 119–137). Thousand Oaks, CA: Sage.

Yin, R. K. (1982). Studying phenomenon and context across sites. *American Behavioral Scientist, 26*(1), 84–100. https://doi.org/10.1177/000276482026001007

Yin, R. K. (2009). *Case study research: Design and methods* (4th ed.). Thousand Oaks, CA: Sage.

Chapter 7
"My Treasure Box": Pedagogical Documentation, Digital Portfolios and Children's Agency in Finnish Early Years Education

Kristiina Kumpulainen and Najat Ouakrim-Soivio

Introduction

In Finland, early years education (ECE) is a universal public service that is based on the principles of social justice and equity. Its primary goal is to support every child's holistic development and learning together with parents/guardians (Kumpulainen, 2018). High-quality Finnish ECE implements well-planned pedagogical practices and their systematic documentation via participatory work between teachers, children and their families. It thrives to recognising children's unique interests and developmental needs, appreciating the characteristics of the local contexts in which children learn and develop (National Board of Education, 2016). Quality in pedagogical practice and documentation is supported by the national ECE curriculum guidelines as well as by an educated and skilled ECE workforce.

The goal of pedagogical documentation in the Finnish ECE is to support inclusive participatory work entailing interaction and knowledge exchange among the people in children's lives, and joint reflection on the quality of ECE and its connection to children's learning, development and wellbeing (see also Edwards, Gandini, & Forman, 1998). Pedagogical documentation is embedded in the values of the Finnish ECE, which consider childhood a unique and precious phase in human life that must be cherished in its own right. From this perspective, each child has the right to be heard, seen, recognised and understood as a unique individual and as a member of his or her community (National Board of Education, 2016).

In the research literature, pedagogical documentation is defined as a tool for participatory work that can enhance the quality of ECE that is reflexive, interactive and based on social justice and equity (Dahlberg, Moss, & Pence, 2007). Pedagogical documentation strives to make ECE practices visible and is especially interested in the child's participation and perspective. Pedagogical documentation can offer

K. Kumpulainen (✉) · N. Ouakrim-Soivio
University of Helsinki, Helsinki, Finland
e-mail: kristiina.kumpulainen@helsinki.fi; najat.ouakrim-soivio@helsinki.fi

© Springer Nature Switzerland AG 2019
A. Eckhoff (ed.), *Participatory Research with Young Children*, Educating the Young Child 17, https://doi.org/10.1007/978-3-030-19365-2_7

teachers, other ECE personnel and parents/guardians information about the child's interests as well as his or her self-image as a learner and as a unique individual. This knowledge can be harnessed for the development of ECE pedagogy to meet each child's interests and needs. Observation and documentation of the child's perspectives, experiences and knowledge can make each child and his or her activity and thoughts meaningful and important (Cook & Hess, 2007; Karlsson, 2012).

In the Finnish ECE, pedagogical documentation is conceptualised as a collective and co-constructed endeavour between the child, teacher and parents/caregivers for enhancing participatory knowledge exchange, reflection and learning. The main principle is to consider children as active agents in documenting and reflecting upon their interests, strengths and learning progressions in collaboration with their teachers and parents/caregivers in multimodal ways (Kumpulainen, Lipponen, Hilppö, & Mikkola, 2014). Overall, the Finnish ECE resonates with participatory research methodologies and childhood studies in general that position children at the centre of pedagogical attention and practice (Christensen & James, 2008). Thus, the child can be viewed as an active agent and a recognised participant in ECE.

Earlier research has pointed out that an important dimension of pedagogical documentation is the collective interpretation and reflection of the documented material (Rinaldi, 1998). In fact, reflection distinguishes pedagogical documentation from mere archiving of documents (Rintakorpi, 2018). According to Dahlberg et al. (2007), pedagogical documentation should not be confused with standardised observation methods, as pedagogical documentation emphasises the situated nature of human activity. Thus, pedagogical documentation can be seen as an effort to make children and their activities and worlds visible in multiple ways and modes situated in the sociocultural context.

In this chapter, we are interested to make visible the opportunities and challenges associated with the practices of pedagogical documentation in the everyday life of Finnish ECE. We are particularly interested in how digital portfolios are used in ECE classrooms for inclusive participatory practice. Our work aligns with efforts to understand and design for inclusive documentation practices in the everyday life of ECE classrooms.

Digital Portfolios as a Means of Pedagogical Documentation

Digital portfolios are attracting increased attention as a means of pedagogical documentation of ECE practices (Kumpulainen & Ouakrim-Soivio, 2018). These portfolios can consist of multimodal content of the processes and products of children's activities, learning and development created via various textual, visual, digital and audio procedures (Anttila, 2013). The content of digital portfolios typically stems from children's life worlds, including home, ECE centres, field trips, hobbies and leisure time. Visual methods and artefacts, such as, the creation of drawings, photographs and videos, have gained popularity among Finnish educators and researchers as potential means for participatory work in pedagogical documentation (Kumpulainen, 2017). Visual methods are regarded as natural, child-sensitive means that can potentially communicate children's perspectives in multiple and authentic ways in their full complexity and that provide knowledge about the world as experienced by children that would be difficult, and even impossible, to gain in other ways (Clark, 2005). Visual methods are also linked to other creative and aesthetic forms of self-expression that help the narrator find his or her voice and identity (Bragg, 2011; Brushwood Rose & Low, 2014). Lorenz (2010) defines visual artefacts as metaphors that can animate emotions and personal experiences and help children share and reflect upon their worlds. Overall, visual methods and artefacts for education are considered important in a world that is largely based on pre-described performance and accountability and in which there is little room for emotions, creativity and collective interpretation (Kumpulainen, 2017).

Altogether, digital portfolios are considered dynamic tools that can potentially capture and enhance and make visible the multidimensionality of children's learning and development in ways that more traditional educational methods cannot (Niikko, 2000; Wagner, Brock, & Agnew, 1994). Children's personal digital portfolios also offer the child an opportunity to reflect on and evaluate one's learning, development and wellbeing. Consequently, in the Finnish ECE, digital portfolios are considered to enhance the child's self-evaluation skills while the child can engage in organising, documenting and making sense of his or her activities, thoughts, feelings and learning via portfolio work (Ouakrim-Soivio, 2016).

In Finland, research on pedagogical documentation and the use of digital portfolios in ECE is surprisingly restricted and limited, considering that they are considered important methods of participatory ECE pedagogy in the curriculum documents and in teacher education. Kankaanranta (1998) investigated the use of portfolios to support children's transitioning to first grade and active interaction between teachers, parents/guardians and children (see also Kankaanranta & Linnakylä, 1999). Rintakorpi (2010, 2018) investigated the ways in which pedagogical documentation in the Finnish ECE centres responds to the ECE curriculum and how ECE personnel approach pedagogical documentation in their work, which refers to the meanings and purposes that ECE educators attach to pedagogical documentation.

In this chapter, we aim to extend current research knowledge on the use of digital portfolios as means of participatory work in pedagogical documentation in Finnish ECE. We ask how digital portfolios are used in the Finnish ECE centres and how children's participation, agency and reflection manifest themselves in the contents and forms of digital portfolios. To this end, we draw on empirical data from the research and development programme of three Finish municipalities and their ECE centres. We demonstrate how the construction of digital portfolios as a means of pedagogical documentation in these ECE communities produced a dynamic tension between the adults' and children's agency; between digital archiving and narrative documentation of the children's lived experiences; and between documentation and reflection.

Sociocultural Theorising on Children's Agency

Lately, more researchers, scholars and educational providers are underscoring children's agency and involving children in educational processes and research. Childhood and children are seen as worthy of investigation in their own right and as important participants in pedagogical work as teachers and researchers in education aim to learn more about children's worlds from children themselves (Einarsdottir, Dockett, & Perry, 2009). The underlying rationale for the interest is manifold. From one perspective, it stems from initiatives that stress children's visibility and position in society and entail respecting their right to express opinions and have a say in matters that affect their lives (Lundy, 2007). Another perspective holds that listening to children's voices, that is, their meanings, experiences, opinions and perspectives in relation to their life worlds, creates avenues for educators to learn about children and, hence, to support their holistic learning and wellbeing. Researchers have suggested that weaving children's voices into the educational process promotes educational equity and opportunity (Kumpulainen et al., 2014; Niemi, Kumpulainen, & Lipponen, 2014).

The sociocultural framework that guides our research work on participatory work with children foregrounds agency as a social construct that derives from context. Accordingly, we conceptualise children's agency as socially constructed, meaning that children's agency is the result of a dynamic interaction between the child's life history, prior experiences and the social context in a given activity (Valsiner, 1998). Hence, there exists a relational interdependence between agency and social context. We also hold that agency can manifest itself in various actions that encompass discursive, practical and embodied relations to the world (see also Archer, 2001, 2003). Hence, agency should be analysed by focusing on the manifestation of agency in social practices, as well as on the children's interpretations, meanings and purposes in relation to their agentic actions in different social contexts.

Sociocultural theorisation of agency underscores the importance of conceptual (e.g. language) and material (e.g. artefacts) tools in mediating human interaction and sense-making (Bakhtin, 1986; Wertsch, 1991). Vygotsky (1978) explains the mediating role of tools in human interaction using the concept of double stimulation, in which an external tool is employed or created for intentional, voluntary problem-solving activities. In other words, to redefine situations, control their own actions and transform the contexts in which they act, people develop and use artefacts (Virkkunen, 2006). Using this line of thinking, we can approach digital portfolios as material tools that mediate and create opportunities for children's agency and reflection, and that can at an organisational level foster inclusive participatory practices in ECE. We can also view digital portfolios as creating a potential social context for collective reflection between the child, ECE educators and parents/guardians.

Description of Research Study

Our study uses empirical data from a one-year development project (conducted throughout 2017) of three Finnish municipalities and their ECE centres (Kirkkonummen kunta, 2018). The project was designed by the municipalities themselves to offer ECE teachers professional support and portfolio tools for the enhancement of participatory work in pedagogical documentation in their everyday work at the ECE centres. The professional support of educators consisted of courses and seminars over one academic year addressing theories and models on pedagogical documentation. These seminars took place on average once a month. The topics covered the introduction of pedagogical models that underscore the importance of documenting and reflecting on children's strengths and interests in their ECE instead of focusing only on children's developmental needs and what they cannot yet do. The education of teachers also focused on the notion of "media play" in which the teachers learned how to harness digital media in participatory, playful, child-centric and transformative ways as part of their ECE practices. Last but not least the professional development program was specifically directed to ECE centre leaders/ heads for managing the change processes in implementing digital portfolios in participatory ways in their ECE centres. In addition to seminar days, the educators who represented these three different municipalities and their ECE centres were also able to share their work with others in the seminar meetings and beyond, thus enhancing peer learning. There was some support at the educators' workplace for the uptake and use of the digital portfolio and digital documentation.

Altogether, the empirical data of our study comprise the digital portfolios of 71 children from six different ECE groups across three municipalities who participated in the development programme. Of these 71 children, 37 were girls (52%) and 34 (48%) were boys. All these children worked in mixed aged groups composed of children aged 3–5 years old. This is a typical arrangement in the Finnish ECE for these age groups. The number of children whose portfolio data were analysed for this study varied from 7 to 18 children per ECE group. These were children who had a written consent to take part in this specific study. According to the Finnish law, the maximum number of children in an ECE group for children over 3 years old is 24, the educator child ratio being 1:8 (Kumpulainen, 2018).

Ethical Considerations

Our research follows the ethical guidelines for research set forth by the Finnish Advisory Board on Research Integrity (http://www.tenk.fi/en) and the University of Helsinki. The study only uses material has been authorised by the municipalities, ECE centres and children's parents/guardians. Children's participation in the research was voluntary, and the children could withdraw from the study at any time.

The digital portfolios we analysed in our study were saved in a peda.net service administered by the University of Jyväskylä in Finland. The municipalities chose this service for their portfolio work, and the ECE centres and their personnel independently archived the digital portfolios into this service without the researchers' involvement. The researchers of this article are not responsible for the service and its use. The analysis of the children's portfolios took place directly from the service to which the researchers were granted access. The research material has not been stored elsewhere. In sum, we paid careful attention to research ethics to respect and honour the integrity of the children and their communities (Sime, 2008).

Methods

The analysis of the data was guided by our research questions, which focused on the content and purposes for which the digital portfolios were used in the ECE groups, and on the manifestation of children's agency in and reflection on the portfolio content. We analysed the data using both quantitative and qualitative methods. The quantitative analyses focused on the general qualities in the content of the portfolios, such as the number of photos and videos in each child's portfolio. The typical quantitative methods, e.g. frequency distributions and measures of central tendency and variation, were used. Differences between the six ECE groups were analysed using a one-way ANOVA test. If there were statistically significant differences, the differences in the variance analysis were also reported using etha's square (h2) (Cohen, 1988; Cohen, Manion, & Morrison, 2002). The correlations between quantitative variables were studied using Pearson's correlation coefficients and coefficients of determination. We recognise the limitations of our quantitative analyses due to the small sample size.

The qualitative analysis of the portfolios focused on the topics and themes depicted in the portfolio content (i.e. written texts, photos and videos) to develop an understanding of the content and purposes of the portfolios in the pedagogical documentation of the ECE centres as well as the nature of children's agency and reflection in relation to their portfolios. The analysis process begun by reading all the data repeatedly to achieve immersion and obtain a sense of the whole (Tesch, 1990). Then, we began our abductive development of overall themes from the data while drawing on sociocultural theories on agency and relevant research findings on pedagogical documentation and digital portfolios (Miles & Huberman, 1994). Altogether, our analysis involved repeated iterations between data and theory (Van Maanen, Sørensen, & Terence, 2007)

Our qualitative content analysis revealed three polarities in the construction and use of the children's digital portfolios in the ECE groups; the adult's and child's agency; digital archiving and narrative documentation; documentation and reflection. Each of these thematic groupings and their polarities provide evidence of the different purposes and ways in which the portfolios were used. They also illuminate the varied opportunities children to exercise their agency and reflect on the portfolio content.

Results

Here, we discuss the findings of our study. First, by drawing on both quantitative and qualitative data, we provide an overview of the content and forms of the digital portfolios in and across the ECE groups and children. Second, we discuss our findings on the thematic dimensions depicted from our data with regards to the ways in which the digital portfolios were constructed and used in the ECE practices, as well as the nature of children's participation, agency and reflection in this process.

The Nature of the Digital Portfolios in and Across the ECE Groups and Children

Our findings show that the children's digital portfolios mostly consisted of photos and videos. At times, these photos and videos were accompanied by written explanatory texts.

No gender differences were identified in the number of pictures and videos in the children's portfolios ($F = 0.07$, df = 1, 3.05; $p < 0.05$). Interestingly, there were significant differences in the number of photos in the children's digital portfolios across the different ECE groups ($F = 18.13$; df = 5, 430, 80; $p < 0.01$). Also, the number of videos in the children's portfolios differed significantly across the children and ECE groups ($F = 5.99$; df = 5, 16.46; $p < 0.001$). The ECE group explained 58% of the differences between the average number of photos per children and the ECE group explained 32% of the differences between the average number of videos per children. The number of photos in the child's digital portfolio did not correlate with the number of videos ($r_{xy} = 0.15$).

The contents of the children's personal portfolios largely documented the children's everyday life and activities in and outside of the ECE centres. For instance, the contents of the portfolios included digital photos on "a theatre trip", "first snow and a snowman", "physical jerks", "recycling", "all about my summer", "my favorite place at the ECE center", "in the forest", "snack", "our play", "playing in the yard", "in the park", "jerk play", "cake bakers", "my picture", "I am good at" and "what I want to learn" (see Figs. 7.1, 7.2 and 7.3).

Moreover, most of the children's digital portfolios included documentation of various learning processes, such as developing a skill or developing knowledge of a certain concept (see Figs. 7.4 and 7.5). Such processes were often documented via videos related to ideas and activities such as "What I want to learn", "making a concoction", "jumping on the trampoline", "water games", "silhouette dance", "singing and music performances" and "future dreams". A child's "achievement picture" served as an example of a picture in which the child shows how he or she designed his or her artefact via chain loops.

Typical to the children's portfolios was the documentation of the children's emotions and social relationships (see Figs. 7.6 and 7.7). These materials were often

Fig. 7.1 Mathematics

Fig. 7.2 Fifteen nights for Christmas

entitled as "the most boring or enjoyable play" followed by a photo of a "shelter play", dodgeball or playing home. Children's emotions were also documented via titles and accompanying photos, such as "This is what I like" and "Happy moments". For these contents, the children selected pictures that depicted things they liked, such as riding a slide, woodwork and cats and dogs. In "Happy moments", the portfolio documents consisted of pictures that depicted everyday life in ECE, favorite play, birthdays and the children's achievements.

Altogether, the contents of the children's digital portfolios resonate well with the goals of the Finnish ECE curriculum, which emphasises children's rights to play, learning by playing, joy and making sense of oneself and the surrounding world via

Fig. 7.3 This is what I like to do the most during my summer

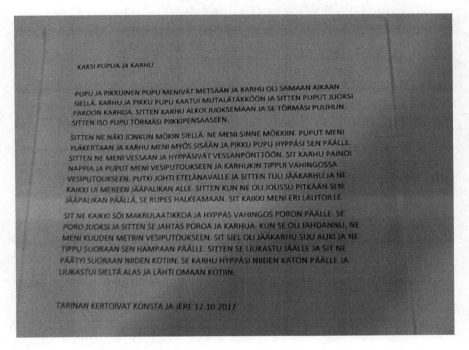

Fig. 7.4 Storytelling was fun. Not boring at all

wonder and investigation. The curriculum also underscores children's rights to express and share emotions in multiple ways and via multiple modes as well as to learn new skills and knowledge independently and in collaboration with others (National Board of Education, 2016). However, the significant differences in the

Fig. 7.5 I was so afraid when I went skating the first time. The ice was slippery. You must stay still and then I skated a little. I could not yet skate

Fig. 7.6 Saara's rule: You must not tease others or take their toys

amount of content in the children's digital portfolios across the children and ECE groups warrants attention, as these suggest inequalities among the children in the ways their lives, learning experiences and emotions were recognised, documented and reflected upon.

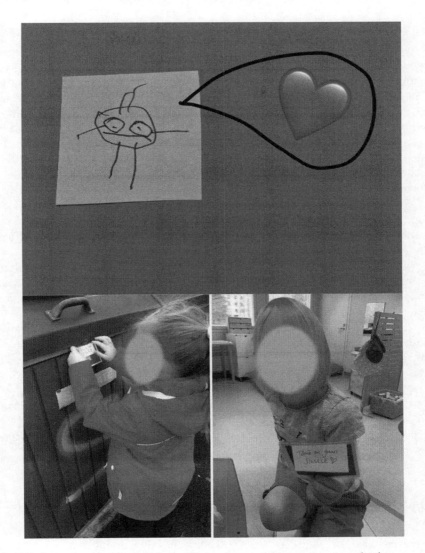

Fig. 7.7 Our praise campaign: passing positive and encouraging messages to each other

Next, we discuss the thematic and contrasting dimensions identified in the contents of the children's portfolios to highlight the possibilities and challenges in the use of digital portfolios as a means of participatory work in pedagogical documentation in the context of Finnish ECE.

Adult's Agency and Child's Agency

While the digital portfolios dynamically captured the children's everyday lives, learning and emotional wellbeing in accordance with the goals set forth by the Finnish ECE curriculum, there was little evidence of the children's own agency in the construction and content of the portfolios. Hence, children's participatory work in pedagogical documentation was not always realised. By large, the content of the documentation was directed by the adult/teacher, hence evidencing strong teacher agency in acting as the prime and oftentimes the only author of the child's portfolio content. Moreover, the data provide evidence of pre-planned situations captured in the digital portfolios, such as singing and exercise time. All the children in the same ECE group had a similar or the same picture or video in their personal portfolio. In sum, the children pictured themselves in many portfolios as passive objects rather than agentive actors in terms of their participation in designing and creating their portfolios.

In a few ECE groups, we found evidence of the children's participation and agency in the design and content development of the portfolios between the educator and the child. For instance, in one ECE group, each child had a folder on emotions that the child had constructed together with the adult. The documentation on the child's emotions took place on a flower-shaped poster. In the middle of the flower poster, there was a text that read, "This is who I am", underneath which appeared the child's name. The following topics were written on the petals of the flower: "The most fun thing at the ECE center is…."; "I will be happy when…"; "This is what I love to do the most…."; "I am good at….."; "This is what I love to do the most with my dad….."; "I will be sad when…"; "These are my favorite plays..."; "My strengths are…"; "I would like to learn more about…."; "My important friends are…"; and "This is what I love to do the most with my mom….". The ECE teacher had written down the child's responses to each of these topics.

Digital Archiving and Narration

From our analysis, we identified two contrasting dimensions in the use of the portfolios. On the one hand, the portfolios were used to archive the photos and videos without narrating the contents in the children's portfolios. On the other hand, there were digital portfolios that created a meaningful storyline from the content.

In its most simple form, narration was visible in the children's portfolios, which were thematically organised. These folders included titles such as "My important moments", "Learning stories and thinking" and "I in a group". In this same ECE group, the teachers edited digital pictures that documented the children's future goals. Using the pictures, each child depicted his or her dream, such as flying with the wings of an airplane, acting as an archaeologist on an excavation or driving a large Land Rover. In another ECE group, the educators created a blog which was available and visible for parents to comment upon. The blog consisted of pictures and short texts explaining the everyday life at the ECE center. The blog contrasted with the archived documentation, in which the portfolios consisted of only pictures with little explanation or attention to storying or reflection processes. Overall, the titling and written descriptions appeared to enhance the narrative potential of the digital portfolios.

The narrative nature of documentation in the digital portfolios was also manifested in the series of visual documents that pictured the processes of the children's crafting activities, watercolour painting or climbing a bunk bed to take a nap. These documents typically ended by showing the outcome and/or end product of the activity. For example, there was a series of pictures drawn by one child that were about herself and her family, as well as pictures that depicted how the child was learning to write her name. These pictures were accompanied by a short and simple title that helped the reader understand how the child was making sense of and developing within his or her sociocultural context. In one ECE group, the teachers constructed a blog that created an interpretative framework and context for the photos and videos and texts, thus enhancing the narrative nature of the digital portfolios.

Videos were also powerful for illuminating the narrative nature of the pedagogical documentation in the children's portfolios. For instance, a video clip could demonstrate the processes of learning to spell the letter R. Also, a child's process of learning how to do a somersault was demonstrated via several videos, thus highlighting how the child was developing a skill. In another ECE center the digital portfolios consisted of videos of singing moments that were later edited to highlight the child's progression.

Documentation and Reflection

Our results give evidence of a dynamic interplay between the use of portfolios for documentation and the use of portfolios for reflection. About two thirds of the 71 children had pictures and videos with explanatory text in their portfolios that demonstrated the child's reflection on their portfolios. One third of the portfolios did not give any evidence of the children's engagement in explaining or reflecting on their portfolios. In these cases, digital portfolios were used to document and archive digital content on children's lives in ECE and not as tools for reflection.

Reflection was evidenced by the children's own narrations of their portfolio content, with the educators acting as reporters of the children's storying. In these cases, the children's portfolios included texts such as, "I drew my dad, mom, big brother, sister and me. And a cat, and a baby cat. And a flower. Dad has a flower." In another portfolio, there was a photo taken from the child's favorite play that depicted a shelter made out of pillows and covers. The child's narration consisted of the following: "The shelter play is fun since we can play hide and seek. And play with soft toys. We can play home too. When the adult puts the roof on our shelter is its fun."

Videos were also effective for capturing the children's reflection activities. For instance, one ECE group developed "Reflection videos", which each lasted for about 5 min, that included the child's own reflection of his or her ECE activity, thoughts and feelings. Here, the adult and child watched, discussed, recalled and reflected upon the digital content together.

One ECE group constructed a joint collage regarding the topic of "All about my summer", and in the video the child reflected upon the major events that occurred during her summer vacation. In the video, the child is looking at the collage and explains its content: "Everything about my summer are demonstrated as well. I had eaten sausage, it was good. The sausage was grilled over a barbeque. V was visiting us overnight. We spent a night at Ähtäri. Sleeping at a hammock. Eating a nut and baking wafers. I like chocolate ice cream. At activity park jumping on a trampoline."

There were also other interesting 5-min videos that demonstrated how the children were developing their reflection and evaluation skills. For example, in one video the adult asks the child which situations she wants to document in her digital portfolio, or "treasure box". The adult and child also discuss and reflect on the content of the digital portfolio together:

Educator:	Are you ok, if we look at your "treasure box" together?
Child:	Jep!
Educator:	Here are exercise videos from this week, do you remember?
Child:	Mmm.
Educator:	What does this picture tell about?
Child:	When we did physical jerks with the rings.
Educator:	And then...what's there?
Child:	A tape.
Educator:	Yeah, they call it a rope... whose there? You are doing so well there. And what did we do yesterday?
Child:	We threw ball.
Educator:	What else?
Child:	Mmm, and then rubber boots.
Educator:	Yeah, we threw rubber boots too.

The conversation regarding the content of the digital portfolio continues, and the adult asks, "How do you feel about watching these memories from these videos?" The child responds, "Good!" The educator then asks, "Have you watched these pictures with mum or dad?" The child's shakes her head, indicating no. Before the child continues, another mother enters the room and the reflection moment ends.

Neither the ECE teachers nor the parents were found to comment or reflect on the children's portfolios. Of the 71 portfolios in total, there was only one portfolio in which one parent commented on a picture of her child's artwork. Also, there was little, if any, evidence of joint reflection and analysis of the content of the portfolio material between the child, parent/guardian and the educator. Only two portfolios showed evidence of such collective reflection. These findings may be explained partially by the fact that the actual service that was used for the digital portfolios was inflexible and cumbersome to use, thus discouraging parents and children from participating, commenting and reflecting on the content. The platform that were chosen to be used in this development project required literacy of some kind. The children could not navigate without any reading skills and they seemed to need very often adult's help for adding pictures or videos. Clearly, the reasons for these findings warrant further research.

Discussion

In our chapter, we have discussed the use of digital portfolios in pedagogical documentation as a form of inclusive participatory practice in the cultural context of the Finnish ECE. Grounding our work in sociocultural theorising, we focused on the opportunities and challenges in the use of digital portfolios with young children in their early years education and specifically focused on children's participation and agency in this work. The empirical research that we drew upon in this chapter stems from a research and development programme initiated by three Finnish municipalities and their early years centres on the use of digital portfolios in their ECE. The development project was motivated by the need to develop ECE pedagogy, specifically the methods of pedagogical documentation for the enhancement of the quality of ECE, ensuring children's participation and equal educational opportunities.

Our research demonstrates how digital portfolios can highlight the richness of children's activities, interests and emotions, as well as learning and development processes. In many cases the digital portfolio content did not entail extraordinary or extreme experiences, but rather, just the opposite. In many cases, the portfolios documented small but seemingly important moments in the lives of the children. In accordance with our earlier research, we can conclude that the events and activities captured in the children's portfolios could have easily gone unnoticed if they were not captured in the portfolios (Kumpulainen et al., 2014).

Our study also shows that digital portfolios have great potential to be more than archiving tools. As illuminated in some cases of our study, portfolios can tell rich and multi-layered stories behind ECE activities and children's participation in these activities. These portfolio contents can capture the narrative and aesthetic dimensions of children's everyday lives, which are situated in sociocultural contexts. In these situations, the children were invited to move between the past, the present and the future to compose their life stories and describe the significant events in those stories. Hence, the narratives of the children's lives and experiences were brought into existence for collective memorisation, analysis and reflection. In sum, we conclude that digital portfolios offer children and adults rich means of bringing light upon the everyday life of their engagement in ECE which, again, can result in new meanings, emotions and experiences for everyone involved.

Yet, at the same time, our research indicates the complexity and challenges of using digital portfolios in ECE for inclusive participatory work. The results of our study show that while digital portfolios created diverse and rich opportunities for pedagogical documentation of the children's everyday lives, learning and emotional wellbeing in accordance with the goals set forth by the Finnish ECE curriculum, there was little evidence of the children's own participation and agency in the construction of the portfolios. Despite the possibilities of digital portfolios, our data show many instances in which the digital portfolios were adult-directed and used for archiving rather than for collective interaction, reflection and learning between the child, ECE teachers and parents/guardians. Altogether, our results show how pedagogical documentation and the construction of digital portfolios entailed a dynamic tension between the adults' and child's agency; between digital archiving and narrative documentation of children's lived experiences; and between digital documentation and reflection.

The results also show major differences in the contents and use of digital portfolios across the ECE groups and children, which suggest that the children were seen and heard differently depending on the child and in which group the child was part of. Hence, the results indicate how the digital portfolios created inequality among the children in terms of the ways in which they were seen and heard and how they could participate in constructing and reflecting upon their portfolios. Our study also gives evidence of quality differences in the ways the ECE educators used digital portfolios as tools of participatory work in pedagogical documentation. Our study emphasises recognising the importance of pedagogical expertise among ECE personnel in the use of digital portfolios as tools of pedagogical documentation for the benefit of every child's participation, learning and development. Recognising every child's agency and opportunities for participation and reflection in the construction and use of digital portfolios, calls for pedagogical expertise, creativity and digital skills from the educators.

In Finland, ECE educators are expected to tailor ECE to each child. Educators are charged to recognise barriers to participation, challenge practices that support inequity and find ways to maximise learning opportunities for all children. Clearly, these expectations require that those working in ECE services are strong and capable professionals. The creation of supportive social contexts based on trust, appreciation and authentic interest in children's experiences and learning lives is of utmost importance in constructing portfolio work and pedagogical documentation in ECE that is based on participatory work.

Educators occupy a central role in creating ECE pedagogy that empowers children's participation and agency for the advancement of children's learning and holistic development (Edwards, 2007; Johnsson, 2008; Lipponen & Kumpulainen, 2011; Pace & Hemmings, 2007). In order to create opportunities for children's participation and agency to document and reflect upon their life worlds, a new type of relationship that grants agency to children and uses children's lived experiences as a starting point for ECE is needed. This calls for the reconfiguration of ECE practices away from teacher-authored activities, and sensitivity in guiding portfolio practices towards enhancing children's participation and agency (Kumpulainen & Lipponen, 2010). The children should not only be positioned by adults, but they should also be granted opportunities for agency in directing and composing their portfolios. This child-centred approach requires strong teacher professionalism to make the shift possible.

Questions for Reflection

- How unique do you feel the Finnish ECE's valuing and support for participatory work with children and families is in light of your experiences working with or researching alongside young children? What benefits does this valuing afford to early childhood researchers?
- How can ECE teachers promote children's and their guardians' participation and agency in pedagogical documentation via digital portfolios?
- What challenges are identified in the construction of digital portfolios for inclusive participatory work in the Finnish ECE?

References

Anttila, P. (2013). Taitojen ja luovien alojen arvioinnin kysymyksiä. In A. Räisänen (Ed.), *Oppimisen arvioinnin kontekstit ja käytännöt* (pp. 89–118). Helsinki, Finland: Opetushallitus.

Archer, M. (2001). *Being human: The problem of agency.* Cambridge, MA: Cambridge University Press.

Archer, M. (2003). *Structure, agency and the internal conversation.* Cambridge, MA: Cambridge University Press.

Bakhtin, M. (1986). *Speech genres and other late essays.* Austin, TX: University of Texas Press.

Bragg, S. (2011). "Now it's up to us to interpret it": "Youth voice" and visual methods in creative learning and research. In P. Thomson & J. Sefton-Green (Eds.), *Researching creative learning: Methods and approaches* (pp. 88–103). London, UK/New York, NY: Routledge.

Brushwood Rose, C., & Low, B. (2014). Exploring the 'craftedness' of multimedia narratives: From creation to interpretation. *Visual Studies, 29*(1), 30–39. https://www.tandfonline.com/doi/abs/10.1080/1472586X.2014.862990

Christensen, P., & James, A. (Eds.). (2008). *Research with children: Perspectives and practices.* London, UK: Routledge.

Clark, A. (2005). Listening to and involving young children: A review of research and practice. *Early Child Development and Care, 175*(6), 489–505.

Cohen, J. (1988). *Statistical power analysis for the behavioural sciences* (2nd ed.). Hillsdale, NJ: Lawrence Erlbaum Associates.

Cohen, L., Manion, L., & Morrison, K. (2002). *Research methods in education.* London, UK: Routledge Falmer.

Cook, T., & Hess, E. (2007). What the camera sees and from whose perspective. Fun methodologies for engaging children in enlightening adults. *Childhood, 14*(1), 29–45. https://doi.org/10.1177/0907568207068562

Dahlberg, G., Moss, P., & Pence, A. (2007). *Beyond quality in early childhood education and care: Languages of evaluation.* London, UK: Routledge.

Edwards, A. (2007). Relational agency in professional practice: A CHAT analysis. *An International Journal of Human Activity Theory, 1*, 1–17.

Edwards, C., Gandini, L., & Forman, G. (Eds.). (1998). *The hundred languages of children. The Reggio Emilia approach – Advanced reflections.* New York, NY: Ablex Publishing Corporation.

Einarsdottir, J., Dockett, S., & Perry, B. (2009). Making meaning: Children's perspectives expressed through drawings. *Early Child Development and Care, 179*(2), 217–232.

Johnson, B. (2008). Teacher – Student relationships which promote resilience at school: A micro-level analysis of students' views. *British Journal of Guidance and Counselling, 36*(4), 385–398.

Kankaanranta, M. (1998). *Kertomuksia kasvusta ja oppimisesta. Portfoliot siltana päiväkodista kouluun.* (Stories of growth and learning. Portfolios as a bridge from kindergarten to primary school). Jyväskylä, Finland: University of Jyväskylä: Institute for Educational Research.

Kankaanranta, M., & Linnakylä, P. (1999). Portfolio tutkimusmenetelmänä lapsuuden kasvu- ja oppimisympäristöissä. In I. Ruoppila, E. Hujala, K. Karila, J. Kinos, P. Niiranen, & M. Ojala (Eds.), *Varhaiskasvatuksen tutkimusmenetelmiä* (pp. 260–261). Jyväskylä, Finland: Gummerus Kirjapaino Oy.

Karlsson, L. (2012). Lapsinäkökulmaisen tutkimuksen ja toiminnan poluilla. In L. Karlsson & R. Karimäki (Eds.), *Sukelluksia lapsinäkökulmaiseen tutkimukseen ja toimintaan* (pp. 17–63). Jyväskylä, Finland: Suomen kasvatustieteellinen seura.

Kirkkonummen kunta. (2018). *Diggaa mun digimatkaa – Digga min digiresa. Digitaaliset portfoliot varhaiskasvatuksen pedagogisen toimintakulttuurin kehittämisessä.* Accessed from https://indd.adobe.com/view/9ce1fc00-a197-48e0-851f-c0d88ee6b402

Kumpulainen, K. (2017). Picturing voice: Visual methods and children's voices in Finnish education. *Image, 3*(1), 210–212.

Kumpulainen, K. (2018). A principled, personalised, trusting and child-centric ECEC system in Finland. In S. L. Kagan (Ed.), *The early advantage 1: Early childhood systems that lead by example* (pp. 72–98). New York, NY: Teachers College Press.

Kumpulainen, K., & Lipponen, L. (2010). Productive interaction as agentic participation in dialogic enquiry. In K. Littleton & C. Howe (Eds.), *Educational dialogues. Understanding and promoting productive interaction* (pp. 48–63). London, UK: Routledge.

Kumpulainen, K., Lipponen, L., Hilppö, J., & Mikkola, A. (2014). Building on the positive in children's lives: A co-participatory study on the social construction of children's sense of agency. *Early Child Development and Care, 184*(2), 211–229.

Kumpulainen, K., & Ouakrim-Soivio, N. (2018). Digitaalinen portfolio varhaiskasvatuksen toiminnan arvioinnissa. In Kirkkonummen kunta (Ed.), *Diggaa mun digimatkaa – Digga min digiresa. Digitaaliset portfoliot varhaiskasvatuksen pedagogisen toimintakulttuurin kehittämisessä* (pp. 50–54). Kirkkonummi, Finland: Kirkkonummen kunta. Retrieved from https://indd.adobe.com/view/9ce1fc00-a197-48e0-851f-c0d88ee6b402

Lipponen, L., & Kumpulainen, K. (2011). Acting as accountable authors: Creating interactional spaces for agency work in teacher education. *Teaching and Teacher Education, 27*(5), 812–819.

Lorenz, L. (2010). Visual metaphors of living with brain injury: Exploring and communicating lived experience with an invisible injury. *Visual Studies, 25*(3), 210–223.

Lundy, L. (2007). Voice is not enough: Conceptualising Article 12 of the United Nations Convention on the Rights of the Child. *British Educational Research Journal, 33*(6), 927–942.

Miles, M. B., & Huberman, A. M. (1994). *Qualitative data analysis: An expanded sourcebook.* Thousand Oaks, CA: Sage.

National Board of Education. (2016). *Varhaiskasvatuksen opetussuunnitelman perusteet* (Määräykset ja ohjeet, 17). Helsinki, Finland: Opetushallitus.

Niemi, R., Kumpulainen, K., & Lipponen, L. (2014). Pupils' documentation enlightening teachers' practical theory and pedagogical actions. *Educational Action Research, 23*(4), 599. https://doi.org/10.1080/09650792.2014.942334

Niikko, A. (2000). Portfolio oppimisen ja kasvun välineenä. In J. Enkenberg, P. Väisänen, & E. Savolainen (Eds.), *Kohti opettajatiedon kipinöitä. Kirjoituksia pedagogiikasta* (pp. 102–119). Joensuun yliopisto, Finland: Savonlinnan opettajankoulutuslaitos.

Ouakrim-Soivio, N. (2016). *Oppimisen ja osaamisen arviointi.* Helsinki, Finland: Otava.

Pace, J. L., & Hemmings, A. (2007). Understanding authority in classrooms: A review of theory, ideology, and research. *Review of Educational Research, 77*(1), 4–27.

Rinaldi, C. (1998). Projected curriculum constructed through documentation – Progettazione: An interview with Lella Gandini. In C. Edwards, L. Gandini, & G. Forman (Eds.), *The hundred languages of children. The Reggio Emilia approach - advanced reflections* (pp. 113–125). Westport, CT: Ablex Publishing.

Rintakorpi, K. (2010). *Lasten toiminnan dokumentointi varhaiskasvauksessa.* Pro gradu tutkielma. Käyttäytymistieteellinen tiedekunta, Helsingin yliopisto.

Rintakorpi, K. (2018). *From documentation towards pedagogical documentation in early childhood.* Doctoral dissertation. Faculty of Educational Sciences. University of Helsinki. Retrieved from https://helda.helsinki.fi/bitstream/handle/10138/229852/Varhaisk.pdf?sequence=1

Sime, D. (2008). Ethical and methodological issues in engaging young people living in poverty with participatory research methods. *Children's Geographies, 6*(1), 63–78.

Tesch, R. (1990). *Qualitative research: Analysis types and software tools.* Bristol, PA: Falmer.

Valsiner, J. (1998). *The guided mind: A sociogenetic approach to personality.* Cambridge, MA: Harvard University Press.

Van Maanen, J., Sørensen, J. B., & Terence, R. M. (2007). The interplay between theory and method. *Academy of Management Review, 32*(4), 1145–1154.

Virkkunen, J. (2006). Dilemmas in building shared transformative agency. *Activités, 3*(1), 19–42.

Vygotsky, L. S. (1978). *Mind in society: The development of higher mental processes.* Cambridge, MA: Harvard University Press.

Wagner, C. L., Brock, D. R., & Agnew, A. T. (1994). Developing literacy portfolios in teacher education courses. *Journal of Reading, 37*(8), 668–674.

Wertsch, J. (1991). *Voices of the mind: A sociocultural approach to mediated action.* Cambridge, MA: Harvard University Press.

Part III
Participatory Research and Challenges to Accepted Practices and Understandings of Young Children

Chapter 8
Participatory Research with Young Children from Special Populations: Issues and Recommendations

Jennifer Urbach and Rashida Banerjee

Conducting Participatory Research: Introduction

Many researchers have argued for student voice and active student involvement in research (e.g. Fielding, 2001; Kellett, 2005). As described in Chap. 1 of this book, Fielding (2001) proposed four levels of student participation which serves to support the understanding of the nuances of participatory work – students as sources of data, students as active respondents, students as co-researcher, and students as researchers. Fielding (2001) uses the term *Students as Researchers* and describes six principles that guide the active student role: (a) partnerships between staff or outside researchers and students that respect each other's strengths and expertise; (b) a positive orientation through the involvement of all researchers; (c) the centrality of learning amongst all researchers as key issues are investigated; (d) equal and authentic access and opportunities provided for all researchers; (e) an assurance of quality in the preparation of student researcher and staff engagement; and (f) a reflection leading to actions such as dissemination and change. He further argues that in order to prepare active and involved student researchers, we must be involved in ongoing evaluations of student voice aligned with these six principles. Kellett (2005) suggests that this concept may require a "new paradigm with a characteristically different methodological approach from others in our research consciousness" (p. 2).

While there is much support for, and many examples of, participatory research with typically developing children, not much has been written that answers the "why" "what", or "how" questions in terms of supporting children with disabilities to become active researchers. The purpose of this chapter is to describe the need for participatory research with this special population and, within a framework aligned with Fielding's principles, discuss issues and recommendations related to various stages of conducting participatory research with children from special populations

J. Urbach (✉) · R. Banerjee
University of Northern Colorado, Greeley, CO, USA
e-mail: Jennifer.Urbach@unco.edu; Rashida.Banerjee@unco.edu

© Springer Nature Switzerland AG 2019
A. Eckhoff (ed.), *Participatory Research with Young Children*, Educating the Young Child 17, https://doi.org/10.1007/978-3-030-19365-2_8

using a strengths-based competency model. We use the term "children" to include pre-K to elementary-aged children with a broad range of disabilities such as physical, social-emotional, intellectual and multiple disabilities.

In addition, because we view children as researchers, we use the term 'outside researcher' to indicate the researcher(s) who partner with the children during the research process. The issues and recommendations in this chapter are organized upon the different steps researchers engage in that are critical to designing, implementing, and analyzing research, understanding research outcomes, and making decision about how to disseminate findings. We particularly emphasize the importance of equity, accessibility, and authenticity when collaborating with special populations in their role as co-researchers.

Participatory Research with Special Populations

Historically, research in special education often focused on behaviorist or process-product approaches, both of which derive from in a medical model of disability or a deficit perspective. In this perspective, the research usually assumed a deficit within the person and tried to provide interventions to fix that problem. This type of research is typically quantitative and maintains a positivistic epistemology. Qualitative research grew in popularity by the turn of the century, however, participatory research was still largely absent. Thus, research still focused *on* people with disabilities rather *with* people with disabilities. More recently, disability advocates argued for a social model of disability, which assumes that deficits impacting those with disabilities lies within the society rather than within the person. This has led some researchers to seek the interpretation and understanding of those with disabilities. As a result, participatory and emancipatory research projects with adults with disabilities have started to emerge. Largely absent from this new branch of research are projects research with children. Much participatory research with children and youth with disabilities is still adult-led, adult-designed and conceived from an adult perspective (Kellett, 2005). However, children with disabilities are members of a sub-culture that gives them a unique perspective and an insider view that is often marginalized and perceived through a deficit model rather than a strengths-based model. Those using a deficit model presume that the barriers of doing research with young children are too great to overcome. Sceptic maintain that children with disabilities are not competent enough to engage in participatory research due to their age and physical and intellectual capacities.

Arguments similar to those promoting participation of children in general, can be used to debunk this myth. Solberg (1996) suggests that children's competence is 'different from' not 'lesser than' adults' competence. Further, Kellett (2005) argues that "if research areas that interest children emanate directly from their own experiences, then no adult, even the most skilled ethnographer, can hope to acquire the richness of knowledge that is inherent in children's own understanding of their worlds" (p. 10). Thus, there is much we can learn from the voices of these experts.

Participatory research recognizes the expert knowledge children bring to the research; therefore, it innately derives from a strengths-based lens regarding children's competence.

Consequently, in a world where children with disabilities are marginalized, it is critical to ensure that the children's perspectives and voices are heard and followed upon. Participatory researchers working with special populations must employ this same strength-based lens. In order to provide authentic participatory research opportunities aligned with Fielding's six principles, researchers need to be aware of the issues ingrained in the research process while recognizing the strengths of the child.

When conducting research with special populations, there are a range of issues that might need to be acknowledged and addressed. These populations might have specific characteristics- such as limited cognitive, verbal, or attention capabilities that must be considered and addressed. Further, since children with disabilities are not a homogenous, other elements such as cultural and language differences or subtle or hidden elements such trauma, homelessness, hunger or emotional difficulties might also impact the young child's abilities to fully engage in the research. Finally, working with special populations often includes the involvement of multiple professionals and family member in caregiving and educational roles that may provide a unique challenge and an opportunity. The unique nature of working with special populations is that there is no 'one size fits all' option; outside researchers must continually be cognizant of the needs and strengths of the population with whom they are working and persistently work to remove barriers that prevent their co-researchers' voices from being heard. In the sections below, we elaborate on specific unique issues that outside researchers may encounter during of the research process and provide recommendations to address these issues.

Issues and Recommendations When Conducting Participatory Research with Special Population of Children

Beginning the research journey with young children from special populations requires that the outside researchers establish a positive orientation towards the research by enriching communication among the researchers and create a partnership that reduces power barriers and respects the perspectives of all researchers. While these values are important throughout the research process, they are essential to the beginning of the research process, which is the assent process and the determination of the key topics to investigate. Below we discuss issues and recommendations related to the assent and determination of the research questions through the lens of positive orientation and partnership.

Issues and Recommendations Regarding Assent We can think of an ethical assent as one that addresses both positive orientation and partnership because, at its core, the assent should make sure that the participants understand the research and freely agree to be in the research partnership. Creating this ethical assent for children from special populations requires thoughtful preparation aligned with the children's strengths and needs. Some children may have difficulties with conceptual understanding, slow processing skills, short attention spans and limited vocabulary to express anxiety, discomfort or distress. Children with disabilities may not feel they have the ability to say "no" to an adult. Finally, there are some children whose disability is so significant that they do not understand the importance and use of assent. There are many questions that must be addressed when creating an ethical assent process for young children from special populations. The following questions may be considered:

- When it comes to creating an ethical assent, how can outside researchers understand all the needs and abilities of their co-researchers and reduce power inequities?
- How can outside researchers present the assent in a way that children who have difficulties with conceptual understanding, language, and attention can understand?
- How can children communicate their assent or dissent even when verbal communication is not their strength?
- What precautions can outside researchers take to make sure children from special populations understand all aspects of the research and feel free to dissent at any time?
- What if outside researchers determine that young children's age or disability impact their ability to understand assent?

Aligning with the principles of positive orientation and partnership, we make four recommendations that outside researchers should employ when focusing on the assent process. The outside researcher must: embed themselves in the community, understand how children digest and communicate information, look for nonverbal signs of assent, and create a multilayered process. (See Fig. 8.1 for a summary of the recommendations.)

Recommendation #1 The outside researcher should embed themselves within the community. When working with special populations the relationship between the outside researcher and the co-researcher is paramount (Aldridge, 2016). Aldridge describes the need for a "close alliance" where outside researchers understand the needs of the co-researchers and keep the co-researchers interests at the heart of the research. Embedding oneself into the community allows the outside researcher to be aware of the strengths and needs of their fellow researchers (i.e. the children). Consequently, the researcher will learn, how to design an ethical assent and how best to work with these specific young children as research partners. Because of the diversity of children's physical and intellectual abilities and limited exposure to research procedures, the outside researcher cannot make assumptions about the children's ability to collaborate in the research process. Learning first-hand about the dynamics within the classroom and its individuals can be incredibly important when working with special populations. Further, it allows outside researchers to develop a rapport with the children. It is important when visiting the site that the

1. Embed yourself into the community

   a. What do families and caregivers say are the best methods to communicate with the child?

   b. Do the children use augmentative and alternate communication methods to communicate? If so, which ones?

   c. How are they being taught?

   d. How do they best learn information and communicate information?

   e. Have I gained the trust of the children?

   f. How do I make sure that I am not seen as an authority figure within the classroom?

2. Create assents based on how children digest and communicate information

   a. How will I use the children's strengths and needs to help create assents?

   b. Can I use the methods within the classroom to help create assents?

3. Identify ways the children can communicate assent or dissent

   a. How will I use the children's strengths and needs to create ways to communicate assent or dissent?

   b. If I use a tool, did I ensure that the children know how to use that tool?

   c. What are the signs of distress, anxiety, or disinterest typically displayed by this child?

4. Create multilayered assents

   a. How will I make sure that the assent communicated in different ways, by different people, in different context?

   b. How will I make sure I provide assent at every stage of the process?

Fig. 8.1 Four major recommendations and questions to pose when creating assent

outside researcher not take on the role of a teacher; young children should not feel that the outside research is in a power position. This will enhance the trustworthiness of data collection and analysis, but it also contributes to the child feeling comfortable dissenting as well.

Recommendation #2 Knowing how a child digests information should be at the heart of creating an appropriate assent. Thus, outside researchers must investigate how the child will best understand the assent. Information gathered from the child's family, educators or caregivers as well as their own observations can help outside researchers best understand the strengths and needs of the child. In her work with young adults with autism, Loyd (2013), used visuals, a strength for her students. Along with this, she examined how they learned within the classroom. Since the class used a symbol system and social stories in their classroom, Loyd presented the assent information in a similar format. While Loyd worked with older students, outside researchers working with younger children with disabilities can explore other options. Similarly, Mayne, Howitt, and Rennie (2016) describe using a narrative approach with young children which outlines the research, what participants are expected to do, and how to assent or dissent. This approach was presented through interactive media to maintain children's attention. Video modeling, a tool used to teach skills such as perspective taking and social skills to young children with autism, could be an effective platform for this narrative approach (Hine & Woolery, 2006). For those with limited language, outside researchers might also focus more on the pictures; a picture pamphlet describing the elements of the study can be developed for the assent and paired with simple oral sentences for children with language or intellectual limitations (Einarsdottir, 2007).

Recommendation #3 Along with how they digest information, we need to decide the best way children can communicate their assent or dissent. Outside researchers cannot assume that all techniques work for all children. For instance, Funazaki and Oi (2013) found that, while answering 'yes' or 'no' questions may work fine for some children with disabilities, children with echolalia may have difficulty responding to 'yes' or 'no' questions; further, age and significant cognitive disabilities may also impact a child's ability to answer these questions. Gray and Winter (2011) suggest offering a myriad of tools to help children communicate assent. These tools could range from 'smiley' face stickers to the use of a communication device. Whatever tools outside researchers choose to provide, they must ensure that the child understands what the tool is communicating; if the tool is not used in the young child's environment, training on how to use the tool may be needed. Finally, even if a child verbally communicates assent, researchers should continuously look for nonverbal cues of dissent. Signs of dissent may be obvious signs, such as facial expressions, crying or pulling away. However, the signs may also be subtle; for example, not responding, ignoring, or decreased levels of engagement may also tell us of a child's unease or anxiety (Kossyvaki, 2018; Skanfor, 2009). Cameron and Murphy (2007) note that agreeing without listening or ambivalent responses should be concerning as well. It is important that outside researchers are tuned into the individual child's normal signs of unease. Ongoing nonverbal signs of unease or distress should always trump parents' consent and the child should be removed from the study (Kossyvaki, 2018).

Recommendation #4 The assent should be considered a multilayered process; one that offers multiple opportunities for assent or dissent. Loyd (2013) argues that one way to alleviate issues with understanding and power inequalities is to have the assent "presented in different ways, by different people, in different context"

(p. 136). As aforementioned, Loyd created the assent in multiple ways by using tools found within the classroom and what she knew of the strengths of people with autism. Outside researchers should also consider giving the assent to the child through different people in different contexts as well. Having several different people, including those with whom the child is most comfortable, explain the research project, solicit and answer questions, and ask for assent offers the repetition that some children need. By having familiar people explain the project, outside researchers cannot only reduce the power inequity between the child and the outside researchers but those people familiar with the child may make subtle changes to their presentation (e.g. more wait time, chunking information, additional hand gestures) that can lead to better understanding.

In addition, a multilayered assent would make sure to check for assent on an ongoing basis. A child's understanding of the project or their willingness to be a part of the study may change over time. Asking for assent at each stage of the process or each stage of data collection provides a more concrete view of what is happening at that point in time. Further, for children with short term memory issues, limited cognitive abilities, or shorter attention spans, it provides smaller chunks of information to digest at one time. Thus, continuously checking for assent every time a child participates in the research is an important element of multilayered assent (Einarsdottir, 2007; Gray & Winter, 2011; Loyd, 2013; Palaiologou, 2014; White & Morgan, 2012).

While the above recommendations address an ethical assent, there is one remaining issue to discuss: what if the young children's age or disability impact their ability to understand assent? There is a debate of whether giving voice to these marginalized groups and learning from their experiences outweighs the fact that these children do not have a full understanding of what is happening. Researchers grapple with the ethical dilemma of whether they providing voice to children from special populations or invading their worlds. Sumsion et al., (2011), whose research involved infants as data collectors, suggests that outside researchers must always weigh this ethical dilemma and if, they foresee that the benefits outweigh the negatives, then they must respect the child's nonverbal responses for dissent.

Issues and Recommendations in Identifying Research Questions While there is a dearth of participatory research with special populations, even more scant are research projects illuminating how or if they identified the research questions with these children. The reasons for this are unknown, but one can hypothesize that outside researchers have a prior topic of interest or feel the children's abilities constrain the type of question that will be identified. Yet, Fielding argues that a positive orientation denotes involvement by all and true partnership involves joint determination of the key topics to investigate. While very few studies with young children from special populations highlight this research phase, there are several studies of adults and youth from special populations which do highlight this process. Most of these studies use focus groups, group interview or individual interviews to define the key issues. Yet, because of age, power imbalances, or individuals' needs, traditional interviews and focus groups may not be the best avenue to listen to the voices of the young children with special populations. Some questions to consider when involving special populations in the development of research questions are:

- What is the best method to encourage children's participation during topic development process?
- Is there a power imbalance between the outside researcher and child researcher that is impacting the process? If yes, how is this power imbalance being addressed?
- What adaptations may be necessary to ensure full and equal participation among children and outside researchers?
- When children cannot participate in the identification of research topics, what is the best way to have their voices heard on issues central to their lives?

In accordance with the principles of positive orientation and partnership, we recommend outside researchers: organize interview sessions in ways that enhance dialogue with all participants, approach interviews as discussions and consider using props, identify non-verbal avenues to get at key topics, and consider 'communication partners' when children are not able to identify key issues.

Recommendation #1 When considering recommendations for young children, it is essential to organize the interview in a way that enhances the dialogue. For some children this may mean individual interviews are the best way to hear their voice while other children's voices may flourish in small groups. Grouping the children with familiar peers in small groups of three children may provide the best interactions (Einarsdottir, 2007). Further, enriched and authentic communication can only happen if children feel safe. This is especially important for newcomers or children who have suffered trauma. Steps such as locating the interview in a familiar place, with smaller furniture, or providing food are simple strategies to make the interview more relaxing. Furthermore, adaptations may be required to ensure that all voices are heard in a focus groups or individual interviews. Some children may be able to participate with alternative and augmentative communication (AAC) devices. If AAC devices are used, the outside researchers should use the same process that is used in the child's home and school setting. In addition, before developing their questions outside researchers must be aware of the type and amount of vocabulary that the child can use (Nind, 2008).

Recommendation #2 Outside researchers must approach interviews as a conversation rather than a formal interview (Einarsdottir, 2007). This reduces the power structure and allows outside researchers to truly listen to the children. Proponents of participatory research with young children with disabilities also suggest that children do something like draw or play throughout the conversation. Props can also reduce power imbalances and facilitate discussions. For instance, Gray and Winter (2011) used a rag doll named Molly to help children in an inclusive preschool identify key research questions. The researcher introduced Molly as a new student and asked the children to think about the questions Molly would most likely ask. The most popular question that emerged was 'What do we like the most and least about our school?' (p. 314). Thus, this became the central question the children researched.

Recommendation #3 Sometimes nonverbal solicitation may be a better format than an interview to help identify key issues. For instance, a concerns report survey may be used to identify key needs and concerns (Balcazar, Keys, Kaplan, & Suarez-Balcazar, 1998). This survey could be easily modified to have children circle pictures of their concerns or questions. A visual and concrete survey with options might be easier for some children to follow and understand. Likewise, using a set of predetermined photographs related to certain topics may provide a choice system.

Recommendation #4 Finally, there are some children, who due to their age or disability cannot participate in identifying key issues. When outside researchers cannot work directly with young children from special populations on identifying the key issues, they may interview a 'communication partner,' such as a family member who is "emotionally and communicatively involved" (Nind, 2008, p. 11). When this method is used, Nind suggests that the communication partners are given a time to express their own views as well; creating questions that differentiates the child's perceptions from the interviewee's perception will help to avoid the intermingling of the two perceptions. Another option is to create an advisory group of parents, caregivers, and or older students from the same population to provide insight into the concerns or interests of the young researchers.

Conducting Data Collection and Analysis: Ensuring the Centrality of Learning, Through Equity and Authenticity

While positive orientation and partnerships undergirds all phases of participatory research, it is important to think about the principles of centrality of learning and equity and authenticity when preparing to collect and analyze data. Fielding (2001) sees centrality of learning as creating a learning community. By its very nature, the data collection and analysis process is a learning process where one is researching and discussing significant issues. Yet the key is that it involves a community of learners. That learning community is only strong if the data collection and analysis process is equitable and authentic and all voices are heard and valued. In the sections below we explore issues related to the next phase of research, namely, data collection and analysis and provide recommendations to ensure equitable and authentic research opportunities resulting in centrality of learning.

Issues and Recommendations in Data Collection Participatory researchers working with children emphasize that data collection follows the lead of the child; it should be with the child rather than from the child. The goal is to capture the child's voice and what is important to that child. This is perhaps one phase of participatory research where we see young children from special populations most involved. However, when working with special populations many ethical and logistical challenges may occur. In order to listen to the voice of the children, outside researchers must be able to provide equitable and authentic methods that allow co-researchers to truly share their voice and their expertise. The following questions should be considered when encouraging children in the data collection process:

- How do you capture the voice of children with different communicative and ability levels?
- Are the data tools we are using easily accessible and understood by children with significant needs or from different sociocultural contexts?
- Do data collection sessions consider the unique needs and abilities of children?
- Can students with the most significant needs participate in data collection?

Below we make four recommendations that promote centrality of learning through equitable and authentic opportunities: consider the Mosaic approach for data collection, align tools with children's knowledge, structure data sessions that align with children's needs, and consider innovative approaches for children with the most significant needs.

Recommendation #1 In order to provide children with equitable and authentic methods of data collection, we must start by looking at the Mosaic approach (Clark, 2001; Clark & Moss 2011). This approach makes use of various data collection tools including traditional tools such as, interviews, observation but also participatory tools such as cameras, drawings, tours, art work and role plays. Tools such as photographs, drawing and role plays allow the young child their preferred way to communicate, and it breaks down the power relationship allowing the child to lead the research. Clark (2001) states that parent and practitioner interviews can also be part of the data collection. They note, however, these interviews do not take the place of the child's perspective but complement their perspective. Gray and Winter (2011) specifically used the Mosaic approach with preschoolers with and without disabilities by providing tools such as drawing, smiley face stickers, verbal explanation, and play.

The Mosaic approach aligns well with special education practices that advocate for Universal Design for Learning (UDL) by providing multiple means of representation, expression, and engagement from the outset thus having to adapt less frequently (CAST, 2011). Similarly, it aligns with the visual and technological methods that have been employed with those with special populations during participatory research. Video logs and voice recorders (White & Morgan, 2012) as well as a visual methods such as Photovoice (Booth & Booth, 2003, Cluley, 2017, Jurkowski, 2008) have been used in participatory research with adults and older students with disabilities. Photovoice, in particular, has been a popular data collection method for participatory research with young adults with mild or moderate disabilities (Aldridge, 2016). By giving co-researchers cameras as data collection tool, Photovoice gives us access to the photographers point of view and can act as a springboard for discussions (Booth & Booth, 2003). It can be helpful for those co-researchers with more limited communication because it makes the research more concrete, provides a different avenue of communication, and it allows participants the ability to exercise choice over what is important to document.

Recommendation #2 When using creative data collection tools we need to make sure that those tools are easily accessible and understood by the children. Due, Riggs, and Augustino (2014) used drawings, photo elicitation, along with a likert scale approach with both a 'smiley face scale' (i.e.. a scale of emoticons from frown to a large smile) to indicate feelings and a 'lolly jar' scale (i.e. empty jar to two jars full of lollies) to indicate importance. This scale provided quantitative information and served as 'springboard' for discussion. While this research study focused on other marginalized children rather than students with disabilities, this rating scale can work for children with disabilities as well; however, the outside researchers must ensure that children have a uniform understanding of the scales. Thus, it important to individually explain the scale to children and confirm their understanding of the scales with questions where the researcher knows how the student will answer. Scales can also reflect what is taught in the classroom. Zones of Regulation, (Kuypers, 2018) a popular classroom curriculum that teaches the self-regulation one's of emotions, links a color coding system to emotions. Those color coded visuals could be used in the scale.

Recommendation #3 Strategies derived from the Mosaic approach can be used for research with children with significant needs that limit their physical and verbal participation or for infants with special needs. Sumsion et al. (2011) used a Mosaic methodology derived from the Mosaic approach; they used multiples sources of data and multiple perspectives to 'piece together fine-grained details of infants experiences' (p. 115). This approach involved consultation with families, caregivers, older students in the setting and the infants themselves. Data collection methods included observations, video, photographs, diaries and vocabulary data. Yet, the most innovative element, which allowed infants to participate in the research, was the use of baby cams. Since observation is an important element in listening to children, the baby cam, a tiny camera worn on the infant's head, allowed the outside researcher see what the infant sees. The authors argue that the baby cam provides "a visual perspective that we can rarely access" and provides insight into what captures an infant's attention by linking the baby cam to eye gaze (p. 120). In addition, video was taken of the infant with traditional cameras. Using video analysis software, researchers used split screen functioning to view footage of the infants' reactions while simultaneously viewing what the infant was watching. While Sumsion et al. used the eye gaze and reactions to help get the infants perspective, they also used outside researchers, parents, caregivers, older children in the setting to share their perspective on the data as well, using a 'collaborative interpretative process' to co-construct the infants' experiences in the video.

Thus, this Mosiac methodology provides an innovative practice that can be used with young children with significant support needs. In addition, the insight of the families and caregivers who intimately know the young children lends itself to the type of work early childhood special educators often focus upon. Researchers using this approach with special populations should also consider working with older children or adults from those same special populations to provide their perspectives as well (Kossyvaki, 2018).

Recommendation #4 Not only should outside researchers consider the unique strengths and needs of their co-researchers when deciding on the data collection tools, but they should also examine what strengths and needs need to be accommodated during data collection sessions. For instance, when working with children with ADHD, data collection periods may need to be shorter or frequent breaks should be given (Gray & Winter, 2011). Visuals schedules may help children who have autism. Determining if data collection should be collected in pairs or individually might be another structural element to identify. Gray and Winter created peer dyads between students with and without disabilities. They found that their students with intellectual and physical disabilities were highly engaged with their peer partner; yet, a child with autism did not stay with his research partner.

Issues and Recommendations with Data Analysis There are many issues regarding data analysis when it comes to young children and special populations. Data analysis, after all, is a rigorous process and lack of data analysis training, immaturity, verbal or cognitive abilities may impact this process. Scholars often question whether or not children from special populations can analyze the data through a theory generating lens. Yet, if we don't include them in this analysis are we truly researching with our young children? While there appears to be more questions than answers in the area data analysis, Nind (2011) suggests that these children can participate in data analysis. Some questions to consider during the data analysis process with special populations are:

- Have outside researchers addressed their own explicit or implicit bias, if any, regarding the co-researchers' competencies in engaging in data analysis?
- How do outside researchers begin data analysis with children from special populations?
- How do outside researcher assure data analysis procedures highlight children's perspectives rather than another's just interpretation?
- Does the data analysis process include all students, including students with limited intellectual and oral communication abilities?

To provide equitable and authentic opportunities that enhance a community of learners, outside researchers must: presume competence, allow students to decide what data should be included in the analysis, assure probing questions clarify children's viewpoint, provide non-verbal options for analysis as well.

Recommendation #1 In a review of data analysis participatory practices with individuals with disabilities of all ages, Nind (2011) found that very few studies explored data analysis and those that did, used a variety of techniques- "informal and formal, trained and untrained, explicit and implicit" (p. 359). Nind does not suggest that one method is better than the other, but she does recommend that the outside researcher must believe in their co-researchers' competence. If the outside researchers do not presume competence, they are unlike to strive to find ways to involve the children in data analysis. Children as researchers are different, not less (Solberg, 1996) and their abilities to contribute to the analysis process must be explored through this lens. This may mean that the researcher has to be reflective, search for their own biases and examining the central purpose of participatory research. Once competence is presumed, it is easier to find ways to provide equitable opportunities for participation in data analysis.

Recommendation #2 Analyzing data with children begins by listening to them on what data should be included in the analysis. This process is often concurrently conducted with data generation and thus ongoing and revisited (Nind & Seale, 2009; Dockett, Einarsdottir, and Perry, 2011). For example, Einarsdottir (2007) empowered children to say which pieces of data were to be kept for the analysis and which were not. During this process, teachers sat down with each child to discuss the artifact and what it meant. Then they were asked if they wanted to keep the photo, hide it behind another photo, or throw it away. The discussion about the organization of the artifacts is an important element to data analysis; it provides children control over what data will be analyzed. By having children explain their artifacts and what it means to them, outside researchers can gain insight into their viewpoints, what they find interesting and what they find important. While Einarsdottir's research did not specifically discuss children from special populations, this method would work well for a variety of students because it provides a visual from which to start the discussion and provides limited but concrete options of what to do with the data.

Recommendation #3 Because discussion of the data is an important part of data analysis, outside researchers must make sure that they are listening to children rather than interpreting their response. Thus we need to we must provide equitable opportunities in the discussion of data. While the interviewing strategies previously mentioned still apply, the outside researcher should also consider questions providing probing or guiding questions that allow children a chance explain their rationale. Darbyshire, MacDougal, and Shiller (2005) suggest that outside researchers probe children with questions such as: Why is it important to you? What else could it say? How are these connected? These types of question clarify their responses rather than have them interpreted. Further, Due et al. (2014) insist that outside researchers may need to provide open ended probing questions multiple times and in multiple ways to elicit children's interpretations rather than the outside researcher's assumptions.

Recommendation #4 The methods discussed have all relied on communication. Yet there are strategies that outside researchers can employ to allow those with limited communication to participate. For instance, when using Photovoice outside researchers can present the printed photos taken and examine the nonverbal reactions of the co-researcher; excitement or interest in the photo versus negative reactions of disinterest can assist in determining if they will keep that photo for analysis (Aldridge, 2016). In addition the outside researcher may also consult with family and caregivers who know the young child well to make sure that they agree with the outside researcher's interpretations. As noted earlier, it is important to avoid intermingling the interviewee's opinions with those of the child. Allow opportunities for the interviewee to express their own opinion and create questions that distinguish the interviewee's opinion from that of the student. With regards to analyzing thematically, Williams (1999) suggest offering a range of themes to the co-researcher, using the research questions as a probe, or simply what they find interesting.

Issues and Recommendations with the Dissemination of Research: From Reflection to Action Fielding (2001) argues that student involvement in dissemination of research is important because it provides a sense of ownership and responsibility as well as offers them the opportunity to see the link between their research and changes that are made. Despite the importance that he puts on this stage, there are very few reports focusing on how the young co-researchers with special needs are involved in the dissemination of research. While we do see evidence with adults with disabilities through presentations, articles, and websites, involving young children in dissemination may look very different. Questions to consider when disseminating research with children from special populations are:

- How can children disseminate research in ways that fit their abilities?
- How do you balance the ethics of confidentiality and privacy of the children with the dissemination of research?

When considering how children should disseminate research, we suggest that outside researchers examine avenues of dissemination that highlight children's abilities to communicate the research and weigh the importance of confidentiality and privacy when considering strategies that could identify an individual.

Recommendation #1 Researchers may use different techniques, such as role play and picture collages, to present research to the stakeholder groups. Those studies that have examined dissemination of research with young children provide suggestions that can often be duplicated with children from special populations as well. Gray and Winter's (2011) research with preschools with and without disabilities focused on what children liked and disliked about school. Dissemination of this research included elements such a role play for parents of the various stages of research they participated and a collage of artifacts disseminating the rules. The collage offers a nonverbal way for children to present researcher and, because it was completed as a group, confidentiality of response was still maintained.

Recommendation #2 Researchers must consider whether or not disseminating research in ways that identify the children are in the best interest of the children. This dilemma is best highlighted in the research of Dockett et al. (2011) who allowed their young co-researchers to present at public forum. In this study, children were given an option for pseudonyms, but the children wanted their names to used. Before agreeing to this, the outside researchers had to reflect on the long-term ethical implications of divulging their names. The authors had to think about how media would represent the children and how the children might feel about their names being reported in a few years; yet at the same time respect the children's pride and rights to share their research. Docket et al. assert that outside researchers should constantly think about the ethics behind their work and the rights of our co-researchers in both the present and in the future. Docket et al.'s study was not conducted with students from special populations; however, when working with special populations this challenge is even more important for possible legal, social, and emotional ramifications. Outside researchers must deliberately think of all possible negative ramifications, present and future, before disseminating research with children.

Conclusion: Quality Assurance in Participatory Research with Special Populations

Fielding's last principle is quality assurance. By this he means that there is an awareness of the importance of engaging in participatory research, thus the outside researcher is invested and engaged in making every attempt to prepare young children to be researchers.

Participatory research is critical to both the field and to children's lives. At the very heart of participatory researcher is an element of advocacy. This research focuses on listening to the issues important to its participants. Children from special population voices are often marginalized; this type of research provides a platform from which they are heard. Thus, participatory research with young children from special population fills a gap in the research. Further, by working with children as researchers, the broader community begins to see the competence of each child. Equally as important is what it does for the children. Participatory research is not only advocacy work, but it teaches self-advocacy skills; students are able to communicate their needs, wants and rights. In addition, when outside researchers teach children to identify research questions, implement and analyze research, and disseminate their findings, they are teaching children to be self-determined learners. In a field where self-determination is seen as a critical skill for one's success, the need for more participatory research with young children from special populations becomes even more paramount. Thus, when outside researchers understand how participatory research can advance the field and create self-determined learners, they are bound to seek quality assurances.

By using Fielding's framework to elucidate issues and recommendations through every step of the research process, we hope to assist outside researchers as they prepare young children from special populations to become researchers. From creating the assent to disseminating research, outside researchers should presume children's competency while examining at ways to remove barriers for their inclusion. This is best accomplished when the outside researcher, first, understands their co-researchers strengths and needs and then providing multiple avenues for co-researchers to engaging in research, expressing their knowledge, and representing their perspective.

As noted throughout the chapter, there is a dearth of research with young children from special populations that elucidates research at every step of the research process. More research is needed with young children from special populations, especially research that highlights working with young children from special populations on all phases of the research process. While there are many issues related to working with young children, the challenges are not too great to overcome. This chapter does not provide a panacea, for the issues in participatory research with special populations; the needs of young children from special populations are too diverse, even within specific groups. It does, however, provide broad recommendations that will allow for strong partnerships, positive orientation, equitable and authentic opportunities, the centrality of learning, reflection leading to action, and ultimately for quality assurances. Using these principles throughout their research with young children from special populations, outside researchers can make a difference in the field and in children's lives.

Questions for Reflection
- The authors of this chapter suggest some recommendations for engaging young children from special populations in participatory research during the dissemination process. Based upon your work, can you suggest any others?
- Develop an outline of the steps you would take to engage young children from special populations in participatory research. In order to do this, consider (a) why would you like to engage in participatory research? (b) the children you will work with as co-researchers—their characteristics, attributes, strengths and needs, and (c) all the necessary steps you will take to ensure equity, authenticity, and reflective participation throughout the different stages of the research process.
- As a researcher interested in work with children from special populations, how will you involve children in participatory research? Drawing from the challenges and recommendations discussed above by the authors, can identify the steps you would take to (a) ensure assent, (b) identify the research questions, (c) collect data, (d) analyze data, and (e) disseminate findings when working with children from special populations?

References

Aldridge, J. (2016). *Participatory research: Working with vulnerable groups in research and practice*. Chicago, IL: Chicago Policy Press.

Balcazar, F. E., Keys, C. B., Kaplan, D. L., & Suarez-Balcazar, Y. (1998). Participatory action research and people with disabilities: Principles and challenges. *Canadian Journal of Rehabilitation, 12*, 105–112.

Booth, T., & Booth, W. (2003). In the frame: Photovoice and mothers with learning difficulties. *Disability & Society, 18*(4), 431–442.

Cameron, L., & Murphy, J. (2007). Obtaining consent to participate in research: The issues involved in including people with a range of learning and communication disabilities. *British Journal of Learning Disabilities, 35*(2), 113–120.

CAST. (2011). *Universal Design for Learning Guidelines version 2.0.* Wakefield, MA: Author.

Clark, A. (2001). How to listen to very young children: The mosaic approach. *Child Care in Practice, 7*(4), 333–341. https://doi.org/10.1080/13575270108415344

Clark, A., & Moss, P. (2011). *Listening to young children: The mosaic approach* (2nd ed.). London, UK: Jessica Kingsley Publishers.

Cluley, V. (2017). Using photovoice to include people with profound and multiple learning disabilities in inclusive research. *British Journal of Learning Disabilities, 45*(1), 39–46.

Darbyshire, P., MacDougall, C., & Schiller, W. (2005). Multiple methods in qualitative research with children: More insight or just more? *Qualitative Research, 5*(4), 417–436.

Dockett, S., Einarsdottir, J., & Perry, B. (2011). Balancing methodologies and methods in researching with young children. In D. Harcourt, B. Perry, & T. Waller (Eds.), *Researching young children's perspectives: Debating the ethics and dilemmas of educational research with children* (pp. 68–71). New York, NY: Routledge.

Due, C., Riggs, D. W., & Augoustinos, M. (2014). Research with children of migrant and refugee backgrounds: A review of child-centered research methods. *Child Indicators Research, 7*(1), 209–227.

Einarsdóttir, J. (2007). Research with children: Methodological and ethical challenges. *European Early Childhood Education Research Journal, 15*(2), 197–211.

Fielding, M. (2001). Students as radical agents of change. *Journal of Educational Change, 2*, 123–141.

Funazaki, Y., & Oi, M. (2013). Factors affecting responses of children with autism spectrum disorders to yes/no questions. *Child Language Teaching and Therapy, 29*(2), 245–259.

Gray, C., & Winter, E. (2011). Hearing voices: Participatory research with preschool children with and without disabilities. *European Early Childhood Education Research Journal, 19*(3), 309–320. https://doi.org/10.1080/1350293X.2011.597963

Hine, J. F., & Wolery, M. (2006). Using point-of-view video modeling to teach play to preschoolers with autism. *Topics in Early Childhood Special Education, 26*(2), 83–93.

Jurkowski, J. M. (2008). Photovoice as participatory action research tool for engaging people with intellectual disabilities in research and program development. *Intellectual and Developmental Disabilities, 46*(1), 1–11.

Kellett, M. (2005). *Children as active researchers: A new research paradigm for the 21st century?* Retrieved from http://oro.open.ac.uk/7539/

Kossyvaki, L. (2018). *Adult interactive style intervention and participatory research designs in autism: Bridging the gap between academic research and practice.* London, UK: Routledge.

Kuypers, L. (2018). *Zones of regulation.* Retrieved from http://www.zonesofregulation.com/index.html

Loyd, D. (2013). Obtaining consent from young people with autism to participate in research. *British Journal of Learning Disabilities, 41*(2), 133–140.

Mayne, F., Howitt, C., & Rennie, L. (2016). Meaningful informed consent with young children: Looking forward through an interactive narrative approach. *Early Child Development and Care, 186*(5), 673–687.

Nind, M. (2008). *Conducting qualitative research with people with learning, communication and other disabilities: Methodological challenges.* ESRC National Centre for Research Methods. Retrieved from http://eprints.ncrm.ac.uk/491/

Nind, M. (2011). Participatory data analysis: A step too far? *Qualitative Research, 11*(4), 349–363.

Nind, M., & Seale, J. (2009). Concepts of access for people with learning difficulties: Towards a shared understanding. *Disability & Society, 24*(3), 273–287.

Palaiologou, I. (2014). 'Do we hear what children want to say?' Ethical praxis when choosing research tools with children under five. *Early Child Development and Care, 184*(5), 689–705.

Skanfors, L. (2009). Ethics in child research: Children's agency and researchers' ethical radar. *Childhoods Today, 3*(1), 1–22.

Solberg, A. (1996). The challenge in child research from "being" to "doing". In J. Brannen & M. O'Brien (Eds.), *Children in families: Research and policy* (pp. 53–65). London, UK: Falmer Press.

Sumsion, J., Harrison, L., Press, F., McLeod, S., Goodfellow, J., & Bradley, B. (2011). Researching infants' experiences of early childhood education and care. In B. P. D. Harcourt & T. W. T. Waller (Eds.), *Researching young children's perspectives: Debating the ethics and dilemmas of educational research with children* (pp. 113–127). London, UK: Routledge.

White, E. L., & Morgan, M. F. (2012). Yes! I am a researcher. The research story of a young adult with down syndrome. *British Journal of Learning Disabilities, 40*(2), 101–108.

Williams, V. (1999). Researching together. *British Journal of Learning Disabilities, 27*(2), 48–51.

Chapter 9
Counternarratives from the Margins: School Stories in Children's Voices

Sheri L. Leafgren

Academic Stories: Three Numbers and Calibrated Children

During a visit to an elementary school in a large urban school district, an administrator boasted to me that, upon request, any child in the school—from the youngest to the oldest—would be prepared and able to share his/her academic story. She then called over two first-graders who happened to be walking by and told them to tell us their academic stories. Always happy to hear from children what they understood as their academic stories, I listened eagerly for what I anticipated to be school stories that would be complicated, enlightening, and full of wonderings and possibilities. Instead, each of the children recited three numbers.

The three numbers for each child represented scores on recently administered standardized tests, and were, according to the school district per the administrator, all one needed to know about the children and their school selves. Deflated, I recognized the dominant narrative of oppression and marginalization as children's school(ed) stories are too often limited to what can be calibrated, demonstrating a misdirection in considering what is possible when children's school stories are voiced. Stories that are more than numbers. Stories that *should* be complicated, autobiographical, and enlightening to those who hear/tell them; stories that would serve to challenge traditional assumptions about children and schooled early childhood practices.

I worry that the harshness of our culture is mirrored too accurately in school places where our children come to learn and be nurtured into adulthood. I worry, as does Jardine (1998), that "children are no longer our kin, our kind; teaching is no longer an act of 'kindness' and generosity bespeaking a deep connectedness with children" (p. 5). It matters to me that children are nurtured as our kin, that they connect with one another and the world and that they learn to be cared for and to care

S. L. Leafgren (✉)
Miami University, Oxford, OH, USA
e-mail: leafgrs@miamioh.edu

© Springer Nature Switzerland AG 2019
A. Eckhoff (ed.), *Participatory Research with Young Children*, Educating
the Young Child 17, https://doi.org/10.1007/978-3-030-19365-2_9

for others. One way in which connectedness is enacted as kinship is through our attention to *seeing* (hearing, knowing, attending to) them. Too often, schools are spaces where "standardized ways of looking at kids are deeply entrenched" [eschewing an investment in becoming fascinated by children that] is "an act of compassion, and a central challenge to teaching well" (Ayers & Alexander-Tanner, 2010, p. 24). Too often in these school(ed) spaces, teachers come to believe that it is their responsibility to standardize their lenses and see children and their stories as tests scores, deficits, and as problems to be solved for the good of school.

What is missing in the rampant practice of standardizing children and their school stories is the humanity inherent in the process of teaching and learning. Consider that determining what to pass from generation to generation is the same as deciding and communicating what really *matters* to us as a people and a society. As noted by Hendry (2011), "when curriculum is our lived experience, history is always in our midst…not [as] mere nostalgia or sentimental reminiscence, but an interpretative, political and creative engagement that asks us to question: what does it mean to be human? How do we know? Who can be a knower?" (p. xi, 4). In this chapter, I contend that children are knowers and that it is incumbent upon us as their kin to attend to their testimonies of their lived experiences, and that through their counterstorytelling, they may lead us to new ways of knowing and being ourselves.

Why Counterstorytelling?: A Telling and Re-telling of Our Stories

This chapter details this researcher's pursuit of children's academic stories/school stories toward disruption of the essentializing and deficit "stories" that children are taught to share as their own. A key component of Critical Race Theory (CRT), counterstorytelling, is employed in this research in response to that permanent, endemic, and internalized racism that characterizes school(ed) spaces (Boutte, 2015). Nearly all of the children whose testimonies are included here are African-American, and suffer the consequences of the permanence of racism in the context of U.S. schools in intersection with the consequent struggle of class and the deficit-driven nature of generationalism/developmentalism. Counterstorytelling is a methodological component of CRT that deliberately centers the voices and lived experiences of marginalized people of color (Cook, 2013; Johnson, 2016) while simultaneously challenging the positivistic and traditional ways of knowing and truth.

In ways similar to grassroots participatory practices, CRT's counternarrative embraces a Freirean notion that "knowledge emerges only through invention and re-invention, through the restless, impatient, continuing, hopeful inquiry [children] pursue in the world, with the world, and with each other" (Freire, 1970, p. 58). Counternarratives can be described as "the narratives or testimonies from marginalized groups—such as children and Freire's farmworkers –whose secondary status in society defines the boundaries of the mainstream and whose voices and perspectives have been suppressed, devalued, and abnormalized" (Hayes, 2014, p. 251). Marginalized and suppressed stories in the context of this work center the voices of children telling and retelling their own stories in the context of their urban school settings in their primary grade (K-3) classrooms. In this interpretation of CRT's counterstorytelling, the children's counternarratives serve to disrupt the consequences of the oppression emerging from an intersection of racism, classism, *and* developmentalism.

In this study, the children were enlisted by the researcher to speak "openly about their lives in unthreatening contexts," thus honoring "children as agentic with the strength and capabilities to shape their childhoods…[and honoring their] competence to share their experiences" (Horgan, 2017, p. 246). It became clear while visiting K-3 classrooms in our university program's partner school, that in the day-to-day interactions among children, teachers and the school(ed) curriculum, children's voices seemed muted and inconsequential. As noted in the opening vignette, the children could be prompted to parrot an academic story representing their schooled identities, but these were clearly not *their* stories.

In the context of school, the intersection of marginalized children via racism complicated by developmentalism and generationalism precipitates that children become "defined by what they are not, and so, are plumbed with a standard metric of development" (Leafgren & Sander, 2019, p. 233) that takes priority over the sense of the child herself as a person and as kin. "Rather, children are deemed incomplete and so, are thoroughly marginalized by their identity as child. Further inflating their marginalized state is the dominant perception of children as not only incomplete, but deficient." (Leafgren & Sander, 2019, p. 233). Diminished by their identity as "child" framed in rigid binaries (big/small, smart/ignorant, powerful/ weak, mature/immature, etc.) that inform their child-state as deficit in comparison to their perceived-improved identity as "adult", children are marginalized by their incompleteness and constructed images as inconvenient problems to be solved.

The children's testimonies included in this chapter—gathered through ongoing one-on-one, and small group conversations about their school(ed) lives—serve as counternarratives to the deficit perspective on children, and provide evidence that marginalizing narratives of racial and generational deficiency are false. The conversations were documented by notes made by the researcher, drawings and notes the children shared, and also included hearsay conversations shared with the researcher by university students who also interacted with the children on a regular basis. The children's counternarratives counteracted what was presumed good and right about the children's school experiences— which were generally based on misconceptions and underestimations of the children themselves. By informing the world of their power and possibility, the children's stories offered a catalyst for change.

Merriweather Hunn, Guy, and Mangliitz (2006) explains that "counternarratives push us to change how we think, to develop 'incredulity toward the metanarrative of race' [and development, and so] have an important, perhaps unique, educational value" (p. 249). There is a caveat that these counterstories can be and should be read on several levels (Bell, 2003); in this case, as testimonies not only of the children but also witnessing the spaces (school) from which they emerge. "They can be a powerful individual testimony of resilience, ingenuity, and pain but can also bear witness to institutionalized and unequal social relations that the dominant culture tends to minimize or deny" (Merriweather Hunn et al., 2006, p. 249). Children's testimonies shared here provide examples of resilience, ingenuity and pain; and because the stories are set in schools, they also bear witness to the institutionalized (as opposed to kinship) relationships that drive the dominant narratives.

In the following sections, elements of the method of counterstorytelling are interpreted toward gathering testimonies of the ways in which children experience and co-create their school lives in resilience, ingenuity and pain. The children's counternarratives detailed below may serve to challenge dominant narratives and truths by centering their marginalized and suppressed voices, stories, and lived experiences. CRT's counterstorytelling is thus engaged toward illuminating the fullness of the children's narratives—school stories and more broadly autobiographical stories. Their school/academic stories are thus *their* stories—their emerging curriculum.

Academic Stories: Children's Words and Estranged Labor

Dominant practices in elementary schools, especially in those schools that serve communities of color, often represent oppressive interpretations of curriculum in relation to children. On seeking insights into what become of schooled stories of calibrated children and how their counterstorytelling provide evidence that the academic stories defined by 3 scores are not only incomplete, but false, this chapter represents findings that have emerged from gatherings of counternarratives of children from primary grade classrooms in urban school settings and how those findings serve to inform and influence discussions of pedagogical and curriculum practices. The counternarratives to presumptive notions of children's academic stories that are shared here are representative of stories heard in the context of:

- Classroom observations and interactions in the context of collaborations in school settings: personal and those reported by teacher candidates
- Conversations with children about their lived experiences in school using the classroom work as context
- Drawings and notes generated by children, sometimes during conversations with the researcher
- Conversations with children about their work as documented by dozens of teacher candidates (early childhood majors) in the context of their field work
- Pondering with children, teacher candidates, and teachers how the children's counternarratives may challenge hegemonic and marginalizing pedagogy and interpretations of content

What follows are representations of the children's counternarratives to disrupt the narrative that their stories can be/should be essentialized and reduced to three numbers. The brief representations of their tellings and retellings illustrate the children's critical perspectives on a dominant curriculum that is often narrow and disconnected from the meaning and "learning" that school promises.

Countering Deficit Academic Storytelling, Children's Perspectives on the Work of School

While spending time in primary-grade classrooms, the teacher candidates in my university classes and I observe children's efforts to complete the tasks provided by their teachers. More often than not—in fact, nearly *always*—the tasks are passive, confined to paper and pencil interpretations of content via worksheets. As the children worked and sometimes after it was over and they were showing us their papers, we asked them questions about the work. We asked them variations of these questions: What was it about? Why did you do it? What did you learn? Do you think this work is about you? What was it like to do this? Did you help anyone? The following (in no particular order) are a small collection of their responses:

- *Mrs. Z said it's to be in charge of our own learning to do this worksheet*
- *It reminds me of the test we took a while ago.*
- *Mrs. N didn't collect them we just put them in our take home folder when we finished.*
- *Nothing.* (What did you learn?)
- *It's supposed to help us get a job.*
- *I learned about the paper*
- *No, because if it was about me it would have said my name or my last name.* (Is this work about you? How so?)
- *To do it.* (What did your teacher tell you about it?)
- *We do it because the teacher told us to*
- *No helping. I can't help; no one can help me*
- *Morning work and our stations we always do.* (What did it remind you of?)
- *She was just giving us the answers. It's easier for her that way because she doesn't have to wait for us to be right. I don't like just getting the answers. I want to learn.*
- *We write something every day, sometimes 2 or 3 pages a day. No one ever reads it.*
- *I did it to be able to go to recess.*
- *If I don't get it done by the time the timer goes off, I don't get a dojo point.*
- *I do it because my teacher tells me to.* (Why else?) *What else is there?*

These samplings of children's testimonies offer evidence that they see right through our bullshit claims that the work of school inherently has value, is good for them, and holds meaning and relevance. This is not merely a recent state of affairs. Jean Anyon studied children's relationship with school knowledge and social class in the late 1970's and noted that, "Indeed, some of the children were already engaged in struggle against what was to them an exploitative group—the school teachers and administrators. They were struggling against the imposition of a foreign curriculum. They had 'seen through' that system" (Anyon, 1981, p. 33). The children's voiced insights into their academic stories (their counternarratives) also reflect closely concepts named by Marx on the alienating labor of the worker:

> If therefore he regards the product of his labour, his objectified labour, as an alien, hostile and powerful object which is independent of him, then his relationship to that object is such that another man—alien, hostile, powerful and independent of him—is its master. If he relates to his own activity an unfree activity, then he relates to it as activity in the service, under the rule, coercion and yoke of another man (Marx, 1975 p. 331).

It is a sad note that children can see and name the emptiness of the tasks they spend their days laboring over, and yet, apparently operate under the assumption that coerced labor on estranged and disembodied tasks are exactly what they deserve. Otherwise, why would caring adults insist that the work is "for their own good"? (Miller, 1983/1990). Why else would caring teachers demand and coerce compliance to soulless tasks? Noddings (2002) joined Miller in naming such tasks as *poisonous pedagogy*: "rigid and coercive; it seeks to substitute the will of the teacher for that of the student…teachers guilty of poisonous pedagogy take a highly moralistic tone, insisting that what they are demanding is right and that coercion and cruelty, if they are used, are necessary 'for the child's own good'" (p. 29). And school and teachers have learned that the "good" is what is measured/quantified and scored on tests, papers, and grades—the academic story of three numbers. A consequence of poisonous pedagogy was articulated profoundly by a third-grader when he offered his insights on the purpose and function of his daily lessons in school: "I just do the work, but why? They are just making me do this for another grade. Grade, grade, grade, grade. Grade here, grade there. Like why? This don't mean nothing to me. What is this even about? What am I actually going to do with this?"

Poisonous Pedagogy and Estranged Labor

This young person's school storytelling provides a counternarrative to the dominant narrative of the goodness of school (*Like why? This don't mean nothing to me*); to the idea that school is the path to success; to all of those public service announcements by athletes and actors to "Stay in school, kids." School is a factory, a business that creates assembly lines of castrated content, and produces scores that then serve to sort the children into categories of worthiness and value. Children are commodities. Curriculum is commodified. The labor of children in school is commodified.

Marx (1844/1968) writes, "Labor produces not only commodities; it produces itself and the worker as a *commodity*" (p. 107) and it is so for the children and their school labor. As they labor over tasks that hold little to no meaning to them, they produce themselves as commodities. And the labor itself is what Marx terms, "estranged labor." Estranged labor is work that is external to the child; it doesn't affirm her intrinsic nature, but requires her to deny herself as she feels outside of her efforts and in her work feels outside of herself. As the children expressed in their words in the list above, they do not feel content or happy in their efforts as their labor doesn't freely develop mental and physical energy, and thus, as Marx would frame it, bodies are mortified and minds are ruined. Cox (1998) explains, "What makes us human is our ability to consciously shape the world around us." (np). However, as the children interviewed made clear, their labor is not their own, it is alien, it belongs to someone else, it's a commodity; and so, it estranges the child from her body, "from nature as it exists outside [her], from [her] spiritual essence, [his] human existence." (Marx, 1844/1968, p. 107). As one of the children interviewed noted, "We write something every day, sometimes 2 or 3 pages a day. No one ever reads it," one hears the plaintive note of purposeless and invisibility. For in the context of estranged labor, the "activity of the worker, far from being a creative activity, where [a child] realizes and affirms [her]self, is an activity that impoverishes her, creating in [her] a feeling of powerlessness and of submission, activity becomes passivity, power becomes powerlessness." (Rose, 2005, np).

But all is not lost. The children rise and there is resistance and power to be found in the classroom. Children demonstrate their awareness of and struggle against exploitative estranged labor through their counternarratives and through their sometimes subversive disruption of commodified curricula. The following section details one little girl's resistance to the alienation that estranged labor requires. In spite of the adults' efforts to alienate and impoverish her from the content, she found a way to respond to a commodified curriculum as species-being, honoring her "need for bonding, for creative activity, for knowledge, for self-consciousness and consciousness of [her] environment" (Rose, 2005). Elasia's story of quiet rebellion challenges the marginalizing narratives of racial and generational deficiency, doing what counternarratives are designed to do: push us to change how we think.

Academic Stories: Elasia and the Island

During an observation of a student teacher, Ms. Truly, in a third-grade classroom, I was struck by a series of events that framed a rich counternarrative to dominant and deficit-driven curricula, essentializing notions of what children are capable of and should be able know and do, and schooled lens of the most basic ideas of what an island is.

On this day, the student teacher was presenting a lesson on landforms. A point was made to the children by both the host teacher and the student teacher that *only* landforms were to be discussed and not bodies of water. Listening, I was confused. Some landforms could not be conceived of without considering their relationship to water (e.g., peninsulas). Notwithstanding my unstated confusion, the lesson progressed with a short power point presentation showing cartoon-ish line drawings of

Fig. 9.1 Representation of a cartoonish worksheet typical of those found in the children's folders

islands, mountains, canyons, deserts, plains, etc., and the children watched and listened.

After the presentation, Ms. Truly distributed to each child a paper plate, and a small ball of gray clay, asking them to open their landform folders—a folder holding worksheets (see similar example, Fig. 9.1), and explaining that their next task was to select three landforms from their lists and form all three from the clay.

As I moved from table to table, the children were happy to show me the papers in their folders—each one representing landforms as line drawings and narrowing the children's tasks to naming and defining the forms (labeling, matching, fill-in-the-blank). Ms. Truly explained to me that her host teacher generally found the blackline masters online to copy and give to the children. A few of the children showed pride in the A's and smiley-faces etched onto their papers by their teachers and this made me feel inordinately sad; I felt that I should have been glad for their satisfaction, but the shallowness of the content as it was provided to them was devastating. I realized, too, that the student teacher was also feeling a sort of sadly misguided pride in her lesson. She glanced at me with a smile as she explained to the children that they would be working with the *clay* to make three landforms of their choice! I knew she was glad to show me that she was bringing hands-on work to the children and that she was letting them choose what to make. I returned her smile, recognizing how hard she was trying to negotiate School in the space of someone else's classroom and after having been schooled so hard herself over the past 15 years.

However, my concern escalated as Ms. Truly's underestimation of the children's intellectual capabilities led her to direct them to basically transfer their blackline-master-understanding of landforms to clay and paper plate. After she had distributed clay and paper plates to each child, she instructed them to begin: to consult the papers in their folders, to determine the three landforms ("no water now!"), and to place them on their paper plate—which she called a "continent" –which further confused me as a continent is a higher-order landform itself and because some of the landforms the children were choosing could not be placed on a continent and maintain their defining characteristics. I felt sure that some of the children must have felt the same cognitive dissonance, but if so, they kept it to themselves. It was not only an underestimation of the children's intellectual power that was in play here, but an underestimation of the richness of the content itself. The clay-and-paper-plate exercise was basically a three-dimensional worksheet of representing objects in simple form and naming them (represented in Fig. 9.2).

One girl, Elasia, had decided that her three landforms would be peninsula, island and canyon. She had been talking to herself as she worked and as I neared her table, I overheard her quietly say, "Puerto Rico." I asked her if the island that she was making was Puerto Rico. She acknowledged that it was and that her peninsula was Florida. I wondered aloud about her canyon and she explained, "I just made this canyon because I had to pick a third landform and it seemed easy, but I wanted the island and the peninsula for sure because I've been hearing about Florida and Puerto Rico on TV." "How so?" I asked, "Is it about the hurricanes?" Elasia replied, "Yeah. Hurricane Maria and Hurricane Irma. Puerto Rico and other islands got really hurt by Hurricane Maria. And I know that Hurricane Irma also got after a peninsula, Florida." She paused, manipulating her clay. "I know we're not supposed to be putting out or talking about water now …but if it wasn't for the fact that islands and peninsulas are surrounded by water, the hurricanes wouldn't be there." Even though the subject matter of her explanation was grim, I was overjoyed to see/hear this child transcend the delivered content to make her choices based on a relationship with the concept of landforms in a context outside of paper and projected images. Elasia resisted the imposed alienation of the imposed task (estranged labor) and powerfully related it to her human existence, and through her willingness to provide a counternarrative to the event, she inspired my own resistance to the task.

Fig. 9.2 Representation of the clay-and-paper-plate exercise, virtually a three-dinemsional worksheet

Later that morning, I sat with Ms. Truly and her university supervisor (a retired administrator from a nearby school district) to discuss her lesson. The supervisor had nothing but praise for her well-designed and very detailed lesson plan and for her clear directions given to the children. I focused on asking Ms. Truly questions about her own relationship with the content of the lesson, landforms. During the three-way conversation, I brought up Elasia's conversation about her landform choices, and how she had piqued my own interest in landforms, especially islands and their possibilities.

I inquired about other representations of landforms they'd seen in class prior to this particular lesson. Because Ms. Truly had indicated that their only other experiences had been toward building those collections of worksheets in the folders, I inquired about the ways that, for example, islands had been represented in previous lessons. I hoped that the children had been exposed to more authentic, varied, and *accurate* images than what I had seen that day. Alas, Ms. Truly informed me that they had been shown only pictures very much like the one in Fig. 9.3: a singular/narrowing/schooled representation of ISLAND as small, deserted, and tropical.

I wondered aloud to Ms. Truly and her supervisor whether it would not help the children build a deeper understanding of the characteristics of a landform such as an island if they were to explore a diversity of islands. And perhaps even argue whether some of the examples were islands or not. I showed on my phone some examples of images of islands that were:

- Not tropical: Greenland for one, and it's *huge*! And also this one (Fig. 9.4) which the children may rightly argue its island-ness:

- Not deserted: for example, Manhattan (Fig. 9.5)

- And some not even on earth: these mysterious "magic islands" on Saturn's moon, Titan (Fig. 9.6)

Ms. Truly seemed taken aback but interested, but the supervisor quickly spoke up to remind us both about what kind of academic stories *these* children were to learn

Fig. 9.3 A schooled representation of Island as small, deserted and tropical

Fig. 9.4 A non-tropical island and catalyst for arguments of island-ness

Fig. 9.5 A not-deserted island, Manhattan

to tell: "You don't understand. I'm a former administrator and I can tell you what is needed." I steeled myself, anticipating that I would not like what I would hear next: something that would indicate that she knew what was in the children's best interest—an expression of coercion as caring (Noddings, 2002)—because she *knows* that these children are "deficient and therefore in need of coercion and manipulation—for their own good—by those who are less deficient" (Leafgren, 2009, p. 147). The supervisor continued, "What you're suggesting is ridiculous. *These children will be confused by extra information. We have to keep it simple so they can pass the test.*" (emphasis added).

Even after preparing myself for her response, I was stunned. This overt and explicit articulation of deliberate deficit storytelling, one that perpetuates the kind of academic stories that enumerate failure and reflect precisely the ways that children are describing their work to us (e.g., "*I learned about the paper*), made my blood

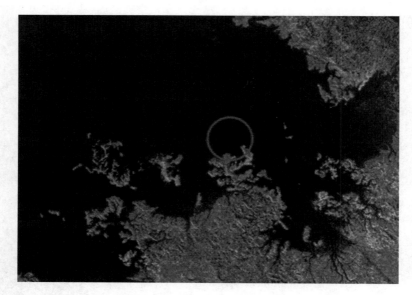

Fig. 9.6 Mysterious "magic islands" on Titan

boil. I responded to the supervisor before Ms. Truly could say a word, "Do you think Elasia was *confused?* So, you think to pass the test, you have to make them stupid?"

I don't recall her stuttered response, but her words did cause me to recall the response of a second grader a few weeks earlier when she had been asked about her time in school and the reasons for her efforts. As if she were channeling the administrator/supervisor, seven-year-old Bre explained, "Well, everything we do is for getting ready for third grade and the third grade test." When pressed about what she's learning and how it will serve her after third grade, she noted, "I am pretty sure that when I am in third grade and do the big test, then everything I have to do will be for fourth grade, and that probably just keeps going until all of the grades run out." When asked if she feels good about what she's learning and what she wonders about, she shrugged and said, "it's just school; I don't think or wonder about anything."

Counterstories as Catalyst for Curricula (Not the Commodified Kind)

I wonder the conversation that would emerge should Bre and Elasia ever meet. In school(ed) spaces where pedagogy is too often poisoned by the rigid and coercive nature of an estranged curriculum. Elasia is one of the many children who by her very nature resists the alienation of the castrated, bloodless curriculum offered to her and instead, shapes her own curricular path—and the paths of all in her trajectory—as she "thinks and wonders" about *everything*. Even in the presence of a rather vapid task, in Marxian fashion, she considers herself the director of her own actions, she determines the character of her actions and defines relationships with nature as it exists outside her, from her spiritual essence, her human existence.

Curriculum as a way to live a life—a "lived curriculum" (Aoki, 1993)—is conceived as "an active force having direct impact on the whole fabric of its human and social context" (Eisner & Vallance, 1974, p. 135), and thus serves to simultaneously represent and produce identities. Grumet (1980) acknowledges a curriculum dialectic shaping the learner as the learner shapes it, capturing the deeply complicated nature of curriculum as it unfolds in living interaction with students, their identities and the social environment.

However, when curricular work bears no relationship to the child's personal inclinations or collective interests, when she is "forced to removes pieces of her[self] to fit," when it is contrary to her nature—her inclinations, desires, logic, her very species-being, when she and "the curriculum collide at the intersection of her socio-cultural, historical, economic, gendered, and racial ways of being…it forces her to make a choice, sometimes to her benefit and others to her demise" (Williams, 2018, p. 16).

In the brilliant book *Death at an Early Age* (1967), Jonathan Kozol tells of such a child whose intensely incandescent resistance to an oppression and alienation still shines bright over 50 years later. He writes:

> After I went in there the first time in November, I began to find my attention being drawn… by a bright and attractive and impatient Negro [sic] girl who showed her hatred for school and teacher by sitting all day with a slow and smoldering look of cynical resentment in her eyes. Not only was she bright but she also worked extremely hard and she seemed to me remarkably sophisticated even though she was still very much a little child…Her eyes, beautiful and sarcastic, told that she understood exactly what was going on. Enough shrewdness and sense of dignity belonged to her that she made no mistake about where to place the blame…Five years from now, if my guess was correct, she would be fourteen and she would be out on picket lines. She would stand there and she would protest because there alone, after so much wasting of her years, would be the one place where her pride and hope would still have a chance. But how could a child like her, with all of her awareness and will of her intelligence, ever in her lifetime find a way to forgive society and the public school system for what it had done to her?" p 37–38.

Pre-dating even Anyon's (1981) school study, the child represented by Kozol struggled against the imposition of "the knowledge of powerful groups on the working class and…[she recognized and resisted] this class-based curriculum" (p. 38). Kozol wrote of being glad that the child was angry and he worried about the children who did not seem to be angry, who seemed to resign themselves to believing their deficiency-driven school experiences were all that they deserved. As cautioned by McLaren and Farahmandpur (2005), school enacts technologies of social control and forced assimilation that is designed to convince children that their interests are served by compliance, that those who are not compliant are untrustworthy, and that their own oppression is inevitable, normal, natural, and ultimately good. To confront this, Anyon (1981) concluded that "really useful knowledge for these students…

would authenticate students' own meanings and give them skills to identify and analyze their own social class and to transform a situation that some already perceive is not in their own interest" (p. 33).

A living, critical pedagogy offers students and workers "opportunities to develop critical social skills that will assist them in gaining an awareness of—and a resolve to transform—the exploitative nature of capitalist social and economic relations of production" (McLaren & Farahmandpur, 2005, p. 53). A critical lived curriculum emerging from counterstorytelling exemplify children's knowledges and wonderings and deep intelligences. Solórzano and Yasso (2002) raise the question, "How can these "stories can be used as theoretical, methodological, and pedagogical tools to challenge racism, sexism, and classism [and developmentalism] and work toward social justice?"

Years of carefully attending to children and becoming engrossed and moved by their powerful and empowering stories, leads to the conclusion that the best way would be to ask the children how to use their own stories—autobiographical and academic. As noted by Grumet (1990), approaching voice "as the medium for the projection of meaning" will allow children to authentically connect themselves and others with their realities, joys, fears, and passions (p. 279).

And so we asked the children. In seeking ways to enrich the curriculum at one of the urban schools involved in this project, we asked the children what mattered to them, what made them mad, what got them stirred up. They told stories about their lives, and worries, and interests, and observations, and from those stories, teacher candidates and I found that these were prevalent themes of their storied curriculum:

- Dangers abound... children talked about shootings, guns, and scary people—often naming police as the scariest
- Concerns about people they care about (some sick, some in danger, some absent...)
- Wonder/worry about where they'll live
- Wonder/worry about who will take care of them (fluctuating family structures)
- Articulated frustration with lame, disconnected meaningless content (school's non-responsive to their experiences)
- Feeling invisible/muted (unseen, unheard, unknown)
- Lack of connection to classmates, teachers, school--antagonism, disrespect, violence
- And another class wants to talk about safety. Being safe. Starting with ways to be/feel safe in school and who's in charge of making sure people are safe and can kids be in charge of that.

This is the way to bring counternarratives that emerge from the children's counterstorytelling of their academic stories and school lives to curriculum. And it's clear upon discussing with children their thoughts about what matters to them in their lives and stories, that the notions of lesser, deficient, and incomplete that too often serve to define them and their school stories are completely uninformed and unacceptable. Solórzano and Yosso (2002) define counterstorytelling as "a method of telling the stories of those people whose experiences are not often told" including people of color, women, gay, and the poor" [and children] (p. 26). Counterstories or narratives stand in opposition to narratives of dominance called majoritarian stories. Curriculum, as narrowly defined in school settings, emerges from and perpetuates a dominant narrative---a series of majoritarian stories. "Just last week, a group of children shared with me that they want to do an analysis of Why Kids Hate School-- with a range of dimensions." (1st grade and SPED).

The children's counternarratives disrupted the dominant school(ed) narrative of school claims that literacy and language lies in other (more important) people's words and stories. The children developed complex and meaningful stories based on their own identities and experiences and thus shaped the curriculum as it shaped them. Their stories were not only academically rich in development of skills and understanding but they were related to issues of fear, hunger, frustration with school and society, discrimination, family separation, housing, and more. Although discussion was just beginning, the children became deeply engaged in telling and re-telling their stories, in hearing and relating to other children's narratives, and were moved by the ways in which they were heard. Each of the children embraced not only opening their world via storytelling, but they were willing to be vulnerable to see their stories read and interpreted by others in ways that sometimes enriched their own narratives.

Questions for Reflection
- As children's talk in school settings is often largely dictated and determined by their teachers, can you envision ways to engage and encourage those working with young children to create the spaces that support children's telling of counter stories?
- Participatory research practices and, particular to this chapter, counterstorytelling offers children a means to authentically represent their lives to others and further their own understandings through the work? This disruption to the status quo can pose challenges to researchers working to continue their research practices in school settings. How can participatory researchers support children's engagement when the expectations from the school site may not be aligned with such work?

References

Anyon, J. (1981). Social class and school knowledge. *Curriculum Inquiry, 11*(3), 3–42. https://doi.org/10.1080/03626784.1981.11075261

Aoki, T. T. (1993). Legitimating lived curriculum: Towards a curricular landscape of multiplicity. *Journal of Curriculum and Supervision, 8*(3), 255–268.

Ayers, W., & Alexander-Tanner, R. (2010). *To teach: The journey, in comics.* New York, NY: Teachers College Press.

Bell, L. A. (2003). Telling tales: What stories can teach us about race and racism. *Race Ethnicity and Education, 6*(1), 3–28.

Boutte, G. S. (2015). *Educating African American students: And how are the children*. New York, NY: Routledge.

Cook, D. A. (2013). Blurring the boundaries: The mechanics of creating composite characters. In M. Lynn & A. D. Dixson (Eds.), *Handbook of critical race theory in education: CRT and innovations in educational research methodologies* (pp. 287–301). New York, NY: Routledge.

Cox, J. (1998). An introduction to Marx's theory of alienation. *International Socialism, 79*(2). Retrieved from https://www.marxists.org/history/etol/newspape/isj2/index2.html

Eisner, E., & Vallance, E. (Eds.). (1974). *Conflicting conceptions of curriculum*. Berkeley, CA: McCutchan.

Freire, P. (1970). *Pedagogy of the oppressed* (M. Bergman Ram, Trans.). New York, NY: Continuum.

Grumet, M. (1980). Autobiography and reconceptualization. In W. Pinar (Ed.), *Contemporary curriculum discourses: Twenty years of JCT* (pp. 24–29). New York, NY: Peter Lang.

Grumet, M. (1990). Voice: The search for a feminist rhetoric for educational studies. *Cambridge Journal of Education, 20*(3), 277–282.

Hayes, C. (2014). What I know about teaching, I learned from my father: A critical race autoethnographic/counternarrative exploration of multi-generational transformative teaching. *Journal of African American Males in Education, 5*, 247–265.

Hendry, P. M. (2011). *Engendering the curriculum*. New York, NY: Routledge.

Horgan, D. (2017). Child participatory research methods: Attempts to go 'deeper'. *Childhood, 24*(2), 245–259.

Jardine, D. (1998). *To dwell with a boundless heart: Essays in curriculum theory, hermeneutics, and the ecological imagination*. New York, NY: Peter Lang.

Johnson, L. (2016). Using critical race theory to explore race-based conversations through a critical family book club. *Literacy Research: Theory, Method, and Practice, 65*(1), 300–315.

Kozol, J. (1967). *Death at an early age*. Boston, MA: Houghton Mifflin.

Leafgren, S. (2009). *Reuben's fall: A rhizomatic analysis of disobedience in kindergarten*. Walnut Creek, CA: Left Coast Press.

Leafgren, S., & Sander, S. (2019). Children, nomads, and queering: Desire and surprise in a wiggly world. In W. Letts & S. Fifield (Eds.), *STEM of desire: Queer theories and science education*. Boston, MA: Brill Sense Publishers.

Marx, K. (1844/1988). *Economic and philosophic manuscripts of 1844*. Amherst, NY: Prometheus Books. Retrieved from https://www.marxists.org/archive/marx/works/1844/manuscripts/labour.htm

Marx, K. (1975). *Early writings*. London, UK: Penguin Books.

McLaren, P., & Farahmandpur, R. (2005). *Teaching against global capitalism and the new imperialism: A critical pedagogy*. Lanham, MD: Rowman & Littlefield Publishers.

Merriweather Hunn, L., Guy, T., & Mangliitz, E. (2006). Who can speak for whom? Using counter-storytelling to challenge racial hegemony. *Adult Education Research Conference*, 243–250. Retrieved from http://newprairiepress.org/aerc/2006/papers/32

Miller, A. (1983/1990). *For your own good: Hidden cruelty in child-rearing and the roots of violence* (H. and H. Hannum, Trans.) (3rd ed.). New York, NY: Noonday Press.

Noddings, N. (2002). *Educating moral people: A caring alternative to character education*. New York, NY: Teachers College Press.

Rose, G. (2005). Species being, social being and class consciousness. *Internationalist Perspective 43*. Retrieved from http://internationalist-perspective.org/IP/ip-archive/ip_43_species-being.html

Solórzano, D., & Yasso, T. (2002). Critical race methodology: Counter-storytelling as an analytical framework for education research. *Qualitative Inquiry, 8*(1), 23–44.

Williams, T. (2018) *Wild and well: An autobiographical manifesto for the love of black girls*. Retrieved from OhioLNK Electronic Theses and Dissertation Center.

Part IV
Analysis and Dissemination
of Participatory Work with Children

Chapter 10
Supporting Children's Engagement in Active Dissemination Practices

Angela Eckhoff

Introduction

At its heart, participatory research holds a transformative agenda where the participants collaborate with the principal investigator throughout all stages of the research process. Ideally, participants' engagement is supported throughout the final stage of the research process: dissemination of findings. Within the field of education, the publication and dissemination phases of research findings are typically concerned with sharing results within a larger community of researchers and practitioners. A central, but often overlooked, aspect of participatory research with children is their sustained engagement in analysis, presentation, and publication phases of the work. These phases pose numerous ethical and logistical challenges that early childhood participatory researchers must carefully consider in order to ensure that children have accessible routes to participation. As a starting point, we must acknowledge the limits of our knowing from the traditional adult-centric publication and dissemination routes.

An important consideration for adult researchers working with participatory methodologies lies within the planning for the final phases of the research process. Traditional qualitative practices of involving participants in the analysis of generated data involve member-checking (Lincoln & Guba, 1985) initial drafts of project findings prior to publication. While member checks ensure a degree of validity, they also mark the end of the participant's involvement in the research process. Involvement of children in dissemination processes would help to support the continued power of their voice and actions throughout culmination of their shared work. This involvement will challenge researchers to move beyond decades of acceptable research procedures and necessitate our negotiation of the inclusion of children's voice during analysis and dissemination in order "...to

A. Eckhoff (✉)
Old Dominion University, Norfolk, VA, USA
e-mail: aeckhoff@odu.edu

© Springer Nature Switzerland AG 2019
A. Eckhoff (ed.), *Participatory Research with Young Children*, Educating the Young Child 17, https://doi.org/10.1007/978-3-030-19365-2_10

produce a range of research outputs that meet the needs of participants and researchers" (Haw, 2008, p. 206).

Passive forms of dissemination – publication in academic journals and books and scholarly presentations – limit the audience for our research to a small group of researchers and educators and serves to primarily benefit the adult researcher. The inclusion of active forms of dissemination – local displays at schools or other community settings, presentations involving children, or policy/practice guidelines for the research setting – can provide a means to continue the participatory roles children assumed during the initial phases of the collaborative work. These active forms of dissemination extend the knowledge generated during the project to the educational organization, community, and to the children, families, and educators involved in the work. Active forms of dissemination can provide opportunities for adult researchers and children to share feedback with one another about the experiences and generated understandings that occur as a result of the children's participation. In addition, active forms of dissemination can extend past the written or verbal requirements of academic work and include non-traditional forms of data including visual arts media, video, and multimedia. Non-traditional forms of data and active dissemination outlets can be particularly valuable when working with young children because such data sources do not solely rely on the child's literacy and language skills. In the section that follows, I present a brief summary of the various active forms of dissemination as they apply to participatory work with young learners.

Active Forms of Dissemination in Early Care and Education Settings

Local Displays of Children's Work

The walls of classrooms for young children are often decorated with children's work samples, artwork, and related visual imagery and, as such, are public statements about the experiences of schooling within each particular classroom. Ultimately, this documentation conveys messages about the relationship between teaching and learning, the image of the child held by the teacher, and the expectations for behavior and social norms within that setting (Gandini, 1998). In many early learning settings adults often hold full responsibility for the creation of documentation displays of children's work (Eckhoff, 2019) but researchers and teacher educators in the field of early childhood are increasingly turning to the theoretical ideas of the environment as third teacher (Strong-Wilson & Ellis, 2007; Tarr, 2004) and pedagogical or classroom-based documentation (Buldu, 2010; Lindgren, 2012) to support higher levels of child engagement in documentation practices.

Documentation practices in early learning settings often center around physical tracings of the child's learning experiences – drawings, writings, audio and video recordings, and observation records to name a few. "These physical traces allow others to revisit, interpret, reinterpret, and even re-create and experience (Krechevsky, Mardell, Rivard, & Wilson, 2013, p. 74). Valuing children's physical traces of learning is an essential part of collaborative work with young children because children's thinking, as part of the process of learning, is largely invisible unless steps are taken to help make student' thinking visible to themselves, to their peers, and to their families (Krechevsky et al., 2013). As children experience pedagogical and documentation practices that open possibilities to exploring the processes of learning, they become more adept at understanding their own thoughts, what knowledge they have, and what they continue to question. Carolina Rinaldi described documentation of children's work as visible listening (2001), which is involves the careful collection of notes, photographs, documents, and artifacts during the course of learning. Visible listening practices differ from traditional classroom or research documentation practices because of the emphasis on listening throughout the process of learning not merely at the conclusion of a learning activity or experiences. Such practices can be extended to participatory research with young children by offering them familiar routes to support their engagement in dissemination practices. Collaborative engagement with data for the purposes of documentation and local dissemination between researchers, teachers, and children can support the processes of exploration and inquiry, offer opportunities for student, researcher, and teacher reflection, support metacognitive thinking by encouraging children to be aware and take ownership of their thoughts and ideas, and also promote understandings and respect for student work that honors the child's thoughts, words, and actions (Rinaldi, 2001).

Presentations Involving Children

Children can take on a variety of roles in local presentations of their work which can be shared within their own community groups, classes, or schools. One of the most frequent occurrences of children's participation in presentations for others within educational settings occurs during student-led, family conferences. While a substantial body of literature depicts the many benefits of such conferences for students, families, and educators (Benson & Barnett, 2005; Little & Allan, 1989; Tholander, 2011) this literature can also be useful in determining the roles, responsibilities, and ethics involved in student presentations of participatory research targeted to various audiences within their communities. Adult researchers interested in facilitating research-based presentations involving children will need to devote the time and supports necessary to encourage children as they reflect upon their work and prepare presentations. Preparation can be done individually, in pairs, or in groups depending upon the goals and the audience for the presentations.

Preparation activities can include:

- selecting visual imagery or other project data to share
- narrating or writing reflections about their experiences

- setting new goals based upon their experiences
- discussing their experiences and working on communication skills
- creating digital presentations or movies to share

Standard practices of ensuring participant anonymity is research dissemination and publication may become blurred as children participate in presentations of the work. Researchers seeking to involve children in such practices will need to account for the children's participation in presentations as part of their institutional project approvals, parent consent, and child assent approvals.

Developing or Redefining Policy/Practice Guidelines for the Research Setting

An important element of contemporary, critical theory frameworks and participatory methodologies is the opportunity for participants to suggest or initiate change. In many early learning environments children are rarely included in decision or policy-making practices. Some participatory research projects may lend themselves to the development of suggestions for policy or practice changes within a particular environment. Inviting and encouraging young children to reflect upon their experiences, work, and ideas can provide adult researchers with a route for children's inclusion in developing such guidelines for change. Researchers should take care to ensure that children do not assume their suggestions or ideas will be implemented or adopted but encourage the children to share their reflections as part of the larger process of disseminating their work. This process can demonstrate for children that their voices, ideas, and understandings can inform adults' and other children's knowledge of their views and experiences.

Steps Towards Participatory Dissemination: A View into a Trip to the Natural History Museum Through *Photovoice*

In the remainder of this chapter, I share my experiences working with a young child in a participatory project that utilized a reflective methodology. His reflections and photographs, as well as those of his classmates, helped to form the documentation of a class-based participatory project which was ultimately disseminated among other classes, parents and families, and the museum staff working at the site visited for the project. Through a participatory design, this research case documents the experiences of an 8-year-old on a field trip to a local natural history museum with his second-grade class. This project was adult-initiated to provide a means for children to extend their classroom-based science learning on animal habitats and the needs of animals into a new setting – a local, natural history museum. Using a variation of the *Photovoice* approach, this project also aimed to further research-based understandings of young children's perceptions, visions, and participation during informal, content-focused classroom fieldtrips. The children on this field trip used digital cameras and tablets to document their experiences throughout their time at the natural history museum. While the majority of the students in the class participated in the *Photovoice* approach, for the purposes of this writing only one child's work is presented as a representative example illustrating the general themes found among the students' imagery. All images that appear in this case presentation are unedited; they are as the child created, choose for inclusion, explained, and labelled.

This research is framed by the use of the *Photovoice* approach – a participatory, action-orientated approach – as the children created, collected, and worked to analyze all data utilized in this project. The use of the *Photovoice* approach is well documented in social science research (Booth & Booth, 2003; Ford & Campbell, 2018; Killion & Wang, 2000; McIntyre, 2003; Wang, 2006). I selected the approach because it held the potential to enable the children to visualize, depict, and reflect on the experiences and spaces that were important to them during the field trip. The use of *Photovoice* with young children can provide unique insights and ideas about their own unique experiences that may differ from those obtained through adult observation approaches using field notes or photography to document the experience for the students. The students in this project were invited to take photographs of their choice during the course of the field trip and, once back in the classroom, select four to six their photographs for inclusion in the class documentation of the project. Using a variation of the PHOTO technique (Amos, Read, Cobb, & Pabani, 2012), I asked the children questions about the photographs they had selected for inclusion.

P: Describe your photo?
H: What is happening in your picture?
O: Why did you take a picture of this?
T: What does this picture tell us about your experiences at the museum?
O: How can this picture provide opportunities for us to tell other children about the museum and the environment?

Photographs, as complex, multi-voiced artifacts, provide an essential means of documenting and sharing an experience by making it concrete. This process of materializing an experience can be conceptualized as reification which is seen as "the process of giving form to our experience by producing objects that congeal this experience into 'thingness'. In so doing, we create points of focus around which the negotiation of meaning becomes organized. ...Any community of practice produces abstractions, tools, symbols, stories, terms and concepts that reify something of that practice in a congealed form" (Wenger, 1998, p. 58–59). Once created, the photographs can be used by both adults and children to communicate understandings and experiences by providing a shared point of reference. *Photovoice*, through its shared use of photographs and explanatory discussion practices offer a means to promote attention to the multiple understandings that children document through photography and ultimately choose reflect upon when narrating understandings of their own experiences (Lipponen, Rajala, Hilppö, & Paananen, 2016).

Following parental assent to participate in the project and as part of the child assent process, I shared with the children that the goal of the project was to see the children's experiences through their eyes and that they were encouraged to photograph what they found to be interesting during their fieldtrip. The children in this project used their school's digital cameras or tablets of which they had previous experience using in their classroom. Each child had their own device to use during the field trip which lasted approximately 3 hours. Devices were passed out to the students during the times of the field trip where they freely explored the museum in small groups guided by a school or parent chaperone. Devices were not permitted for student use on the bus rides or during docent talks in order to adhere to issues of confidentiality with others outside the school setting and to help support the children's attention to the sharing of relevant content or museum information during docent presentations. I informed that children I would view any images or video left on the cameras together with them once we returned to the school in order to engage in the image reflection part of the *Photovoice* process. The children selected and responded to all images included in this writing.

As the principal investigator, I held the primary responsibility for the design and implementation of the project and also took on the responsibility of interviewing each student during the reflection phase of the project and worked collaboratively with the students to develop the final, class-wide documentation book and presentation of the project. A key component of the *Photovoice* approach is the production of final documentation that can be shared in order to impact the knowledge and awareness of others within and outside of the project. I worked alongside the classroom teacher and students to co-create documentation that reflected the children's understandings of the diverse needs of animals in the region related to their expressed notions of caring for and being positive stewards of the earth.

Data Analysis

Following the conclusion of the field trip, all photographed images were downloaded on a computer organized by each child's work. I sat down with children individually to view and reflect upon their captured images using the PHOTO technique described above. I made the decision to work with students individually, rather than in a small focus group, because the process of photographing their experiences and reflecting with the photos was a novel experience for the students. To begin the analysis process, we looked over each of the child's images and talked about similar ideas, issues, or images that repeated themselves or came up frequently. The child then selected 4–6 images to include in the project and went through the PHOTO questions for each selected image. I asked the children the PHOTO questions and the children typed out their responses on the computer under their selected image. Once all of the children had completed that process, I compiled the images and showed them to the class for a whole group reflection. During the class reflection experience, I encouraged the children to look for similarities between the images as a means to begin the identification of overarching themes. The children quickly identified similarities around the themes of Animal Habitats and Needs; Taking Care of Injured Animals; Animals that are Endangered; and Things We Didn't Know. During this viewing session we collectively selected five images and accompanying PHOTO responses for each theme to share with the larger school community via a PowerPoint presentation. From those images and text, a class photo book and online presentation were created to share with parents, teachers and other students within the school setting. Students participated alongside their teacher and myself to create the project's photo book and presentation once the images were chosen for selection. As part of the child consent process, I shared with the children that I would utilize their imagery and interviews in my research writings. A requirement of my IRB protocol was the need to ensure anonymity for all participants so no children could appear in any selected imagery and pseudonyms were needed for all children. As part of the PHOTO interview process, children selected their own pseudonyms.

Overview of Project Findings

The four key themes discussed below and are presented alongside corresponding images from Alex's photographic work on the field trip. At the time of this project Alex was 8 years old and a student in the classroom selected for this work. I selected this Alex's imagery and PHOTO responses for inclusion in this writing because they are representative of each identified theme and also demonstrate how the themes emerged across the majority of the students' photographic documentation.

The first theme, Animal Habitats and Needs, is captured in Alex's image of an otter (Fig. 10.1). Photos and PHOTO questions responses in this theme were most directly aligned to their prior in-class learning. His responses to the PHOTO questions were:

P: Describe your photo? This is an otter who was swimming in the water while I was looking. He had a brother swimming with him.

H: What is happening in your picture? He stopped swimming to come by the window where we were standing so I could take his picture.

O: Why did you take a picture of this? I never saw otters swim. They go under water but come up to breathe air like we do. Also, I like otters they are my favorite.

T: What does this picture tell us about your experiences at the museum? I saw lots of animals in their habitats.

O: How can this picture provide opportunities for us to tell other children about the museum and the environment? Otters need land and water. They need to have space to move on land and then swimming too.

Fig. 10.1 An otter swimming but also posing

Fig. 10.2 An injured bird

The next theme, Taking Care of Injured Animals, can be seen in Alex's photo of an injured bird (Fig. 10.2) and his understandings of the museum's role in supporting injured animals is shared below in his PHOTO responses. The images aligned with this theme and the accompanying student PHOTO responses shared the deep concern that many students experienced on the day of their field trip. This category of images was most closely aligned with emotional responses and documents the feelings of concern and care that emerged as the children learned more about the role of the museum in caring for injured animals.

P: Describe your photo? This is a picture of a bird that got hurt and lives at the museum now in the outside part.

H: What is happening in your picture? He's is sitting on a branch watching me watch him.

O: Why did you take a picture of this? I thought he was cool looking because of his feather thing but I also felt bad because he had gotten hurt.

T: What does this picture tell us about your experiences at the museum? There is a bird part where you can go into and there are birds all around.

O: How can this picture provide opportunities for us to tell other children about the museum and the environment? There is an injured bird center there which is a safe place if they are hurt. So they don't get hurt more.

The third theme, Animals that are Endangered, is depicted in Alex's image of a Bald Eagle (Fig. 10.3) and his responses to the PHOTO questioning. There were just a few species of animals at the museum categorized as endangered but the majority of students included at least one photo of an identified endangered animal. This inclusion across the majority of students signifies the importance the children placed on the animals and their photos in this theme.

Fig. 10.3 Bald eagle in danger

P: Describe your photo? This is a picture of a Bald Eagle sitting still. He never moved while I was watching him. I thought he wasn't real at first.

H: What is happening in your picture? He's is sitting very still.

O: Why did you take a picture of this? I saw the word thing (*exhibit label*) and it said Bald Eagles were in dangered (*endangered*) but more keep getting saved.

T: What does this picture tell us about your experiences at the museum? There are animals there that we must protect because they are in danger.

O: How can this picture provide opportunities for us to tell other children about the museum and the environment? In dangered (*Endangered*) Bald Eagles are a symbol of America and we can't keep making them in danger. Museums can help protect them.

The final theme, Things We Didn't Know, captured images or objects that surprised the students while on their field trip. This category of images represents elements, ideas, objects, or animals that were not known to the students prior to the field trip. It was only through the PHOTO interviews that this category emerged as the student's responses reflected their new knowledge as a result of the field trip. In this sense, the PHOTO questions served to uncover the student's intended purpose for taking the photo which was not obvious when merely reviewing the photos. The images themselves serve as a physical manifestation of the students' acceptance and welcoming of new knowledge, ideas, and understandings. We can see Alex's acceptance of his new knowledge and his desire to share that knowledge in his response to the PHOTO questions. Alex's image of a working bee hive in shared in Fig. 10.4.

Fig. 10.4 New bees

P: Describe your photo? This is hundreds of bees and there is a queen bee in there somewhere.

H: What is happening in your picture? The bees were flying in and out of the window that had a little hole they could go through. They were making honey.

O: Why did you take a picture of this? I saw all the bees flying in and out and it was freaky.

T: What does this *picture* tell us about your experiences at the museum? You won't get stung by the bees and you can go up close to see them moving and crawling all over each other.

O: How can this picture provide opportunities for us to tell other children about the museum and the environment? I didn't know this but these were new bees. There were no bees in the winter in the hive but they come back in the springtime but they have to have a queen. She makes the worker bees do the work.

The themes uncovered during the PHOTO questioning process and during the whole class evaluation of the photos revealed the elements of the field trip experience that the children were able to connect to their previous lessons on animals and habitats. The PHOTO questioning highlighted the objects and situations that interested the students and, thus, also highlighted possibilities for their teacher to extend their understandings once back in the classroom. The last question in the PHOTO questioning protocol – How can this picture provide opportunities for us to tell other children about the museum and the environment? – provided the us, as a collective research group, with a starting point for beginning to design the documentation of this experience to share with others. The children's imagery and reflective responses formed the PowerPoint presentation and class book designed to disseminate their work to the larger school community. The presentation and book focused on sharing the photos and information the children identified as central to teaching others about the museum and the idea of taking care of animals. The text included in their documentation was drawn from the student responses to the PHOTO question protocol.

When explored with a participatory lens, the use of the *Photovoice* approach opens up possibilities for the inclusion of young children in both the analysis and documentation processes directly connected to their previous involvement in the image creation. The participatory framework of this research promotes insight into the ways in which field trips can be part of intentional research practices to empower students to use their experiences, interpretations, and voice to inform and extend the understandings of their experiences to themselves and to others. The use of *Photovoice* provided an accessible means for the children to engage as researchers throughout the data collection, analysis, and the local dissemination work of the study. The students' imagery and explanatory text provide a means to support multi-voiced understandings of their experiences. Through their sustained engagement and participation, the children determined the study outcomes and, subsequently, our understandings of their experiences.

Concluding Thoughts

This research documented the use of digital photographic arts media investigations during during informal, content-focused class field trips. The use of the *Photovoice* approach involved the children as both individuals and a members of a class in the analysis and documentation of their experiences. The *Photovoice* approach also provided the children with opportunties to share their knowledge and understandings in order to advocate for the care of animals to the broader school community. The process of reviewing and categorizing images helped to make the children's knowledge, understandings, and wonderings visible to themselves and others viewing their photographs and explanatory text. At the classroom level, the analysis of their photography and PHOTO responses can be used to scaffold their knowledge through lessons that build upon their questions in an authentic manner. While I, as the adult researcher, developed the design of the research process, this project ultimately promoted high levels of student engagement during all research phases. The children gained new knowledge and skills through their experience with *Photovoice* as an accessible methodology and the various stages of the research process following image/data generation. The structured *Photovoice* protocol offered a scaffolded introduction to research for Alex and his classmates and became an inextricable part of the field trip experience. Their local dissemination work helped to close the research loop by creating an opportunity for the children's findings to potentially inform others about the museum's role in caring for and educating others about the needs of the animals in its care. This knowledge sharing inevitably showed the children themselves that their understandings are valuable and worthy of dissemination to others.

Questions for Reflection
1. Do you find connections and possibilities for active dissemination in your current research? What would you need to modify in your approach to analysis and dissemination to provide children a space for engagement?
2. How could you support or strengthen current supports between children and documentation of learning practices?
3. What ethical issues or classroom challenges do you feel could arise from the collaborative components of the *Photovoice* approach? What steps could you take as the researcher to mitigate any of the potential issues or challenges you've identified?
4. As a researcher, how will you balance your need for passive research dissemination and publication practices with opportunities to engage children in active processes of documentation and local dissemination practices?

References

Amos, S., Read, K., Cobb, M., & Pabani, N. (2012). *Facilitating a photovoice project: What you need to know*. Retrieved from http://www.foodarc.ca/makefoodmatter/wpcontent/uploads/.../VOICES_PhotovoiceManual.pdf

Benson, B. P., & Barnett, S. P. (2005). *Student-led conferencing using showcase portfolios*. Thousand Oaks, CA: Corwin Press.

Booth, T., & Booth, W. (2003). In the frame: Photovoice and mothers with learning difficulties. *Disability & Society, 18*(4), 431–442.

Buldu, M. (2010). Making learning visible in kindergarten classrooms: Pedagogical documentation as a formative assessment technique. *Teaching and Teacher Education, 26*(7), 1439–1449.

Eckhoff, A. (2019). Public displays of children's work in early learning and elementary school settings as documentation of children's learning experiences. *International Journal of Early Childhood, 51*, 73–91.

Ford, K., & Campbell, S. (2018). Being participatory through photo-based images. In I. Coyne & B. Carter (Eds.), *Being participatory: Researching with children and young people* (pp. 127–146). Cham, Switzerland: Springer.

Gandini, L. (1998). Educational and caring spaces. In C. Edwards, L. Gandini, & G. Forman (Eds.), *The hundred languages of children: The Reggio Emilia approach—Advanced reflections* (pp. 161–178). Westport, CT: Greenwood Publishing Group.

Haw, K. (2008). 'Voice' and video: Seen, heard and listened to? In P. Thomson (Ed.), *Doing visual research with children and young people* (pp. 192–207). London, UK: Routledge.

Killion, C. M., & Wang, C. C. (2000). Linking African American mothers across life stage and station through photo voice. *Journal of Health Care for the Poor and Underserved, 100*, 310–325.

Krechevsky, M., Mardell, B., Rivard, M., & Wilson, D. (2013). *Visible learners: Promoting Reggio-inspired approaches in all schools*. Hoboken, NJ: Wiley.

Lincoln, Y. S., & Guba, E. G. (1985). *Naturalistic inquiry* (Vol. 75). Thousand Oaks, CA: Sage.

Lindgren, A. L. (2012). Ethical issues in pedagogical documentation: Representations of children through digital technology. *International Journal of Early Childhood, 44*(3), 327–340.

Lipponen, L., Rajala, A., Hilppö, J., & Paananen, M. (2016). Exploring the foundations of visual methods used in research with children. *European Early Childhood Education Research Journal, 24*(6), 936–946.

Little, A. N., & Allan, J. (1989). Student-led parent-teacher conferences. *Elementary School Guidance & Counselling, 23*(3), 210–218.

McIntyre, A. (2003). Through the eyes of women: Photo voice and participatory research as tools for reimagining place. *Gender, Place and Culture: A Journal of Feminist Geography, 10*(1), 47–66.

Rinaldi, C. (2001). Documentation and assessment: What is the relationship? In Project Zero & Reggio Children (Ed.), *Making learning visible: Children as individual and group learners* (pp. 78–89). Reggio Emilia, Italy: Reggio Children.

Strong-Wilson, T., & Ellis, J. (2007). Children and place: Reggio Emilia's environment as third teacher. *Theory into Practice, 46*(1), 40–47.

Tarr, P. (2004). Consider the walls. *Young Children, 59*(3), 88–92.

Tholander, M. (2011). Student-led conferencing as democratic practice. *Children & Society, 25*(3), 239–250.

Wang, C. C. (2006). Youth participation in photovoice as a strategy for community change. *Journal of Community Practice, 14*(1–2), 147–161.

Wenger, E. (1998). Communities of practice: Learning as a social system. *Systems Thinker, 9*(5), 2–3.

Chapter 11
Learning to Become Researchers: Towards Participation?

Annamaria Pinter

Introduction

A great deal has been written about initiatives where research has been conducted *with* children or *by* children (e.g. Alderson & Morrow, 2004, 2011; Bucknall, 2012; Christensen & James, 2008; Green & Hogan, 2005; Punch, 2002; Prasad, 2013, 2014) rather an *on* and *about* children. Getting children to participate actively in research projects alongside adults has become a popular approach to working with children thanks to the influence of work conducted within the 'New Childhood Studies'. At one end of the scale adult researchers have used various participatory activities (e.g. O'Kane, 2008) to help children be involved more meaningfully in research and to mitigate against the power imbalance between adults and children, and at the other end, some children have been enabled and encouraged to do their own research.

Scholars have been writing convincingly about the potential benefits children may gain when they conduct their own research (e.g. Kellett, 2010a; Lolichen, Shenoy, Shetty, Nash, & Venkatesh, 2006; Roberts & Nash, 2009) and participate in research as partners or co-researchers but at the same time criticism has also been forthcoming about child-led research in terms of its quality, whether it can ever be judged according to the same criteria as adult research, whether adult support may be seen as adult influence, and whether child-led research in fact promotes 'true' participation (e.g. Hammersley, 2015; Kim, 2016a, 2016b).

A. Pinter (✉)
University of Warwick, Coventry, UK
e-mail: Annamaria.Pinter@warwick.ac.uk

© Springer Nature Switzerland AG 2019
A. Eckhoff (ed.), *Participatory Research with Young Children*, Educating
the Young Child 17, https://doi.org/10.1007/978-3-030-19365-2_11

177

Types of Research

Some of the controversy with regard to child research hinges on how 'research' is conceptualized. Research in everyday discourse is often used to refer to looking up information on the Internet while at the highest end it refers to rigorous academic work undertaken by highly qualified experts in universities. However, I would argue that there are many layers and levels in between. For example, research is done by students who are learning to become researchers in different fields of study working on their undergraduate or post-graduate projects, or by teachers who use more informal approaches to exploring their classrooms, such as exploratory action research, in order to gain local understandings (e.g. Smith, Connelly, & Rebolledo, 2014), and research can also be undertaken by children. I would argue that all these examples would fit on a continuum from research with a small 'r' to research with a capital 'R', and each and every researcher, whatever their level of expertise, is situated on this continuum somewhere, but always moving forward, i.e., learning more about research through research.

The children in this study are novice researchers and the aim of the intervention was to shed light on how they react to being introduced to the experience of social research albeit on a basic scale.

Child Research

Children can contribute to the research process in many different ways, such as by suggesting alternative research focus, by helping with data collection and analysis and in some cases by disseminating data (Chen et al., 2010; Coppock, 2011; Ergler, 2011; Johnson, 2008; Kellett, 2010a; Kellett, Forrest, Dent, & Ward, 2004; Kirova & Emme, 2008; Mayers & Groundwater-Smith, 2010; Morrow, 2005). Kellett (2010a), referring to Hart's ladder of child participation (1992), proposes that children as researchers or co-researchers may be involved in research to a lesser or larger extent ranging from tokenistic to genuine, full involvement. Kellet (2010a, p. 49) explains that co-researching is more than just active participation in one or two stages of the research process; in fact it is a role that children maintain throughout the whole of the project:

> 'the *co-researcher role is a partnership where the research process is shared between adults and children. A distinguishing element is that co-researchers can be involved in any number of the research phases from design to dissemination. If we were to think of a sandwich as a metaphor: participant researchers always form part of the filling, co-researchers also form part of the bread.*

In Kellett's (2010a) view the greatest barrier to children being able to engage in research is not their competence or their age but their lack of research knowledge. Once some research training is provided for them, conducting their own research becomes a possibility and it can be a transformative experience. Through the example of an 11 year-old girl's research project about wheelchair users Kellett (ibid) illustrates that not only can children's research influence their immediate environment but it can also impact positively on their 'self-development, confidence and agency'. These children when they 'realize that their research is valued and listened to by adults, will have an increased sense of personal worth, of childhood as an important stage in life, and of their ability to influence the quality of that childhood.' (ibid, pp. 201–2).

Another reason for promoting child research is that children often get responses from their age group that tend to be different from responses given to adults, and thus their work adds to the body of knowledge about childhood as reported by children themselves (Kellett, 2010b). Another forceful argument in favour of the child researchers' movement is related to the political influence of the UN Convention of the Rights of the Child (UNCRC, 1989) which introduced the concept of the child's right to *participation*', i.e. the right to be involved in decisions made about important aspects of their lives. Even though the original UN document does not actually talk about the right to undertake research, the right to participation has been interpreted widely, including the right to active participation in research as well.

'Child Research' and Its Benefits

When offered the opportunity to be involved in research in an active way, some children can take genuine and spontaneous interest in aspects of research, and can gradually take more and more responsibility for the research process (e.g. Pinter & Zandian, 2014). Children may take interest in issues and questions that seem unexpected from adult perspectives and they can offer insights that may help to sharpen the adult research focus (Kuchah & Pinter, 2012). Mann, Liley, and Kellett (2014) also emphasize a range of benefits that affect the self-development of young researchers. These include: raised self-esteem, increased confidence, development of transferable skills, sharpening of critical thinking, heightened ethical awareness, enhanced problem-solving abilities, more effective communication and the development of independent learning skill, among others.

Despite the growing literature illustrating the various benefits of child-led research, critics continue to argue that both child research and the underlying concepts are problematic. Questions arise about the academic rigor of child-led research (Hammersley, 2016; Kim, 2015/2016a, b). Dyson and Meagher (2001), for example, comment that research has inherent quality standards that children will find hard to meet because of a general lack of required competencies. In addition, the fact that child-led research is always initiated by adults in the first instance (Kim, 2016b) means that children's research occurs, 'within the overarching agendas, methodological perspectives or normative aspirations that these adults or organisations they represent bring with them' (ibid: p. 238).

There is also an ongoing debate about the true purpose of child-led research. Claims that children's research should at least to some extent be about true *participation* (rather than just a pedagogical activity) seems like a valid principle (e.g. Kim, 2016b) for those who see child-led research as a political and emancipatory activity. Kim for example, argues that school based research undertaken by children inevitably focuses on adults' agendas. She further states that

'as children's research is vulnerable to being subsumed under the pedagogical intentions of adults, and given the ethical questions that arise when that happens, it seems necessary not to fuse conceptually children's research as a tool for their participation and pedagogy. If so, tensions arising from balancing these objectives seem inevitable, as are those concerning children's status as 'beings' and 'becomings' (2016b, p. 2).

On the other hand, many would agree that child-led research is indeed a beneficial pedagogical activity on its own right and it should be undertaken at school (Bucknall, 2012).

Whilst these debates are interesting from a conceptual point of view, the stark division between pedagogy as undertaking research at school for a pedagogical purpose or undertaking research for participation is over-emphasized. Rather than looking at pedagogy and participation as two opposing positions, we need to focus more on a possible journey children might take from school based research experiences to research outside school contexts.

Different Child Researcher Roles

In fact, this fits with Alderson's (2008) view which highlights three distinct ways in which children can take on roles as researchers. The first role is associated with being exposed to research at school. In this case children's research is unpublished and can be considered as the 'practising' stage. The second possibility is for children to become involved in research designed by adults. In this case, "besides providing data in their traditional role as research subjects, increasingly, children can help to plan questions, collect, analyse and report evidence, and publicize the findings". (Alderson, 2008, p. 279). These tasks fit with the research partner or co-researcher roles. Finally, the third option is research that is initiated and directed by children or young people alone and this corresponds to research for true participation according to Kim (2016b). However, since children cannot become researchers overnight, it seems logical to assume that getting to the third stage - as described by Alderson above, and, as suggested by Kim – presupposes some involvement in research as 'practice' at school, and/ or practice in research having been involved as partners alongside adults, or both. Longitudinal studies illustrating how children may be able to move from one stage or another are currently acutely missing from the literature.

Children who encounter research for the first time may have only limited interest and understanding of the concept of research and what it is for, but it is through practice that they come to appreciate what research is all about, what shapes it can take and what it can achieve. With practice over time some children who stay interested, will acquire new skills and more sophisticated understandings in research.

The small scale study described in this paper focuses on children's very first experiences of research. In particular, I explore the reactions and experiences of a group of mixed ability children in terms of what they notice, what experiences stand out for them and what confusions and dilemmas occur during their first ever encounter with research in the roles of researchers. The main research question that this paper is focused on is:

> Without any formal experience as co-researchers or partners in research, how do a group of mixed ability children (aged 9) react to the experience of carrying out their own research into an issue of their own choice?

Description of the Study

This study was conducted in a primary school in the UK where I volunteered to run an informal research club once a week for 1 h and 15 min, for six consecutive weeks. At the time of the project these children had never come across the idea of conducting their own research.

I introduced the idea of the research club to the headteacher first who was immediately keen for me to proceed with it because he saw the pedagogical value/ potential of the research club. The headteacher selected a group of 8 volunteer children based on my request that I wanted to work with a mixed group (mixed ability, mixed language backgrounds and mixed in terms of being high and low achievers in their class). As a first step the parents of the children were sent letters inviting them to give their permission for their children to participate. It was only after the parents' letters were signed that I was able to gain access to the children, and we could begin discussions about the idea of the research club and about negotiating their own consent to participate. Given that the Research Club ran at school during school hours, many would argue that the children's participation could not be conceived as purely voluntary because of them being a 'captive audience' (Robinson & Kellett, 2004). However, steps were taken to ensure that the children understood about the voluntary nature of their participation in the study. I followed Gallagher's advice on focusing on consent as an ongoing activity (2009). Gallagher (2009) recommends that 'ethical practice might be seen as an ongoing process of questioning, acting and reflecting, rather than the straightforward application of general rules of conduct'. In line with this principle, and in order to confirm the voluntary nature of the children's participation, each session started with briefly re-visiting the children's consent, the aims of the whole project and a review of how far everyone had progressed and whether everyone still wanted to continue. Every attempt was made to explain to the children that their participation was entirely voluntary and they were free to go back to their regular classrooms at any time without negative consequences and even without a need to explain their reasons.

The Participant Child Researchers

The group comprised eight children (four girls and four boys) and four of the eight children were speakers of home languages other than English (i.e. EAL speakers). This EAL status meant that even though these children were learning at school via the medium of English, at home and in their communities they communicated using another language/ languages. This paper does not permit a discussion of EAL learners' difficulties as documented by research however it should be noted that these learners are often at risk academically (for a recent review see Murphy, 2015). In addition to the language diversity in the group, three out of the eight children were also identified by the headteacher as weaker/ 'at risk' learners, and one boy in particular had severe learning difficulties.

The particular composition of the group is noteworthy because in most research where children are enabled and encouraged to become researchers, it is often middle class, articulate and exceptionally high achieving children who are selected by gatekeepers to participate (Horgan, 2016; Kellett, 2011). This group, though small, was much more representative of the mixed population of an average classroom.

The Research Schedule

For the 6 sessions I followed a plan where my aim was to enthuse the children about the idea of research via sharing with them some real, published examples of child research, and then got them to select a topic they might like to research themselves using questionnaires. Research training was provided (see Table 11.1 below) and within the 6 sessions all children designed a questionnaire, analyzed their data and presented their findings in an oral presentation based on their powerpoint slides. In addition, they were interviewed at the beginning about their expectations and at the end about their experiences of completing their research projects.

Ideally the research training should have involved a focus on what tools are appropriate for what types of research questions but because of the time limitation (only 6 sessions in total) questionnaires were selected as a compromise. In the first few sessions some research terminology was taught and practiced using games and interactive tasks. In addition, question types that typically appeared in questionnaires were introduced and discussed with the children. Then the children were invited to fill in and evaluate a real questionnaire that had been designed for other children of the same age by a graduate student as part of her Masters dissertation (Zandian, 2011). This gave the children some exposure to and experience with the tool (questionnaire) and specifically the opportunity to notice and comment on different types of questions (such as Likert scale, or yes/no question examples). This was seen as a necessary step because some of the children had never actually answered/ completed questionnaires, let alone designed any. Next, the children decided on their own research questions by filling in a skeleton sentence '*What do*

Table 11.1   The detailed description of the week-by-week schedule

Session 1	Introductions;
	Interviews about expectations;
	Card games to introduce some terminology such as *research questions, methodology, data collection, data analysis, conclusion*;
	Examples of a child research project;
	Game: A child research presentation taken from the web spread out on the floor: children are asked to move/ step to the correct part of the presentation after hearing terms such as *methodology, interviews, conclusion, bar charts, pie chart, research ethics;*
Session 2	Game: Matching definitions with explanation related to terminology in two groups;
	Learning about questionnaires: questions types, such as *biased questions, yes/no questions, Likert scale questions*; examples on posters displayed;
	Looking at another example of child research
Session 3	Team game about research terms (whispering game; guessing game)
	Completing a revised version of a questionnaire designed for children; guessing the research question; commenting on question types;
	Choosing own Research Questions
	Completing the skeleton sentence: What do…. think about ……?
	All children start work on a draft questionnaire;
Session 4	All children carry on working with the questionnaires, adding questions;
	Adding 'thank you' notes, introductions and decorating questionnaires;
	All start drafting their PPT presentations on the computer;
Session 5	Over the weekend we get some help with typing up the questionnaires and distributing them at school;
	Short demonstration of PPT for presentations including how to make graphs;
	All children conduct analysis;
Session 6	All children complete and decorate their PPT presentations;
	All children are interviewed about the whole process;
	All video or audio-record their presentations;

…….. *think about* ………?*'*. Having selected their topics and research questions they started designing their own questionnaire items. Some children wanted to work in pairs and some individually, and eventually the group split into three pairs and two individuals, 5 projects in total. All completed questionnaires were typed, decorated, printed, and distributed within the school to be filled in by either teacher respondents or other child respondents from different classes. Some questionnaires were designed to be distributed in two different classes with the aim to compare the responses from two groups of children. The topics were about homework, uniforms, online games, horror films and reasons why younger and older children liked/disliked school. These were all topics that the children selected because of their own interests, and some of them were also inspired by child research they came across on the Internet. When the completed questionnaires were returned to the children, they analysed their data and after a brief introduction to the features of Powerpoint, they completed their presentations on the computer. Finally, they all video or audio-recorded (either on an Ipad/ tablet device or an mp3 player) their research presentations orally, and reflected on their experience of being 'first time research-ers', making references back to the first interview when they had talked about their initial expectations.

Parts of the 6 sessions were audio-recorded and a research diary was kept for reflections noting down any observations that seemed relevant. Interviews with the children in the first session and the sixth session were conducted with the aim to reflect on the whole process of their research experience and to compare their initial expectations with the final ones (before and after the project). These interviews were conducted in pairs (three interviews in pairs with children who worked together and the two individuals together as another pair) in order to encourage more talk in a comfortable environment where peers could support each other and build on each other's input (e.g. Lewis, 1992; Mayall, 2008). This also allowed those children who worked on their research project together with a friend to jointly construct and re-construct their shared experiences.

The Role/Status of the Adult Researcher/Facilitator

My role and status as a researcher was that of an interested outsider, not their ordi-nary teacher but someone with a hybrid identity (Kuchah & Pinter, 2012). Reflexivity, or in this case dual reflexivity (i.e. Christensen & James, 2008), is viewed as the need to stand back and constantly reflect on the children's and my own understand-ings and perspectives of what was going on was crucially important. I explained to the children candidly that I was trying to learn from them about what it was like for children to do research for the first time, and explained that my own research ques-tion was something like this: 'What do children, like you, think about becoming a researcher? ' This mirrored their own research questions (*What do ...... think about..........?*) and seemed to make sense to them. Throughout the period of 6 weeks they made frequent references to my research and my research question, asking me how it was going and commenting to each other that we were all engaged in research. I emphasized throughout that I did not expect 'right' answers and also reassured them that any insights, opinions and reactions, both positive and negative, were going to be genuinely useful and much appreciated.

Approach to Analysis

In the interviews in in the first and sixth sessions I asked them about what they expected research to be like and in the last interview the focus was also on what if anything they enjoyed about the research process and why, what they might report about it to others when they explain their research (to parents and grandparents at home for example). All interview data and my research journal were transcribed and analysed thematically. First initial codes were applied (Braun & Clarke, 2006) and then after re-visiting the data several times, the codes were grouped into categories and themes. In what follows I will present some major themes with some comments from the children focusing on their developing understandings of social research. This is my own interpretation of the children's comments, the children themselves have not contributed to my data analysis.

Given that children's views and voices are always embedded in the local interactional and institutional contexts and they are by nature multi-layered and messy (Komulainen, 2007; Spyrou, 2011, 2016), the children's articulations about research must be viewed as a product of our ongoing collaboration in the given school club context. Their enthusiasm is of course coloured by the fact that this research club was a novel experience and it was different from the ordinary lessons they were used to. In this sense their overwhelmingly positive responses need to be taken with caution. Nonetheless, overall, their spontaneous comments on specific aspects of their experiences and the contrast between their initial expectation and their comment at the end seem to outline a process of qualitative change in their understanding about social research.

Analysis and Findings: The Main Themes

Early, Rudimentary Understandings of the Concept of Research

All the children mentioned at the beginning that real research was something carried out by scientists working in laboratories. The children also told me that they all did research at school and at home. One of the children said:

(S4): I think research is about Google, it is going to be about looking for information on the Internet. You do not know and you Google it.

This is of course entirely congruous with the use of the word 'research' at school: Another child at the end said:

(S6 N) I thought at the beginning it was going to be much different, like just searching the Internet for facts and writing down what we find.

Several children also commented that they thought at the beginning that research was going to be something that I myself, i.e. the adult would eventually do, not the children:

(S1) I expected for you to do it all, we tell you some ideas but then you write it all, all very complicated; that is what I thought.

The children were surprised to realize that asking people questions in a questionnaire could be labelled as 'research'. Compared to their original understandings as discussed above, after experiencing this project, they began to appreciate that 'social research' was also a type of research in addition to scientific experiments in labs:

(S7) I thought it was going to be researching stuff like scientists do but we were just talking about what people thought about different things.

(S4) I did not know that research could be about asking people questions.

These comments reflect that the children began to 'demystify' research, by attaining a slightly different, perhaps a multi-layered understanding compared to what they had originally started off with.

In their reflections, the children in this project also referred to the fact that at the beginning they thought research was going to be boring and really hard to do. One of the EAL speakers, the least fluent speaker of English, who had been in the UK only for 8 months at the time of this project, mentioned in the interview at the beginning that she was not sure she could do it at all.

(S5) I am not sure I can do this as I usually can't do many of the tasks so I will see.

Other children also mentioned at the end that they had been anxious at the beginning and they expected the research club to be too 'hard'.

(S2) I thought at the beginning that it was going to be hard but it wasn't hard.
(S8) At the beginning I thought I did not like this because I am not very good at English but I made this questionnaire with my friend, A, and it was well, not hard and I really liked it.

By the end all children reported positive changes in their general attitudes towards research and they all concluded that it was very different to what they had expected at the beginning.

(S5 B) Yes, it was fun and I would like to do it again, times 20 million!

Newly Acquired Technical Skills

Children learnt some technical knowledge and skills related to research and many of them enjoyed this aspect of the research process. They were proud to be using adult terminology and show off their knowledge.

Several children commented on the importance of ethics in research:

(S2) Ethics is important, ethics is if you don't want to do it, you don't have to.
(S4) I did not know this word before, ethics, even though my dad does a lot of questionnaires for his work. Ethics is important because for those filling in the questionnaire it is completely fine not to write their names.

All children also talked about various types of questions in their questionnaires and explained technical terms when I asked them what they might tell others about research:

(S4) Well bias is important. Let's assume you really like pizza. Bias is when you ask: Pizza is great, isn't it and you expect people to agree with you.

(S2)Yes, a biased question is pushing the person to say 'yes';

Other children have mentioned Likert scale questions:

(S7) In Likert scale questions you have to have the same amount of positives and negatives;

One of the academically weakest children in the group who repeatedly approached me in the sessions and warned me that he was not going to be able to do much because of his 'learning difficulties' – as noted in my research diary, reflected about his experience spontaneously in the interview during the final session like this:

(S6) We, I learnt a lot of things to tell others, like ethics, data collection, pie charts, research questions and questionnaires and also interviews, which is what we are having now!

First Experience with Data from 'Real' People

A further theme that emerged strongly was related to the authenticity of the experience in terms of working with 'real data from real people'. The moment the data arrived (i.e. the completed questionnaires), the children's excitement levels increased and the purpose of the research suddenly made real sense. I noted down in my research journal:

> Everyone is keen to read and digest the responses in their questionnaires. Some are still completely absorbed in the task of reading through their responses even though it is now time to stop and pack up for today.

In the final interview several children commented on enjoying reading the responses in the questionnaires.

(S3) We were very interested to see what the other children said.

(S7) We were excited when we got them [the questionnaires] back; wanted to know what everyone said.

One pair had 45 questionnaires back from two classrooms and even though they were overwhelmed with the sheer amount of data, they insisted on completing all the analysis. They spread their questionnaires on the floor and spent all afternoon sorting the answers and entering the data into the computer. I tried to talk them into analyzing just half of the questionnaires, those from one of the classes, but they insisted on completing the analysis of both data sets. They seemed to have a strong commitment to their own data. Some children mentioned that the teachers were very surprised to have received these questionnaires and some said that they had never filled in questionnaire given to them by children before:

(S4) ...and when we gave it to the teachers they said 'Oh, is that for me?' No one has ever done that.

One child also commented that the unexpected responses were motivating to read:

(S3) Why I enjoyed it because what the children said. It might be different from what you think they might say.

Working with Technology

When asked about what was most enjoyable about the research process, all children commented that they enjoyed to work with the computers and the tablet devices. Children particularly enjoyed working with Powerpoint and many said it was the most fun part of their experience. Closely related to working with technology, one of the children also made a point about having ownership of the task, i.e. about being able to work on the computer doing one's own thing, without much intervention from adults:

(S1) Very very enjoyed the computer work...The best thing was that you let us go on the computer and we could write our own questionnaire.

(S4) We could use the I-pads that was best.

All the children commented on the pie charts and the bar charts as the most fun elements of their work within Powerpoint. At the beginning of the data analysis stage they were introduced to these two types of charts and were shown how to enter data to create charts.

(S3) I loved the charts because when you type it, it just goes up and down on its own;

(S5) I liked the bar charts and other charts in Powerpoint. I did not even know you could do a bar chart in Powerpoint. Now I do.

Another child explains here vividly why the completion of the charts was so much fun:

(S4) Really enjoyed making the bar charts, that feeling when finally you finish the bar chart and it comes up, and there is a massive explosion that is the best.

Discussion: First Time Researchers

In line with Mann et al. (2014) the children in this project clearly benefited from the process of undertaking a small questionnaire study. They learnt transferable skills such as recognizing a biased question or a Likert scale question; they gained some insights into what research ethics were, how to write a research question, how to write a questionnaire, analyze the data and present findings. These are technical skills that can be built on over time relatively easily if the children have further opportunities to continue their 'apprenticeship' as researchers. Indeed, if the adult facilitator can continue working with the same group of children, their initial skills can be easily built on for subsequent projects.

In this project, in my role as adult facilitator I assisted the children and modeled for them the steps to take in a small scale questionnaire study. They did not make decisions on their own but rather they were following guidelines and models such as the layout and the format of the sample child research projects downloaded from the Internet which served as excellent sources of motivation and inspiration, and which rang true because they had been produced by children of similar age and similar background.

The six sessions that have taken the children through the steps of conducting and analyzing research were just a set of pedagogically useful activities that allowed them to learn about questionnaires and have a direct experience of working with this research tool. The children had complete freedom to decide who they wanted to work with, what topic area they wanted to research, what specific questions they wanted to ask in their questionnaire and who they wanted to target with their questionnaires. Beyond this freedom, though, a clear structure was also provided guiding them every step of the way and helping them progress through the stages of a research project. This was a deliberate, slow and careful approach with a great deal of structure and scaffolding provided but one which also gave the children a great deal of freedom to make their own decisions and enjoy their own discoveries and findings. This experience- being the first 'taste' of research can serve as a strong motivator to do more research and to want to understand more about research. At the end of the project all children agreed that they wanted to do more research. Most expressed pride and satisfaction with the outcome such as this learner:

(S 3) We are very much proud especially because we did most of it alone. I would like to do some more.

Kim (2016a, 2016b) argues that promoting children's research mainly for its educational benefits seems conceptually inappropriate because the purpose of child research is about supporting their participation rights as 'beings' rather than 'becomings' (Qvortrup, 1994). I would argue that taking children through the research process in a highly structured framework, as described here, is an essential foundation for becoming independent. Practice with research, whether it is in the role of a co-researcher or as child researchers working through a whole project from beginning to end with some guidance and support, will have the potential to facilitate children's progress towards research for participation outside the classroom.

It is reasonable to suggest that engaging children with the idea of conducting research for themselves is a process which has to start from a pedagogically focused set of activities initiated by an adult facilitator, but over time, in some cases, when children are keen to continue, it may have the potential to develop into the type of activity that Kim (2016a, 2016b) labels as more 'authentic' and more true to the core principle of 'participation'.

Returning to the question 'Can what the children have done be referred to as research?' Hammersley's (2016, p. 10) view would be that it could not:

> In methodological terms, I think it is important to recognise that social research is a specialised activity that demands knowledge and skills that a very small proportion of adults – and hardly any children- have, and ones that cannot be acquired quickly. It requires high levels of expertise.' … 'Research involves responsibilities, both as regards seeking to ensure the validity of the findings and respecting ethical considerations – and researchers must be in control of research decisions if they are to live up to these responsibilities.

The children's work cannot of course be compared to academics' sophisticated work at the highest levels of research with a capital 'R'. However, I argue that these children have taken their first steps on the continuum from zero or very limited understanding of social research to a new level.

Children's understanding of what research is, what it is for and what it can achieve will have the potential to grow further if they can be involved in projects like this, if and when they have repeated opportunities to take more and more responsibility while adult facilitation is phased out gradually. Unfortunately, to-date, the literature does not offer examples of studies that would describe children's development as researchers across a number of small scale projects in a cumulative manner. In fact, sustained involvement of children in research so far seems rare, as commented on by Tisdall, as well:

> There is too little research, and particularly too little large-scale and sustainable models of research that involve children as researchers or other deep levels of involvement. (Tisdall, 2012, p.188)

Perhaps with sustained participation and offering multiple opportunities for research in schools we can begin to build up a better picture of how children develop as researchers. However, research undertaken by children in schools is rare and even if it is encouraged, not all children take an interest in it.

Conclusion

Initial encounters with research cannot by definition be mature or sophisticated and it is practice and repeated opportunities to participate in research that help child researchers to develop their skills. At a very different level, adult researchers also need practice and repeated opportunities to undertake research to develop their skills and research expertise.

In this study children responded overwhelmingly positively to the opportunity to do their own research and they did so in a mixed-ability class where some of the children were English as a second language speakers and several children were at risk learners. These children began their journey, learnt some technical skills and knowledge and they expressed an interest in moving forward on their journeys as researchers. This is a modest but positive start and a solid basis that can be built on. The challenge facing adult facilitators is to find ways in which initial motivation to want to do research can be maintained and fostered in children so that they can move forward on the continuum of becoming more 'established' researchers.

Questions for Reflection

- How would/ could you encourage children to take a more active part in your research project, moving beyond simply acting as data sources?
- Given your focus and research questions, what different ways can children contribute to your study? Can they play a part in planning the project, deciding the research questions and the methodology and /or analysing the data? Which, if any of these, phases might be realistic for them to contribute to?
- Familiarising children with research is a beneficial activity. Guiding them through the steps they should take in research in a deliberate manner is one way of introducing research to children. Can you think of others ways?

References

Alderson, P. (2008). Children as researchers: Participation rights and research methods. In P. Christensen & A. James (Eds.), *Research with children* (pp. 276–290). Abingdon, UK: Routledge.

Alderson, P., & Morrow, V. (2004). *Ethics, social research and consulting with children and young people*. Ilford, UK: Barnado's.

Alderson, P., & Morrow, V. (2011). *The ethics of research with children and young people*. London, UK: Sage Publications.

Braun, V., & Clarke, V. (2006). Using thematic analysis in psychology. *Qualitative Research in Psychology, 3*, 77–101.

Bucknall, S. (2012). *Children as researchers in primary schools: Choice, voice and participation*. London, UK/New York, NY: Routledge.

Chen, P., Weiss, F. L., Johnston Nicholson, H., & Girls Incorporated. (2010). Girls study girls Inc.: Engaging girls in evaluation through participatory action research. *American Journal of Community Psychology, 46*, 228–237.

Christensen, P., & James, A. (Eds.). (2008). *Research with children: Perspectives and practices*. London, UK: Routledge.

Coppock, K. (2011). Children as peer researchers: Reflections on a journey of mutual discovery. *Children and Society, 25*(6), 435–446.

Dyson, A., & Meagher, N. (2001). Reflections on the case studies. In J. Clark, A. Dyson, & N. Meagher (Eds.), *Young people as researchers: Possibilities, problems and politics* (pp. 59–76). Leicester, UK: Youth Work Press.

Ergler, C. (2011). Beyond passive participation: Children as collaborators in understanding the neighbourhood experience. *Graduate Journal of Asia-Pacific Studies, 7*(2), 78–98.

Gallagher, M. (2009). Ethics. In E. K. M. Tisdall, J. M. Davis, & M. Gallagher (Eds.), *Researching with children and young people* (pp. 29–64). London, UK: Sage.

Green, S., & Hogan, D. (2005). *Researching children's experiences: Approaches and methods*. London, UK: Sage Publication.

Hammersley, M. (2015). Research ethics and the concept of children's rights. *Children and Society, 29*(6), 569–582.

Hammersley, M. (2016). Childhood studies: A sustainable paradigm? *Childhood, 24*(1), 113–127.

Hart, R. (1992). *Children's participation: From tokenism to citizenship*. Florence, Italy: UNICEF International Child Development Centre.

Horgan, D. (2016). Child participatory research methods: Attempts to go deeper. *Childhood, 24*(2), 245–259.

Johnson, K. (2008). Teaching children to use visual research methods. In P. Thomson (Ed.), *Doing visual research with children and young people* (pp. 77–94). London, UK: Routledge.

Kellett, M. (2010a). *Rethinking children and research: Attitudes in contemporary society*. London, UK: Continuum.

Kellett, M. (2010b). Small shoes, big steps! Empowering children as active researchers. *American Journal of Community Psychology, 46*(1–2), 195–203. https://doi.org/10.1007/s10464-010-9324-y

Kellett, M. (2011). Empowering children and young people as researchers: Overcoming barriers and building capacity. *Child Indicators Research, 4*, 205–219.

Kellett, M., Forrest, R., Dent, N., & Ward, S. (2004). "Just teach us the skills, please, we'll do the rest:" Empowering ten-year-olds as active researchers. *Children and Society, 18*(5), 329–343.

Kim, C.-Y. (2015). Why Resercah by children: Rethingking the assumptions underlying the facilitation of children as researchers. *Children and Society, 30*(3), 230–240.

Kim, C.-Y. (2016a). Participation or pedagogy? Ambiguities and tensions surrounding the facilitation of children as researchers. *Childhood, 24*(1), 84–98.

Kim, C.-Y. (2016b). Why research by children? Rethinking the assumptions underlying the facilitation of children as researchers. *Children and Society, 30*, 230–240.

Kirova, A., & Emme, M. (2008). Fotonovela as a research tool in image-based participatory research with immigrant children. *International Journal of Qualitative Methods, 7*(2), 35–57.

Komulainen, S. (2007). The ambiguity of the child's 'voice' in social research. *Childhood, 4*(1), 11–28.

Kuchah, H., & Pinter, A. (2012). Was this an interview? Breaking the power barrier in adult-child interviews in an African context. *Issues in Educational Research, 22*(3), 283–297.

Lewis, A. (1992). Group child interviews as a research tool. *British Educational Research Journal, 18*(4), 413–421.

Lolichen, P., Shenoy, J., Shetty, A., Nash, C., & Venkatesh, M. (2006). Children in the driver's seat. *Children's Geographies, 4*(3), 347–357.

Mann, A., Liley, J., & Kellett, M. (2014). Engaging children and young people in research. In A. Cark et al. (Eds.), *Understanding Resrearch with children and young people* (pp. 286–304). London Sage.

Mayall, B. (2008). Conversations with children: Working with generational issues. In P. M. Christensen & A. James (Eds.), *Research with children: Perspectives and practices* (pp. 120–135). London, UK: Falmer Press.

Mayes, E., & Groundwater-Smith, S. (2010, December). *Year 9 as co-researchers: "Our gee'd-up school."* Paper presented at conference of Australian Association for Research in Education, Adelaide, SA, Australia. Retrieved from http://s3.amazonaws.com/academia.edu.documents/31395813/1723bMayesGroundwaterSmith.pdf?AWSAccessKeyId=AKIAJ56TQJRTWSMTNPEA&Expires=1476898127&Signature=10Zmpdlv6soUZuW1mntqqPgITFE%3D&response-content-disposition=inline%3B%20filename%3DWith_Groundwater-Smith_S._Year_9_as_Co-.pdf

Morrow, V. (2005). Ethical issues in collaborative research with children. In A. Farrell (Ed.), *Ethical research with children* (pp. 150–165). Maidenhead, UK: Open University Press.

Murphy, V. (2015). *Second language learning in the early school years: Trends and contexts*. Oxford, UK: Oxford University Press.

O'Kane, C. (2008). The development of participatory techniques: Facilitating children's views about decisions which affect them. In P. Christensen & A. James (Eds.), *Research with children: Perspectives and practices* (pp. 125–155). London, UK: Routledge.

Pinter, A., & Zandian, S. (2012). *'I thought it would be tiny little one phrase that we said, in a huge big pile of papers':* Children's reflections on their involvement in participatory research. *Qualitative Research, 15*(2), 235–250.

Pinter, A., & Zandian, S. (2014). I don't ever want to leave this room: Benefits of researching with children. *ELT Journal, 68*(1), 64–74.

Prasad, G. (2013). Children as co-ethnographers of their plurilingual literacy practices: An exploratory case study. *Language and Literacy, 15*(3), 4–30.

Prasad, G. (2014). Portraits of plurilingualism in a French international school in Toronto: Exploring the role of visual methods to access students' representations of their linguistically diverse identities. *Canadian Journal of Applied Linguistics, 17*(1), 51–77.

Punch, S. (2002). Research with children: The same or different from research with adults? *Childhood, 9*, 231–341.

Qvortrup, J. (1994). *Childhood matters: Social theory, practice and politics.* Aldershot, UK: Avebury.

Roberts, A., & Nash, J. (2009). Enabling students to participate in school improvement through a students as researchers programme. *Improving Schools, 12*(2), 174–187.

Robinson, C., & Kellett, M. (2004). Power. In S. Fraser, V. Lewis, S. Ding, M. Kellett, & C. Robinson (Eds.), *Doing research with children and young people* (pp. 81–96). London, UK: Sage.

Smith, R., Connelly, T., & Rebolledo, P. (2014). Teacher research as continuing professional development: A project with chilean secondary school teachers. In D. Hayes (Ed.), *Innovations in the continuing professional development of English language teachers* (pp. 111–129). London, UK: British Council.

Spyrou, S. (2011). The limits of children's voices: From authenticity to critical reflexive representation. *Childhood, 18*(2), 151–165.

Spyrou, S. (2016). Researching children's silences: Exploring the fullness of voice in childhood research. *Childhood, 23*(1), 7–21.

Tisdall, E. K. M. (2012). The challenge and challenging of childhood studies? Learning from disability studies and research with disabled children. *Children and Society, 26*(3), 181–191.

United Nations. (1989). *United Nations conventions on the rights of the child.* New York, NY: United Nations.

Zandian, S. (2011). A personal reflection on the impact of researching children on my own professional development. *ELTED Journal, 14*, 32–36.

Chapter 12
Then and Now: Reflections on Arts-Based Participatory Research with Young Children

Marissa McClure Sweeny

Faith in the existence of a singular determinant origin and the uni-linear nature of time itself—that fact that only one moment exists at a time—is waning
– Karen Barad, 2018

Introduction

Recently, I have considered the lens of 'then' and 'now' in my arts-based participatory research with young children. My daily encounters with the young children with whom I have worked over the past decade have provoked a continual re-examination of my positionality as an artist, a teacher, and a researcher who works *with* young children. That *with* is especially significant for me. Even in my early years of work with young children, I did not feel that my research was *about* children or that my teaching was *to* children. I always felt as if we were working together, and I saw my work as an artist as work that was done in collaboration with children. This placement was always an uneasy one, as I was simultaneously so keenly aware of the powerful position that I occupied as a teacher. Was it even possible within the academic systems in which I worked to work *with* children? Was it desirable? How could it be ethical?

M. M. Sweeny (✉)
Indiana University of Pennsylvania, Indiana, PA, USA
e-mail: marissa.mcclure@iup.edu

© Springer Nature Switzerland AG 2019
A. Eckhoff (ed.), *Participatory Research with Young Children*, Educating the Young Child 17, https://doi.org/10.1007/978-3-030-19365-2_12

Then: Mapping My Journey to Participatory Arts-Based Research with Young Children

I have worked with young children as an artist/teacher/researcher for more than 10 years. While I do not wish to focus this chapter biographically, I do feel it is important to share my *then* in order to frame the *now* so that I might begin to consider the question of what participatory arts-based research with young children is and why we do it. I have worked in multiple roles in diverse educational settings including as an art specialist teacher in three public and parochial elementary schools, a reading teacher in a bilingual elementary school, a lead preschool classroom teacher in a parent cooperative independent preK-8 school which was a magnet site for children with special needs, a children's studio teacher in a large art museum, a teaching artist in a Reggio-inspired bilingual preschool near the US/ Mexico border, a studio educator in two Reggio-inspired campus-based childcare centers, and now as a teaching artist in a community-based art studio program for infants and toddlers and a university professor working with undergraduate pre-service art educators. Each of these contexts has influenced the perspectives that I share in this chapter, and the situation from which I approach working as an artist, teacher, and researcher with young children.

While it is tempting to take the 'now' for granted in working with young children, it is important to consider this *now* in relationship to my *then*. In fact, it was the magnetism of the 'now' that drew me to work with children. As a new teacher, I found children's interests much more compelling than my own ideas about what they might *learn* from my teaching. Even though I felt deeply attracted to the children's interests in my classroom, I clung to a teacher-directed version of myself leading a classroom of young children. This vision quickly blurred when I encountered the daily practice of caring for the young children my classroom. Beyond that, I felt so *free* lingering in that now, in that relentless presence so familiar to adults who work or live with young children. The intensity of that feeling became the catalyst for my research. I wanted to dwell as much as possible in that comfortable expanse of the now with the children who were in my care as a teacher. It was here that my teaching, and subsequently research, practice shifted from what I could teach *to* young children to *my wanting to learn* what they *knew*.

When I recently began to reflect on those first teaching, researching, and art-making experiences with young children, I realized how my initial 'then' was not about the 'now' but about 'the future.' My very first teaching position was in a bilingual elementary school in Colorado. I was not certified. My educator preparation was a 2-week summer crash course in lesson planning and classroom management taught by an especially charismatic principal and populated by nine other new teachers fresh from liberal arts programs. Only one of us, not me, was a graduate of an educational preparation program.

The expectations the Title 1 school had for my Federal grant-funded teaching position were clear. The children with whom I would be working were identified as having a reading proficiency in English of at least two grade levels behind their peers. Some of my third grade students were reading in English at a pre-primer level. The expectation for me was that my students would be reading two grade levels ahead of where they tested at the start of the school year. Their progress would be assessed through standardized tests.

Then. Framing Teaching Through Research with Children

I began research with children very practically. I did not even realize I was doing research: I was trying to survive a first year of teaching for which I was distressingly under-prepared. I wanted to learn about the children's interests to engage them in reading in English. I worked to learn to speak some Spanish so that I could better communicate with the children and their families. Since we could not speak together at first, we began by drawing together. I made a sketchbook for each child from donated materials, and brought one of my own. As we drew together, sitting side-by-side, the children shared invited me into their worlds. We pasted almost every surface of our classroom—a small shared space carved from carpeted room dividers within a larger room—with watercolor paintings of local butterflies, Crayola marker reproductions of Pokémon, and cut-paper homages to the Denver Broncos. I had two simultaneous feelings pull at me: First, I felt very strongly that *this* was why I wanted to be a teacher: This incredible pleasure in being with children each day, what Davies (2014) has described as affective and *intra-active* (original emphasis). Second, I struggled to reconcile what I felt to be such meaningful experiences with the rigid testing expectations of my school system. I felt that there was something more *there* in the *now* and in the children's drawings and making—what I later learned could be called their voluntary artwork: the artwork that children create when adults provide materials and time for artistic work but do not provide suggestions of content or subject matter. At the end of my first year teaching, I joined a graduate program in Art Education at the University of Arizona and became an elementary art specialist teacher in Tucson.

Then: Research Relationships Between Young Children's Art as Artifact or as Social Process

I pressured myself to think about the children's art as instrumental. I wanted to prove to others that it was as meaningful as I felt it to be. I tried to do this by situating the children's art making within the educational language that I thought was most powerful. For example, I wondered how an art teacher could use art to enhance literacy? Like others before me, I found little evidence of 'transfer' between art and other subject areas. When sharing those findings, I thwarted by common-sense and polarized assumptions that surrounded young children's art as either a series of unfolding developmental stages or unfettered self-expression. I had yet to find an eloquent methodological approach to including the children's conversations about their work within traditional qualitative research processes. I tried to do so but several senior scholars in my field suggested that this work was *not research* but merely a recounting or documentation of the children's work. I struggled to assert my process with my Institutional Review Board: They had never encountered a proposal in which preschool children generated their own research questions. I was crushed by this. I first read Brent Wilson's article, "The Second Search," in which he conceptualized research as **re-search**, a literal *second* search. He asserted that, "one of the distinguishing characteristics of education research is that it relates what is with what might be and what ought to be." What seems like moments later, a teaching colleague of mine suggested that I might like the artwork that young children were making in the preschools and infant toddler centers in Reggio Emilia, Italy. I viewed the documentary *To Make a Portrait of a Lion* in which a group of young children from the *Diana* preschool visit a well-known statue of a lion and make an assemblage of various portraits of the lion using clay and paint. I was incredibly fortunate in Tucson to be connected to a US-based site through the Tucson Children's Project that was particularly inspired by the Reggio Emilia approach to early childhood education and to a richness of resources and conversations that supported me in a journey of reinventing my work with young children as an artist/teacher/researcher.

Now: What Is Participatory Arts-Based Research with Young Children and Why Is It Important?

Together, these experiences buoyed the confidence that I needed re-search, and to undertake participatory arts-based research with young children I will now refer to this as 'our work together' throughout the rest of this chapter. The first step in beginning this work together was for me, as the adult and teacher/researcher, to let go of the idea of finding out of what children's art could do and what children might learn and to embrace what children's art was already doing and what children *know*. Participatory research re-conceptualized my view of what research is and what our work together could be. Instead of research suggesting implications for future changes, the research process became the change itself. The participation is the action. As Alderson and Morrow (2011) explain, participatory means "treating children as experts and agents in their own lives," "including children, practitioners, and parents in reflection on meaning and interpretations of the data," and "*focused on children's own experiences and views*" (p. 14, original emphasis). In turn, as I embraced participatory research with the children in my classrooms, I moved from traditional qualitative data collection methods like field notes and observation to arts-based approaches like inviting children to create their own digital documentation of our time together and our work together. As Knowles and Cole (2008) explain, "[a]rts-based research can be defined as the systematic use of the artistic process, the actual making of artistic expressions in all of the different forms of the arts, as a primary way of understanding and examining experience by both researchers and the people that they involve in their studies" (p. 29). Our practical work together, then, lies in the intersection of these two methods: Participation as action and artwork as data collection, data analysis and data sharing. Post-developmental and post-human theoretical perspectives support our theoretical work together and inform the ways in which I situate the work on our behalf within art educational dialogues. The pedagogy of listening and pedagogical documental provide further methodological support.

Embracing the intersection between participatory and arts-based research does not mean that I have let go of the idea of deeply considering the responsibilities of the researcher toward pedagogy or what ought to be—in fact, it means that I have turned even more closely to this question as I have thought about and attempted to enact the processes of pedagogy, research, and art-making in our work together. Thompson calls this practice "being there" with children. It is a process-based practice deeply related to a pedagogy of listening. It is the intra-active movement in which the children, myself, and the media create ourselves through our interaction with one another and with our environment.

We undertake this work together because it is transformative in and of itself, and because within it, we position ourselves and young children, together, as rights-bearing citizens and full participants within pedagogical contexts. This, in turn, has radical political implications which are especially crucial to the most vulnerable populations of young children among us and within our care.

Now. How Can We Design Participatory Arts-Based Research Projects with Young Children?

Considering these definitions of participatory research and arts-based research and their intersections shapes how we may design or co-design participatory arts-based research projects with young children. I would like to share one example of our work together from the long-term project *Amigos en el Jardin: Friends in the Garden* in order to illustrate one possible approach to this kind of collaborative work.

Amigos en el Jardin began as part of a larger research project entitled *Children's Digital Visual Culture*. That project was funded by a faculty professional development grant from the University of Arizona. Its premise was to document ways in which young children approach using digital technologies in their art-making. Within the proposal, young children's use of digital technologies was framed as art-making with new media. This assumption was based in previous collaborative work that I had undertaken with young children using digital technologies in my preschool classroom. In that space, I was the classroom teacher and was with the same group of twenty-two three, four-, and five-year-old children each day from approximately 8:00 AM–3:00 PM (often earlier or later). I began in that Reggio-inspired situation working with digital technologies as a technique of pedagogical documentation. During the course of our documentation together, the children increasingly began to turn the digital cameras on themselves, and to create not only their own documentation of their work together but to generate new works. So, the tools of documenting their making became their making tools. I felt that in this way, the children had incorporated digital technologies as new media in their art-making. I began a blog that was shared with families to document our work together, and to invite dialogue about it. I situated the children's making with new media art as divergent from general understandings of instructional technologies. New media art generally refers to artworks created with new technologies including digital art, and interactive art. New media art often involves interaction between creator and observer. While I understand the category of new media art is evolving in contemporary artistic practice, it is still useful for understanding our work together in this context.

Following this, I proposed the project *Children's Digital Visual Culture* in order to specifically provide young children with an opportunity make art using digital technologies including digital photography and digital video. I wanted to formalize what I had seen occur organically in my classroom. My research goals were to consider how young children made art with new media. As a teaching artist, I would meet with the children once or twice weekly for 2–3 h. One classroom of sixteen 4-and 5-year-old children in a Reggio-inspired preschool program chose to participate. We began the research process with a meeting with children and their families. The families were already intimately involved in the children's classroom, and so would be participants in the project, as well. During this meeting, I shared that I would be inviting the children to use the digital cameras and video cameras in their classroom. I shared written consents with the families, and verbal consents with families present with the children. The consents were offered in both Spanish and in English, as all of the families and children were Spanish speakers. I established a password-protected blog site that families and children could visit at any time to review what had happened during the day's work together in both languages. All of the families chose to participate in the project, and to share their child's work. One family elected not to share their child's work initially but later chose to do so.

On our first day of work together, the classroom teacher and I introduced the children to the digital cameras at the beginning of the school day, before we had breakfast together. We allowed the children to handle the cameras and explained how to use them to frame and to create photographs. We shared the basic photography concepts of angle, framing, and light. Many of the children already had experience using smartphone cameras but did not have experience using more traditional digital cameras. On this day, we invited the children to use the cameras in and around the classroom, and with one another. Our first blog entry follows:

> we worked with the camera for the first time today: j* and k* spent quite a bit of time with
> me, learning to turn the camera on and off; looking through its viewfinder; attaching it to

our tripod; and learner to rotate the camera to better frame the objects, people, and places they chose. here are a few photographs to share:

hemos trabajado con la cámara por primera vez hoy en día: j* y k* pasó un poco de tiempo conmigo, aprender a encender la cámara y fuera, mirando por el visor, lo coloca a nuestro trípode, y aprende a girar la cámara para enmarcar mejor los objetos, personas y lugares que eligieron. aquí están algunas fotos para compartir:

On that first day together, I also chose to document the children's work together with the cameras. I showed my documentation of their working in a separate blog post after sharing their photos. I wanted to offer two different views of what was happening as we worked together. I later found that this became increasingly difficult for me to simultaneously document as the children worked, and to be as fully engaged in our work together as I would have liked to have been. In this case, several of the family members who joined us on our excursions, and the classroom teacher also used their cameras to document. Our number of cameras and lenses grew as the project grew.

As I shared in our blog, a few months into our project:

the children have become so adept at using the camera that it has become nearly impossible for me to edit their photos for documentation. today, b*, k*, d*, r*, and k* worked with me in the garden. i had proposed that they take photos in this special place, which will be planted tomorrow with summer plantings. here are just a few of the many [304!] photographs the children made.

los niños se han vuelto tan hábil en el uso de la cámara que se ha vuelto casi imposible para mí, para editar sus fotos para la documentación. hoy en día, b*, k*, d*, r*, y k* trabajó conmigo en el jardín. yo había propuesto que tomar fotos en este lugar especial, que serán plantados mañana con las plantaciones de verano y aquí son sólo algunos de los muchos [304!] fotografías de los niños hicieron.

Our process for analyzing our photographs and videos began during the following visit. I would spend the rest of the day after our mornings together uploading and cataloguing the photographs according to who was using the camera, and I put them in desktop folders. This also became increasingly complex as the project grew because often children were using the cameras collaboratively and staging photographs and playscapes together in order to photograph and to video record them. I also transcribed the video pieces during this time, sometimes juxtaposing videos and photo recordings of the same events. I would then share this documentation with the children, who would offer their own recollections or insights into what would happen, and who would return to photographs and to video pieces that they found particularly compelling. We chose together, to focus the research that I would share publically, on these events. Our focus was on the images that the children felt were most compelling: Those they created of themselves, and those they created of one another.

Our blog explains:
throughout their time with the camera, the children delighted in making photographs of themselves, sometimes looking down, or holding objects in front of the tripod while composing a frame.

largo de su estancia con la cámara, los niños encantados de hacer fotografías de sí mismos, a veces mirando hacia abajo, o sostener objetos delante del trípode mientras compone un cuadro.

And:

the children's images, too, show them together—reflecting the good cheer and camaraderie that exists within this very close group of friends, and between the adults that support them.

las imágenes de los niños, también las había show juntos—que refleja la alegría y la camaradería que existe dentro de este grupo muy cercano de amigos, y entre los adultos que los apoyan.

Amigos en el Jardin: Friends in the Garden

As our work together grew, that first year's focus drew increasingly toward the children's art-making in their community garden. The school-based community garden was at the center of their classroom life, so this seemed to be a natural progression for many of the children. As the children were working in a Reggio-inspired classroom, they were simultaneously working on the long-term Hunger Project, where they would grow food not only for themselves but also for a nearby free kitchen, *Casa Maria*. As I shared with families in our blog:

as i begin to know the children better, and they begin to work with me for a second time, i have noticed that there are places to which they continually return to photograph. one of these 'favorite' places seems to be the garden, and the areas that surround it. on this day, r* and j* were deeply engaged with making photographs that document the garden, especially the fruit trees that surround it.

como empezar a conocer mejor a los niños, y empiezan a trabajar conmigo por segunda vez, he notado que hay lugares a los que continuamente volver a fotografiar. uno de estos 'favoritos' lugares parece ser el jardín, y las áreas que la rodean. en este día, r* y j* estaban profundamente comprometidos con la toma de fotografías que documenten el jardín, especialmente los árboles frutales que lo rodean.

We decided, together, to title our first year of work *Amigos in el Jardin*, or *Friends in the Garden*. We used a self-publishing platform called Blurb to publish our blog as a photo book that could be shared with others. We chose a selection of the photographs most-loved by the children to print as large-scale prints to exhibit at a local gallery and to host an opening for families and friends. In 2014, our photo book was selected as part of a juried exhibition at the Phoenix Museum of Art, and photographs from the book have since been shown in various art and research venues.

Now: What Are the Ethical Concerns we Collectively Face in Creating Participatory Arts-Based Research Projects with Vulnerable Populations of Young Children?

As I certainly found in our work together, then always exists within now. And that now is variable and created intra-actively. In this way, I would like to consider what became of the many versions of now that I did not include in the research story that we shared in *Amigos en el Jardin*. These decisions, made in collaboration with children, illustrate some of the ethical responsibilities of arts-based participatory research.

In the work I shared, and in my current work together with a new group of young children, I have begun to think more carefully about research with children as other/than—as making something that is other than child art and other than adult art, as Wilson first explained in 2007. If, following Wilson, the term child art and modernist notions of childhood artistic creations are outmoded, then our work together is not young children's art. My very presence in this context with children means that our work is at least made collaboratively between adults and children, if not between the several other teachers, and many family members that joined us on our varied excursions and encounters. It is wholly intra-active, in this way. So, sharing our work together as art invites another kind of intra-action, and propels the research and who its participants are in various lines of flight (Davies, 2014).

So, here, one part of the *now* with which I am engaging in my second and many subsequent searches is one that I had left out of our first search. While I was focused on the complexity the children experienced in the situation, I was not focused on the complexity that the adults, including myself, experienced *with* the children—our transactional experiences. Theoretically, I have been reflecting upon the pieces that were chosen for our exhibitions and those about which I have written more extensively—why did we choose those pieces? What shared resonance did they have for us, when I can very clearly see that there are a number of pieces that we have passed over for others. How does this passing over impact our shared research process? Practically, I am considering how 'being there' with young children and the now that this practice generates are devalued within the standardization sought by many contemporary pedagogical contexts for young children. I also consider and what roles arts-based participatory research may play in sharing what ought to be— in re-searching and in making visible the value in the now.

These considerations, in turn, make visible the broader ethical implications of working together with vulnerable populations of young children. When our work together, *Amigos en el Jardin*, began, it was in the aftermath of the passing of Arizona's Senate Bill (SB) 1070. Since its passing, the ACLU and a number of civil rights organizations have been continually challenging the bill which allows for racial profiling against Latinos, Asian-Americans and others presumed to be 'foreign' based on how they look or sound. The bill also authorizes police to demand papers proving citizenship or immigration status from anyone they stop and suspect of being in the country unlawfully.

SB 1070 caused tremendous anxiety in a community already facing the daily impact of immigration enforcement. Many of the children who participated in our project and their families live within this community, and were rightfully concerned about exposing the children to danger through the sharing of photographs of them, especially online. Such considerations are especially pertinent to artists, teachers, and researchers who work together with young children using digital media for artwork and for documentation. At the same time, losing the ability to share our work together in appropriate ways could lessen its impact on the very pedagogical practices we are working to reform. In the case of this shared work, we chose to limit our use of the children's images and access to our blog to those who were initial participants in the project. This poses several ethical questions for those of us who work in this way with young children.

Questions for Reflection
- What are some practical steps that we might take in ensuring that the ways in which we engage with young children in participatory arts-based research are ethical?
- How can we use reflection to redefine our roles as researchers when we undertake participatory work with young children? What aspects of our roles do we need to interrogate and to reflect upon as we work together with young children? What are the power dynamics at play?
- If we determine that it is both ethical and beneficial to exhibit images of children, how do we decide which venues for sharing are appropriate?
- What challenges and what possibilities within participatory arts-based research does the rise of digital media, especially digital photography and video, pose?
- What challenges to new media art-making with children does the media itself generate?
- What are our roles as artists, researchers, and teachers in this shared space?

References

Alderson, P., & Morrow, V. (2011). *The ethics of research with children and young people: A practical handbook*. Thousand Oaks, CA: Sage.

Davies, B. (2014). *Listening to children: Being and becoming*. New York, NY: Routledge.

Knowles, J. G., & Cole, A. L. (2008). *Handbook of the arts in qualitative research: Perspectives, methodologies, examples, and issues*. Thousand Oaks, CA: Sage.

Wilson, B. (2007). Art, visual culture, and child/adult collaborative images: Recognizing the other-than. *Visual Arts Research, 33*(2), 6–20.

Index

© Springer Nature Switzerland AG 2019   205
A. Eckhoff (ed.), *Participatory Research with Young Children*, Educating
the Young Child 17, https://doi.org/10.1007/978-3-030-19365-2